P9-CDH-096

Privatizing Poland

Culture and Society after Socialism

a series edited by BRUCE GRANT *&* NANCY RIES

The Unmaking of Soviet Life: Everyday Economies after Socialism
by CAROLINE HUMPHREY

Russia Gets the Blues: Music, Culture, and Community in Unsettled Times
by MICHAEL URBAN with ANDREI EVDOKIMOV

The Vanishing Hectare: Property and Value in Postsocialist Transylvania
by KATHERINE VERDERY

Privatizing Poland

This book belongs to:
Karlia Brown
karlia.n.brown
@vanderbilt.edu
2013

*Baby Food, Big Business,
and the Remaking of Labor*

Elizabeth C. Dunn

Cornell University Press   Ithaca and London

Copyright © 2004 by Cornell University

All rights reserved. Except for brief quotations in a review, this book, or parts thereof, must not be reproduced in any form without permission in writing from the publisher. For information, address Cornell University Press, Sage House, 512 East State Street, Ithaca, New York 14850.

First published 2004 by Cornell University Press Printed in the United States of America
First printing, Cornell Paperbacks, 2004

Library of Congress Cataloging-in-Publication Data

Dunn, Elizabeth C., 1968–
   Privatizing Poland : baby food, big business, and the remaking of labor / Elizabeth C. Dunn.
       p.   cm. — (Culture and society after socialism)
Includes bibliographical references and index.
   ISBN 0-8014-4225-7 (cloth : alk. paper) — ISBN 0-8014-8929-6 (pbk. : alk. paper)
   1. Privatization—Poland.   2. Industrial relations—Poland.   3. Power (Social sciences)—
Poland.   4. Corporations, Foreign—Poland.   I. Title.   II. Series.
   HD4215.7.D86   2004
   338.9438′05—dc22

                                                                    2003024996

Cornell University Press strives to use environmentally responsible suppliers and materials to the fullest extent possible in the publishing of its books. Such materials include vegetable-based, low-VOC inks and acid-free papers that are recycled, totally chlorine-free, or partly composed of nonwood fibers. For further information, visit our website at www.cornellpress.cornell.edu.

Cloth printing   10 9 8 7 6 5 4 3 2 1
Paperback printing   10 9 8 7 6 5 4 3 2 1

Contents

Acknowledgments, vii

1 The Road to Capitalism, 1

2 Accountability, Corruption, and the Privatization of Alima, 28

3 Niche Marketing and the Production of Flexible Bodies, 58

4 Quality Control, Discipline, and the Remaking of Persons, 94

5 Ideas of Kin and Home on the Shop Floor, 130

6 Power and Postsocialism, 162

Notes, 175

Bibliography, 187

Index, 197

Acknowledgments

Many people helped me with the intellectual, practical, and emotional complications of doing an anthropological project like this one. None of them can be held responsible for any errors I commit or opinions I express, and all of them have my gratitude.

Deepest thanks go to friends and supporters in Poland. From finding me a field site to teaching me how to make pierogies, these people taught me how to make a life for myself in a strange place: Anna Orzińska, Piotr Paliwoda, Elżbieta Dzierdzak, Michelle Austin, Peggy Simpson, and Bogdan Stręk. *Dziękuję serdecznie!* Lucyna and Krzysztof Kiedrzynscy, Paweł Bulanda, Izabela Napiórkowski, and Józefa and Ryszard Zarębscy taught me how to be a friend and family member in ways I never imagined. My thanks and love also go to Irena and Marek Rzucidło, and their daughters Patrycja, Paulina, and Karolina.

At Alima-Gerber, I thank those who paved the way and bothered to explain how to do the job right: Daniel Kortlan, Aleksander Bialec, Jacek Oniszczuk, Renata Szczeczewska, Maciej Ładno, Grażyna Tomaszek, Renata Markowska, Anna Ożyla, Władysław Piech, Elżbieta Majchrowicz, Józef Grzesiakowski, Barbara Zięba, Jacek Kotula, and other AG employees who I do not name to protect their privacy. In particular, I thank a group of people on the factory floor—Ula, Ala, Wojtek, Gosia, Zdzidza, Teresa, Stanisław, Genofewa, Janusz, Grazyna, Grzegorz, Marysia, Irena, Renata, Monika, Ania, Józia, Bogusia, Helena, Ewa, Basia, Zosia, Krysia, and Kazia. I am not using their last names here, and I do not use their real first names anywhere in this book, but I hope they know how grateful I am to them. I also thank the people I spoke with at Gerber in Fremont.

Many academic colleagues provided intellectual assistance and emotional sustenance, both in Poland and in the United States. First and foremost, I thank Katherine Verdery, for all she has taught me. Among Polish academics, Kazimierz Doktór, Włodzmierz Panków, Krystyna Janicka, Bogdan Mach, and Michał Buchowski were always helpful. David Ost, Nikki Townsley, Erica Schoenberger, Ewa Hauser, and Martha Lampland helped in the field and back home. I am also grateful to Sidney Mintz, Erik Mueggler, Elizabeth Ferry, and Sarah Hill.

Research for this dissertation was supported in part by a grant from the International Research and Exchanges Board (IREX), with funds provided by the National Endowment for the Humanities and the U.S. Department of State, which administers the Title VIII Program. The research was also aided by a Fellowship for East European Studies from the American Council of Learned Societies, a grant from the SHRM Foundation, and funding from the National Science Foundation. The *Wissenschaftskolleg zu Berlin* provided me with a wonderful year in which to write this book and the intellectual contributions of Wolf Lepenies, Jürgen Kocka, Yehuda Elkana, and Matthias Bergmann. The interpretations, conclusions, and recommendations are mine, and do not necessarily represent these organizations' views. I am grateful for their support.

Finally, thanks to the people I love most: Barbara and George Miller, Bryan and Kris Dunn, and Jason and Lisa Dunn. I dedicate this book to the memory of Olive Dunn, who through the beauty of her everyday life taught me the true meaning of the gift.

Privatizing Poland

1 The Road to Capitalism

Gerber Products Company, the baby food company, is headquartered in the tiny town of Fremont, Michigan, population four thousand. It is an hour away by car from the nearest airport, in Grand Rapids. Gerber is a major player—some might say it was *the* major player—in the jarred baby food industry, which Dan Gerber and the Fremont Canning Company pioneered in 1901. Gerber dominates the U.S. baby food market. Every year, across America, it sells more than four hundred jars of baby food per baby.

Despite its American dominance, declining birthrates and market saturation have forced Gerber to seek markets outside the United States. In 1992, soon after the fall of the Berlin Wall and the end of state socialism in Eastern Europe, Gerber bought the Alima Fruit and Vegetable Processing Company of Rzeszów, Poland, and formed the new Alima-Gerber S.A. baby food company. Alima, Gerber officials imagined, could follow the same developmental trajectory that transformed Dan Gerber's small Fremont Canning Company into the multinational baby care firm, Gerber Products, and reinvigorate the mature parent firm back in Michigan.

Driving from Grand Rapids to Fremont, one easily sees why Gerber officials were struck with the similarity of Alima and Gerber, since their settings look so much the same. Like Rzeszów, Fremont is a fairly small town surrounded by other small towns and villages. The rural landscape is one of rolling hills, fields, and brown scrubby brush punctuated with evergreen trees. The road from Grand Rapids to Fremont is lined with small farmhouses with peeling faded paint, grain silos, and small apple orchards. The names of the streets crossing the two-lane road to Fremont, like Fruit Ridge Road and Peach Ridge Road, refer to the region's agricultural base. Alongside the road, the signs and the billboards give the area a small-town feel and testify to rural religiosity: "Rose of Sharon Market and Garden Center: Say Yes to Jesus," and "T.J.'s Cafe: Happy Birthday Travis" are two of many. In

mid-November, old VW buses and pickup trucks pass by with stiff deer carcasses tied to the top or lying in the truck bed.

The road to Rzeszów from Warsaw is much the same. The November climate has the same gray skies and chilly air. The brown scrub, the vegetable fields, and the small villages, one after the other, are like those in Michigan. There are small roadside cafés and small farmhouses with peeling paint similar to those near Fremont. Small shrines punctuating rural roads are marks of everyday religious sentiment, much like the biblical reference in the "Rose of Sharon" sign near Fremont. The road to Rzeszów has fewer gas stations and fewer McDonald's than the road from Grand Rapids to Fremont. Rzeszów has more factories, more people (a population of 250,000), and the occasional horse-drawn wagon to hold up traffic. Nonetheless, the road to Rzeszów *feels* a lot like the road to Fremont. These are two communities shaped by a common industry, surrounded by apple orchards, and full of small farmers who love the outdoors.

The two factories are also quite similar. Each depends on produce from farms around the plant that is cooked and canned by local people working inside the factory. The most important products in each factory are the same: apples and carrots, the major ingredients for the baby food and juice. Like socialist-era Alima, Gerber was—and, to some extent, still is—a local company with close ties to the surrounding agricultural community. Generations of workers from the same family, both in Fremont and in Rzeszów, have supplied the fruit, vegetables, and labor to make baby food. The two factories appear so similar at first glance that Alima's own "Vademecum," a compendium of products and methods, uses pictures taken in Michigan to illustrate a text about the Rzeszów operation. Few people at Alima-Gerber have noticed the switch.

Given how similar the two firms and their settings look, it is no wonder that Gerber executives believed they could duplicate their firm's phenomenal rise, in the new Polish setting. They assumed that Poland was a case of arrested development and that somehow both the firm and the country were developing along the same lines Gerber followed in the early twentieth century. Gerber's CEO, Al Piergallini, made the comparison explicit: "This country reminds me a lot of the United States in the 1920s" (Perlez 1993). Seeing the firm and the nation as similar also led Gerber executives to assume that Polish rural entrepreneurs, factory workers, and consumers were like the ones they had come to know in Fremont. Since they believed the people were similar and the places were similar (except that Poland was somehow ninety years behind Fremont), Gerber managers believed Alima could follow Gerber's road to capitalist success.

This, in microcosm, was the same set of assumptions governing the privatization and economic transformation process in Poland at the national level. The designers of postsocialist economic reform believed the people of Poland were essentially the same as people in Western capitalist countries. If only the constraints of communism could be removed, natural tendencies toward capitalist economic rationality, profit maximization, entrepreneurship, work ethics, and consumption patterns would ensure that a market economy would develop spontaneously. According to neoliberal reformers like Leszek Balcerowicz, Poland's first post-Communist minister of finance and the architect of Poland's "shock therapy" plan for economic reform, privatization in all its forms would allow those natural tendencies in persons to be expressed in economic behavior. In the best liberal tradition, the designers of economic reform assumed that the aggregate of these natural human behaviors would create a market economy. As Balcerowicz put it,

> A private market economy is the natural state of contemporary society. Indeed, whenever a country lacks private firms, this is due to state restrictions and not due to a lack of potential entrepreneurs. Removing these prohibitions always leads to the development of private enterprise. (Balcerowicz 1995, 133; translation mine)

Balcerowicz and other post-Solidarity neoliberal reformers believed that once fundamentals of capitalism such as private property were established, the Polish economy would resume its place on the path to capitalist development. They assumed that this path was the same one followed by the Western market economies, which Central Europe left in 1945 (and Russia much earlier). According to this ideology, Eastern Europe may have been "backward in time," but with the advent of privatization, it would be back on the road to a capitalism identical to that found in the West. As economist Janoś Kornai phrased the problem for the whole Eastern European region:

> The "first road" of capitalist development was abandoned first by the peoples of the Tsarist empire, and later by the other peoples that came under communist-party rule, in favor of a new, "second road" that led to the development of the socialist system. Some decades later, it became increasingly plain that socialism in its classical form was a blind alley. . . . The termination of the sole rule of the Communist Party removes the main road block, so that society can return to the first road, the road of capitalist development. (Kornai 1995, vii–ix; italics in the original)

But Poland is not the United States, and Rzeszów is not Fremont. The apartment blocks, the smokestacks of the town's airplane engine factory, and the huge concrete monument to the "heroes" who helped the Russians invade the city during World War II are all reminders that Rzeszów's people experienced more than forty years of socialism. While their apple orchards and rural roads may look the same, the two towns were part of systems with vastly different social relationships that gave those orchards and roads widely differing meanings. Rzeszovians and Fremonters might both grind carrots, pack baby food, go to church, and go fishing, but they do not experience the world in the same way. This discovery came as a surprise to Gerber's managers. As AG's director of human resources said several years later:

> The Americans who bought [Alima] took over its management with the best of intentions, but at the same time, incomplete knowledge of Polish

realities, customs, and workers' attitudes. Not surprisingly, it was hard [for Gerber's managers] to understand why not all their orders were implemented immediately. (cited in Gestern 1996)

When Gerber discovered that Alima employees and Rzeszów area farmers were not the same as the people of Fremont, the company began to try to *make* the people it deals with in Poland into the kind of people it is familiar with. Because Gerber believed Alima was *like* the Gerber of the 1920s, it applied the same kinds of management techniques to Alima that it had used upon itself in recent decades to transform itself into a "new," "global," and more "flexible" corporation. Whether by applying Western management techniques like audit, niche marketing, and standardization to its employees, by reorganizing the relationships between the farmers and the firm and actively changing their farming practices, or by advertising to Polish mothers in order to change the way they feed their babies, Gerber actively sought to reproduce the system of relationships between the firm, its suppliers, and the customers that it had in the United States in the 1990s. In a sense, the underlying assumption of Gerber's Polish venture, like that of many American companies in Eastern Europe, is that to make the kinds of products it knows, the company first has to make the kinds of people it knows: shop floor workers, managers, salespeople, and consumers like those in the United States.

But why pay attention to the management strategies of a small, not-very-important factory in an out-of-the-way Polish town? What do Alima's experiences have to say about larger, more widespread issues? In the first place, Alima-Gerber's experiences illuminate much bigger questions about the transformation of state-socialist societies. How does a society carry out massive economic change in such a short time? Alima's answers to that question—which hinge on the privatization of the firm and transforming the employees who work in it—prefigured some of the central issues surrounding privatization and economic transformation in Poland.

Soon after the "big bang" of 1990, it became obvious even to supporters of radical economic liberalization that privatization was a necessary but not sufficient condition for economic restructuring (McDonald 1993; Kozminski 1992; Johnson and Loveman 1995, 32). A "culture change" was called for, or so it was thought (Fogel and Etcheverry 1994, 4; Tadikamalla et al. 1994, 216). Some argued that "the socialist mentality is basically at odds with the spirit of capitalism" (Sztompka 1992, 19–20; see also Kozminski 1993). While most efforts focused on restructuring both privatized and state-owned enterprises by reeducating managers, employees of all types and consumers were also subjected to more and less subtle forms of "reeducation." To get a

Western-style capitalist economy and to participate in ever more rapid flows of capital and goods around the globe, it seemed that new kinds of persons and subjectivities had to be created. In management texts and fashion magazines, in business schools and on shop floors, a variety of methods were employed to promulgate the habits, tastes, and values of postmodern flexible capitalism (Dunn 1996; cf. Harvey 1989).

Alima-Gerber's attempts to reeducate and reconstruct its managers, employees, and customers thus illustrate one of the most fundamental aspects of the "transition" from socialism. They show that the successful creation of a market economy requires changing the very foundations of what it means to be a person. The case of Alima-Gerber highlights how important workplaces are in transforming economies. Firms not only change patterns of production and investment, but also instill new ideas about different kinds of people and what they like, transform notions about what kinds of actions people of different ages, classes, and genders supposedly can do, and change the ways that people regulate their economic behavior.

A close study of Alima also shows that the transformation of state socialist societies is not merely a question of changing political parties, building democratic institutions, or even shifting property regimes, as difficult as all those tasks may be. Rather, the "transition" is a fundamental change in the nature of power in Eastern Europe. Observing new forms of management and the inculcation of new forms of personhood shows that *governmentality* in Poland has undergone a sea change in the years since 1989. In this book, I argue that if we define "technologies of government" as arrangements of artifacts, practices, techniques, dispositions, and bodies, then the Warsaw Pact countries and the Western market democracies had radically different forms of governmentality between 1945 and 1989. As much as the early architects of socialism might have wished to engage in the same modernizing projects as capitalist powerhouses like the United States, state socialist modernity never operated in the same way as the capitalist modernity of the United States and Western Europe.

The postsocialist transformation is a conscious effort to make the systems of governmentality in the former Soviet Bloc and the capitalist "First World" alike—that is, to put Eastern Europe back on the "road to capitalism" by making its steering mechanisms the same as those in Western Europe or the United States. Poland's transformation is not just a transition to ideal-typical capitalism but part of a much larger process of globalization that entails the adoption of many of the same systems of governmentality and regulation used in countries like Germany, the United States, or Japan. Just as in these countries, politicians and managers in Poland are trying to make the leap to a more flexible, "post-Fordist," or neoliberal form of capitalism. It comes as no surprise, then, to discover that many of the ideas and techniques for transforming people and economies in Poland are based on techniques developed in Japan, Western Europe, and the United States.

Just as in Poland, changes in labor discipline have been a key technology for changing the economies of the First World. Techniques like niche marketing, accounting, audit, and quality control have been used in firms throughout Western Europe and the United States, including at Gerber. These techniques are used to make people into flexible, agile, self-regulating workers who help their firms respond to ever more rapidly changing market conditions. Although popular business writers praise them as "liberation management" (Peters 1992), these techniques also have a starkly disciplinary, and often discriminatory, side. They force some workers to work ever harder to comply with the firm's demands for flexibility, while excluding those they deem inflexible and incapable of self-regulation from working at all (Martin 1994). These doctrines of flexibility—and demands that both workers and firms become "self-regulating selves"—mark the advent of a fundamentally new form of power in postsocialist Eastern Europe.

For many American and Western European workers, it is difficult to critique the new "flexible management" or even to criticize the "flexible economy" that threatens their job security whenever there is an economic downturn. Fundamental tenets about what it means to be a person—an individual, "accountable," responsible, self-managing person—mean that many workers blame themselves, not their firms or the national economy, when they are unhappy about discipline at work or when they become unemployed (Newman 1999). Polish workers, however, have a stronger standpoint from which to criticize these changes in management and in personhood, because the shift in governmentality is not total. Polish workers spent more than forty years under socialism, which organized both production and personhood in very different ways. While Poles accept many of the changes that global capitalism brings—and eagerly welcome some of them—their historical experience of socialism and the cultural system built, and sustained in those decades also allow them to contest, modify, and reinterpret many initiatives of multinational corporations. Certainly, their sense of themselves as persons has been drastically altered by their contact with the ongoing dramatic changes in world capitalism. However, their history, religious background, concepts of gender and kinship, and ideas about social relationships all ensure that their sense of themselves as parts of a capitalist system is not the same as that found in the United States.

How, then, do Polish workers respond to attempts to make them into the new, "flexible" workers of late capitalism? How do Polish workers, managers, and consumers contest and rework the categories of persons imported by American management, and how might those contestations form the basis of a critique of contemporary capitalism? Do their attempts to block, modify, and circumvent new managerial technologies change the system of relations emerging in Poland into a distinct form of capitalist economy? Do struggles and negotiations on the shop floor turn the disciplinary power of flexible accumulation into something new and unrecognizable, just as they warped and weakened socialist authoritarian power?

In this book I explore how Polish workers use experiences of socialism and Solidarity union activism, as well as Catholic, kin, and gender ideologies, to redefine themselves and negotiate work processes and relationships within the firm. By deploying alternate concepts of value, Solidarity's expectations of the relationship between worker and enterprise, and webs of acquaintanceship developed in the shortage economy, workers seek to develop other subjectivities and to become subordinated in a way they can live with. Their struggles offer a new lens through which to see the ways that power is distributed inside the "flexible" firms of the new global economy and which kinds of people are excluded from it. They frame changes in political economy as changes in the moral economy of work. Hence the challenges workers face open up an opportunity to critically examine changes in the lived experience of global capitalism as well as the more narrowly defined "transition" in Eastern Europe.

Alima in Global Context, or, Why Rzeszów and Fremont Are Nowhere Near the Same Place

In an article entitled "Gridded Lives: Why Kazakhstan and Montana Are Nearly the Same Place," Kate Brown looks out over the streets of both Karaganda and Billings. She argues that "by straining away the mountains of verbiage produced during the Cold War, we may find the Soviet Union and the United States share a great deal in common" (2001, 21–22). In a courageous move, Brown asks how these places, once set up as polar opposites, might be alike. She wants to reveal how power was produced in both places through forms of Foucauldian discipline and to show how both capitalist and socialist spaces were artifacts of a common modernity. By examining how managers of large enterprises in both places sought to ensure the "regimentation and subjection of labor," she hopes to show how they created "corresponding patterns of subjection" (2001, 23).

But was work really organized in the same way in both capitalist and socialist enterprises from the early 1920s, when the Soviets first began to create socialist industrial society, until 1989? Did state socialism's factories and collective farms produce the same kinds of subjectivities that American manufacturing plants and corporate farms did? Were there so few differences between working in Billings and Karaganda or Fremont and Rzeszów? The stakes in answering these questions go beyond a theoretical debate about whether capitalism and socialism were merely variations on a theme (although that has been a steady argument in the literature on work—see Braverman 1974; Van Atta 1986; Burawoy and Lukács 1992). Rather, the questions go right to the core of the postsocialist transformation project. Like Brown, Poland's early neoliberal reformers and privatizing managers also assumed that capitalist and socialist factories organized work in similar ways. But if they were incorrect, the map they drew of the road to capitalism was, from its very inception, flawed.

The idea that Eastern European socialism and American capitalism shared specific ways of organizing industrial work comes from a peculiar historical conjuncture. Ironically, given that the early Soviets were trying to create a society antithetical to capitalism, it was the innovations of Henry Ford, a pathbreaking American capitalist, which inspired early models of Soviet production systems. Planners argued that the utopian values of efficiency, rationality, and industrialization would lift Russia out of backwardness, and they grouped those values under buzzwords like *Amerikanizatsiya* (Americanization). *Fordizatsiya* became a metaphor for the speedy industrial tempo, high growth, and productiveness that characterized the Soviets' ideal modernity (Stites 1989, 149). Ford's memoir, *My Life,* appeared in eight translated editions in the USSR in the 1920s, and peasants went so far as to name both their tractors and their children after Henry Ford (Stites 1989, 148).

The cult of Henry Ford that emerged in 1920s Russia went beyond metaphor and imagery. Ford not only shaped the Soviet imagination, but he also exercised a profound influence on the organization of state socialist industry. Between 1920 and 1926, the Soviet regime ordered more than twenty-four thousand Fordson tractors, as well as Ford motorcars (Stites 1989, 148). Fascinated by the technology, both Lenin and Stalin became great admirers of Henry Ford's River Rouge plant in Michigan, which at that time was the largest industrial enterprise in the world. Seeking to emulate the assembly line, which he saw as the centerpiece of capitalist economic power, Stalin invited Henry Ford himself to design the Gorkovskiy Automotive Plant and arranged for American engineers and skilled American workers to train the Soviets in the proper administration of production (Dyakanov 2002).

The huge, vertically integrated enterprise, along with the gridded cities and large industrialized farms that Brown (2001, 38) describes, became the centerpiece of the Fordist vision of modernity. Vertical integration was already in wide use in the United States by the 1950s—including at Gerber's Fremont plant—when the newly socialist states of Eastern Europe began replicating it at the end of World War II. Socialist planners hoped to spur development by using vertical integration to achieve economies of scale. In the early 1960s, Polish planners began reorganizing the Alima factory along Fordist lines as part of a plan to rationalize the food system. Although Alima had been built as a candy and jam factory before World War II, socialist planners in the 1960s ordered Alima to specialize in the production of a standardized range of baby foods. Although fruit and vegetable production had to be geographically dispersed in order to be close to producers, rather than being spatially concentrated like Ford's River Rouge plant, Alima became a part of a socialist corporation known as *Zjednoczenie Przemyslu Owocowo-Warzywnego* (ZPOW, the United Fruit and Vegetable Industries), which was run directly by the Ministry of Food and Agricultural Industries as if it were one vast, vertically integrated enterprise. With vertical integration and with assembly-line technology imported from Western Europe, socialist Alima modeled itself on the basic Fordist model as much as capitalist Gerber did.

Large enterprises organized along Ford's assembly-line model—whether state socialist or capitalist—demanded a distinctive form of labor discipline. In the United States, Ford's River Rouge plant and Gerber's Fremont Canning Company, like other enterprises of the 1920s, used a form of discipline known as "Scientific Management" and organized their shop floors along the lines sketched out by efficiency expert Frederick Winslow Taylor.[1] Fordist firms used Taylor's methods to separate mental and manual labor, to wrest control of the production process out of the hands of skilled craftsmen and to centralize control of the production process in the hands of managers. Managers using the Taylor method applied engineering principles to workers to improve their efficiency. Since Ford's assembly line had already broken the production process down into simple, repetitive jobs that each worker did over and over, Taylorist industrial engineers focused on breaking those jobs down even further. They hovered over workers with stopwatches, timing each worker's tiniest movements, and then tried to recombine those movements in ways that would to increase the amount of output per shift. The Taylor system aimed at making workers into parts of the machines they controlled: passive objects performing the same motion over and over, in a rhythmic and efficient fashion. To spur workers to pro-

Fig. 1. Advertising for Bobo Frut brand juices, circa 1979. The label and the logo remained virtually unchanged until after Gerber acquired Alima (formerly ZPOW) in 1992.

duce more and to goad them into accepting the dictates of the industrial engineers, Fordist firms paid employees on the shop floor by the piece rather than by the hour. The result of this system was a radical deskilling of industrial work—and the advent of a uniquely mind-numbing and backbreaking form of labor (Taylor 1947; Aglietta 1987, 113–16; Hirsch 1984, 15–16; Aitken 1960, 13–48; Brenner and Glick 1991, 76).

Workers in Taylorized plants often rose up against the system, demanding that managers put away their stopwatches and give workers back their abilities to decide how best to accomplish their tasks. The Taylor system of labor discipline was never implemented in its entirety anywhere in the United States (Aitken 1960; Van Atta 1986, 330). However, elements of scientific management found their ways into Fordist factories in the United States and around the world, where they shaped factory life for decades. In an Oregon fish-canning factory in the early 1970s, Barbara Garson observed factory managers watching women gut salmon and using the bones from the picked-over fish, rather than stopwatches, to determine the women's rate of work (Garson 1975). In a factory in Chicago in the 1970s, Michael Burawoy observed machinists "playing games" and racing to overfill their quotas in an attempt to raise their piece-rate wages (Burawoy 1979). In a Japanese-owned semiconductor assembly plant in Malaysia in the 1980s, Aihwa Ong observed the minute control of working women's bodies in space. Managers noted and controlled the women's every movement from the shop floor to the bathroom or the prayer room, and conducted elaborate surveillance of the movements of their "small" and "nimble" hands to ensure high production rates (Ong 1987).

Also in the 1980s, Maria Patricia Fernandez-Kelly discovered the unbearable pressure to complete a single simple task over and over at high velocity as she worked in an apparel factory on the Mexican border. In the *maquiladora,* she was expected to sew a pocket to the leg of a pair of blue jeans every nine to ten seconds—that between 360 and 396 pockets per hour or about 3,000 pockets per shift. The perfect coordination of eyes, hands and legs that it took to accomplish this feat was continually monitored by managers, who carried out constant surveillance of the workers' while they worked and checked to ensure they met piecework quotas (Fernandez-Kelly 1983, 114–16).

These examples, each of which demonstrate a Taylorist disciplinary technique in action, highlight the fact that Taylor's ideas were "the intellectual framework within which the capitalist firm was reconstructed in the twentieth-century United States" (Van Atta 1986, 327). As incompletely as Taylor's ideas were implemented, the drive towards increased efficiency and the impulses towards managerial control they provided changed the way capitalist firms operated and drastically reduced workers' autonomy on the shop floor.

State socialist factories attempted to use similar disciplinary techniques. That Taylor became an explicit model for industrial organization alongside Ford came as no great surprise, as V. I. Lenin himself was a great admirer of scientific management in general and *teilorizatsiya* in particular. Taylor's system, he wrote,

> like all capitalist progress, is a combination of the refined brutality of bourgeois exploitation and a number of the greatest scientific achievements in the field of analyzing mechanical motions during work. . . . The Soviet Republic must at all costs adopt all that is valuable in the achievements of science and technology in this field. . . . We must organize in Russia the study and teaching of the Taylor system and systematically try it out and adapt it to our needs (cited in Braverman 1974, 12).

As new, vertically integrated megafactories were being built across Eastern Europe, managers attempted to install Taylorist labor practices in order to discipline the peasants who were becoming urban workers. Labor discipline was a particularly important element in the socialist drive to industrialize, because the Eastern Bloc countries were largely impoverished. Without the resources to invest in the technology that was state of the art in the capitalist world, the socialist countries tried to drive development by producing a highly disciplined and efficient workforce. Man-as-machine became a dominant metaphor, as Communist Party leaders and industrial managers held up the Taylorized worker as the image of the New Socialist Man (Stites 1989).

Inside factories around the Eastern Bloc, managers tried to improve efficiency and meet the production quotas set out for them by taking control of the labor process. They broke jobs down into simple steps, specified which tools workers should use, described in minute detail how the job should be done, and told workers how fast to produce. In many factories, workers were not paid per hour but per piece, which sometimes drove them to "fury and panic" as they "risked life and limb to make the rates" or to produce the specified number of pieces per hour (Burawoy and Lukács 1992, 40; Haraszti 1978). The norms, or the time that management determined should be spent on each task, were often ratcheted down along with the wage paid per piece, forcing workers to struggle ever harder to produce more and earn a living wage.

Echoing Harry Braverman's critique of thirty years before, Kate Brown argues that these shared disciplinary techniques meant that the *experience* of labor was the same in capitalist and socialist enterprises. She says they shared

> the same machines, the same hierarchies and rush for production, the same endless days and fatal accidents, clogged air, ragged lungs, fragmented bodies and flat, beaten stares. It comes as no surprise that in the realm of labor history, the names, dates, and places begin to blur into one long, muscle-aching sigh. A sigh that indicates the physical experience of industrial labor differs little whether in capitalism or in communism, because the same [disciplinary] grid stretched over not only space but time, the process of production, and, consequently, lives. (Brown 2001, 42; bracketed word mine)

Like factory workers in the capitalist world, state socialist workers struggled against a form of discipline that promised to rob them of control over their labor and the performance of their jobs (cf. Braverman 1974, 116). Yet, there was one element that a focus on shared disciplinary techniques and poetic descriptions of the agonies of labor misses but which made the physical experience of industrial labor dramatically different in capitalist and socialist factories: *the Plan*.[2] The Plan—the key element in the socialist economy—so fundamentally changed Eastern European economies that it made the daily experience of factory work into something distinct both from the Fordist/Taylorist vision and from the actual realities of factory work inside capitalist firms.

In basic terms, the difference has to do with the scale at which power was centralized. In a Fordist factory, the power to organize the labor process was taken away from the workers and centralized in the hands of management. In a socialist economy, the power to plan production was centralized at the level of the nation-state rather than the firm. Planners at the ministry level took on the role of enterprise managers. It was the central planners, not the enterprise managers, who were supposed to decide what kinds of goods would be produced, how much raw material was needed, and how the material would be transformed into the desired product. This generated a logic of work organization that was different from both the Fordist/Taylorist model and the lived experience of work in capitalist factories.

In a vertically integrated Fordist corporation like Gerber, upper-level managers decided what each division would produce and then prepared budgets that detailed how the firm's resources would be allocated among the divisions. Gerber's managers decided whether to invest in making jarred baby food or boxes of cereal. They decided how much to invest in new capping machines, how many jars of strained peas to produce and how many jars of strained apricots, and how much produce to buy from local farmers.

At Alima, by contrast, central planners at the _national_ level usually took over this function. In the late 1960s, during a wave of consolidation, planners at the Ministry of Agriculture decided Alima would specialize in baby food. As a member of ZPOW, Alima became a single specialized division in a large, geographically dispersed socialist corporation—much as if it were a single plant in a large capitalist agrifood corporation. Central planners decided on whether to invest in the company's physical plant and what kind of machinery to buy, set targets for how many jars Alima would produce of what, and decided how many tons of vegetables Alima would receive from local peasants. The degree to which the center carried out such detailed planning later varied. Alima and other state socialist enterprises in Poland were granted more autonomy during the reform period of the 1970s but were placed back under central control in the 1980s. Nonetheless, even during the most sweeping reforms, the party/state always retained some control at the central level. This meant that while the planning process was similar in capitalism and socialism, the _scale_ at which major decisions were made was always different.

Centralizing managerial authority at the level of the national government eliminated competition between multiple firms in an open marketplace. But it also eliminated the need for an enterprise to make any profit. Unlike capitalist enterprises, state socialist enterprises had _soft budget constraints._ Since the state owned the firms, they did not have to worry about losing money or going bankrupt. There were no penalties for demanding—and using— as many resources as socialist enterprises could convince central planners to give them (Kornai 1992). In aggregate, however, this constant hunger for more inputs led to extreme shortages. Central planners simply received more requests for inputs than they had goods to allocate (Verdery 1996, 21). Shortage, in turn, led managers request even more goods, in the hopes that they might be able to stockpile enough resources to produce the amount specified in the plan and perhaps have enough left over to trade with other firms for inputs they could not get from the state.

The ability to gain control over these resources and to reallocate them became the most important form of power in the centrally planned economy. Both managers and central planners struggled to hoard more goods to allocate later to their allies in the hopes of creating political alliances (Verdery 1996, 22). This constant hoarding created more shortage, which spurred managers and planners to hoard even more. The resulting downward economic spiral in most of the Eastern European countries was periodically broken by reforms or large-scale borrowing (such as Poland's massive loans from the West in the 1970s) but was never permanently halted.

The shortage-hoarding cycle drove socialist factories away from the classic American Fordist model and made the experience of factory work in them different. Because the dedicated machinery used in assembly-line production was so expensive, Fordist managers sought to keep the line running around the clock. This necessitated a steady flow of supplies into the factory (Schoenberger 1997, 35). But under socialism, shortage made a smooth flow of material through the plant impossible. In the early weeks of a planning period, the line might sit idle for days, while managers scrambled to assemble all the inputs needed for production. At Alima, the line would often grind to a halt while wagonloads of fruit and vegetables quietly rotted in the sun, waiting for the arrival of glass bottles or sugar or some other good that was in shortage. Far from being watched at all times or clocked with a stopwatch, or being subjected to endless days of muscle-aching labor, workers often had time to leave the factory and stand in the eternal lines in front of food shops or go home to work in their fields. Toward the end of the planning period, however, the tempo of work changed dramatically. Once all the necessary inputs were assembled, workers "stormed," or labored furiously to meet the Plan's targets before the end of the period. Management's careful specifications about how to do the job, which were supposed to ensure consistent product quality, were discarded as workers worked frantically to produce the quantities the Plan demanded. Socialism did not share the steady machine-rhythm of work that the Taylorist disciplinary grid gave to Fordist enterprises but rather proceeded in fits and starts.

Shortage also reversed Fordism's tendency to centralize authority and drove control of the work process down through the hierarchy and back onto the shop floor. At Alima, central planners assigned specialties to firms within larger socialist corporations or industrial sectors and set targets specifying precisely how many jars of strained carrots were supposed to be produced. But the realities of shortage often made it impossible for Alima to produce just strained carrots or even just baby food. From the late 1960s onward, Alima's production managers responded to the irregular supply of inputs by taking control of the product array. They flexibly switched production among a wide range of products, trying to make use of what was available. The Plan might have specified apricot baby food, for example, but if no apricots were available, Alima's procurement specialists would obtain tomatoes for making tomato paste or find some cabbage and ground meat to go with the tomato paste and make *gołąbki* (stuffed cabbage rolls) for adults. At one time or another, depending on the season and the availability of materials, Alima made marmalades, compotes, fruit drinks, mineral waters, carbonated drinks, ketchups, canned dinners, and frozen vegetables, all in addition to baby food (Welc 1994, 25). Instead of producing long runs of standardized product, as Fordist managers did and as state socialist planners wanted to do, managers of state-owned enterprises in Eastern Europe had to take control away from central planners and scramble to produce a diverse array of goods in small batches.

On the shop floor, shortage at least partly undid Taylorism's separation of mental and manual labor. To compensate for the variable quality of inputs, workers often had to circumvent the recipes and instructions provided by management and continually adapt their work procedures. Fruit, for example, would arrive in varying degrees of ripeness, depending on when peasants had been able to marshal the labor needed to pick it and how long it had been sitting outside the factory waiting to be used. Riper fruit was sweeter, which meant that the quantity of sugar, the cooking times, and the temperatures in the official instructions had to be altered. Varying qualities of bottle caps and glass jars meant workers had to change the fill temperature and the torque of the capping machine. And always, aging machines were breaking down. With parts in shortage, workers had to use their ingenuity to improvise solutions and get the freezers, cooking vats, labelers, and palletizers back online. Just as in most state socialist enterprises, Alima's workers and shop-floor supervisors—not upper-level managers—had to deploy craft knowledge in order to make the necessary adjustments in real time and ensure that the line continued to run smoothly (cf. Burawoy and Lukács 1992, 103; Verdery 1996, 23).

Finally, central planning and the economy of shortage gave workers political power that workers in Fordist enterprises could not have marshaled. The Communist Party premised the legitimacy of one-party rule on the notion that that through rational planning, it could provide worker-citizens with what they needed, including food, housing, and medical care (Verdery 1996, 63). Because the source of the state's power was its ability to reallocate what workers made, workers gained considerable leverage over the party/state. Polish workers used it to their advantage. Unhappy with the state's incapacity to provide basics, like bread and meat, and displeased by the state's continual attempts to wrest power away from the shop floor, workers sometimes coordinated large-scale strikes (such as those under the banner of the Solidarity movement), which threatened the party's ability to rule society. Even during periods of what seemed like labor peace, workers used the ability to withdraw their labor as a tool against the state and against the managers of state-owned enterprises. Using implicit threats to work to rule or to slow down production, workers parried managers' attempts to impose stringent labor discipline and negotiated the organization of work on the shop floor.

The Plan, the shortages it created, and the often innovative ways that managers devised to cope drove socialist factories away from the classic Fordist model of industrial organization. Although the Fordist system was the basis of the initial design for socialist factories, as managers and planners worked out the contradictions in the political economy of socialism they left the classic Fordist attempt behind for more contemporary economic strategies. Planners shaped and reshaped the economic systems of each country by trying series of reforms. Those reforms made the economic environments of countries like Poland, Hungary, and Romania quite different from one another. Responding to the constraints of socialism and the reforms, managers tried out formal changes in factory management (like implementing Workers' Councils) and devised hosts of stopgap measures necessary to keep the line running. In places like Karaganda and Rzeszów, the Plan created an institutional context for labor completely unlike the one found in Billings or in Fremont. Capitalist Fordism and state socialism may have started out with similar visions and even initially deployed similar disciplinary grids, but the presence of the Plan ensured that by the late 1980s, power was distributed quite differently in socialist workplaces than in capitalist ones. While Fordism and state socialism may have shared the same *modernizing project*, they resulted in two different *modernities*, which led to both radically different experiences of labor and the construction of workers as different types of persons.

Meanwhile, Back at the Ranch: From Fordism to Flexible Accumulation

In the United States and other capitalist countries in the 1970s, the Fordist system was also changing. Capital, which under Fordism largely stayed within the boundaries of a single domestic economy, began to circulate at a greater rate across national boundaries. Whereas only $50 billion of capital was "multinational" in 1973, more than $2 trillion was circulating transnationally by 1983 (Harvey 1989, 163). Goods, too, were circulating across national borders more rapidly and in ever greater numbers. Increasingly, corporations shipped semifinished goods to production plants in different countries and sent finished goods to be sold in foreign markets.

These changes in world capitalism were given a variety of names: flexible accumulation (Harvey 1989), disorganized capitalism (Offe 1985), post-

Fordism (Amin 1994), neoliberalism, or simply globalization (Dicken 1992). Whatever name it was given, it was clear that a shift within capitalism had both intensified its processes and opened new spaces—including Eastern Europe—to the penetration of capital. Although varying theories of the shift made different prognoses for the direction of change, all of them agreed on the catalyst of the change: the rigidity of the Fordist system (Harvey 1989, 142). As Emily Martin sums up the change:

> The preeminent model of industrial organization of the decades before 1970, which has been called "Fordist," has undergone radical revision. Gone is the linear work sequence of the moving assembly line, its machinery dedicated to mass production and mass marketing. Instead, the organization is a fleeting, fluid network of alliances, a highly decoupled and dynamic form with great organizational flexibility. (Martin 1994, 208)

Martin perhaps overstates the case—assembly lines, after all, still exist. But the shift to "flexible production" did require dismantling many of Fordism's key tenets. Factories struggled to shift from long production runs to making small batches of different products, each tailored to a niche market (Harvey 1989, 155). Product differentiation meant producers had to turn their attention to quality rather than quantity. So they introduced audit-based, quality-control systems like Total Quality Management (TQM) and ISO 9000 (Casper and Hancké 1999). Since rapidly shifting product arrays required an ever-changing list of inputs, vertically integrated corporations broke themselves apart, sold off their subsidiaries, and entered into new, loose networks with geographically dispersed independent suppliers.

Big organizational changes meant substantial changes in labor discipline, as well. Management gurus drew a parallel between Fordist firms, which had been diagnosed as too rigid, and what they believed were the passive bodies of workers disciplined by Taylorism (Kanter 1989; Peters 1992; Hammer and Champy 1993; cf. Zuboff 1988). The attempt to make workers more "flexible"—which often translated to teaching them to tolerate risk and job insecurity—was first done by having them "experience the metaphor" of flexibility in a bodily sense. Experiential education programs took employees to the tops of teetering poles, made them rappel off cliffs, and provoked so much fear in them that some literally soiled their pants (Martin 1994, chap. 11). But transforming employees from the supposedly passive and unthinking bodies of Fordism to active, thinking subjects took more than metaphors and adventure courses. Tools to inculcate and institutionalize flexibility soon appeared in workplaces, from factory floors to university departments. Through many of the techniques also described in this book—standardization, accountability, audit, quality control, participatory management, and ideas about private property—managers tried to turn their employees into self-directed, self-activating, self-monitoring workers (Strathern 1999, 2000; Shore and Wright 2000; Wasson 1993; Hoskin 1996). Where Taylorism had promoted the separation of mental and manual labor, this new form of labor discipline pushed workers into "continuous learning," an endless process of reskilling to meet changing production requirements.

What are the broader effects of this sea change in labor discipline? More than just an increase in productivity or a change that facilitates new organizations of work, changes in technocratic management may shape employees as human beings:

> For it is in work, as much as in "private life," that human beings have been required to civilize themselves and encouraged to discover themselves. It is around work, as much as around sexuality, that truths about the nature of humans as persons have been elaborated, and that norms and judgments about the conduct of individuals have crystallized. . . . And it is in work, as much as in some realm outside the factory gates, that we have been taught the techniques of life conduct, of fashioning and monitoring ourselves in order to become a laborer, a worker on the production line, a foreman, a manager. A genealogy of subjectivity needs to address the intrinsic links among these attempts to create and recreate the identity of individuals in the sphere of production. (Miller and Rose 1990, 461)

The question is, then, how do new forms of management shape not only the performance of work but also the kinds of persons that workers become? What fundamental assumptions about human beings' capacities for action does "flexible" management incorporate? How is the value of work and the people who do it changed by new disciplinary techniques? And why does it appear that regulating subjectivity—creating new forms of personhood—is such an integral part of making capitalism?

Studying workers who are in the midst of a transition not only from socialism to capitalism but also to a distinctive and emerging form of capitalism helps to shed light on anthropological questions about personhood, as well as on more general problems of market economy and democracy that face both First World countries and Eastern Europe. At the center of market democracy is the idea that individuals are autonomous, self-creating, and endowed with the ability to choose. This is the central element in post-Fordist workplace management in Eastern Europe, Western Europe, and

North America. Yet the apparently self-evident nature of that idea, made natural over the centuries in which capitalist democracy developed in the West, was not at all self-evident in socialist Eastern Europe. There, people were very visibly *not* entirely autonomous, and choice was highly constrained. Most analyses of workplace relations in Western Europe or the United States assume that self-reliance, independence, rights, and decision-making capabilities are innate properties of human beings. Some writers see management reforms relating to empowerment, participation, and so on as liberating these innate qualities of employees from the heavy hand of corporate hierarchy (while, of course, harnessing the productive capacities of these human qualities to serve the interests of the firm). Others see nouveau management styles as obscuring the fact that workers check their independence at the office door. But in both cases, these qualities are assumed to exist prior to the moment an employee enters a firm. What all these perspectives miss—and what the Eastern European experience makes explicit—is that the workplace is one of the most important places in modern society where agency, the ability to choose, and the right of self-determination are produced. As those who preach work as a form of self-fulfillment grasp intuitively, work is one place where identity and subjectivity, including the idea that human beings are endowed with autonomy and rights, are forged (Miller and Rose 1990; Burawoy 1985).

The creation of the working subject as a being with the right to choose is obviously a centerpiece of political democracy, no less so in the United States than in Poland. The notion of "attitude" and its centrality to both electoral politics and industrial management highlights the issue. When attitudes are taken as elements of consciousness that determine the activity of individuals in the social world, measuring and managing attitudes becomes one of the most important means of governing in a market democracy (Rose 1998, 125). Measuring public opinion, understanding how to mold the attitudes of voters through "spin control," surveying employees' attitudes toward their work and their workplaces, and managing the attitudes of employees in order to ensure better performance are all modes by which "modern" subjects are governed.

"Government" in market democracies, then, is the art of managing choosing subjects without violating their ability and right to choose. Both democratic governments and industrial managers address this problem not by limiting choice but by altering the field of alternatives and the method of calculating costs and benefits. Particular choices come to be seen as logical and rational (Miller and Rose 1990). Governments, of course, have a wide variety of social policies, tax incentives, interest rates, and so on with which to achieve this aim. So, too, do industrial managers. Armed with hiring procedures and performance evaluations, department audits and management consultants, industrial managers create a system of incentives and costs that make particular forms of behavior the logical and natural choice for employees.

But the choosing self of post-Fordist market democracy is more than a person with an attitude and the right to choose. The "enterprising self," a person who actively seeks to construct him- or herself by actively choosing and assembling the elements of a life, is now as important in the definition of a citizen as it is in the definition of the employee (Miller and Rose 1990, 455; Rose 1998, 123). Persons who are "entrepreneurs of themselves" flexibly alter their bundles of skills and manage their careers, but they also become the bearers of risk, thus shifting the burden of risk from the state to the individual (Maurer 1999). In Eastern Europe, transforming persons into choosers and risk-bearers soon became the project at the heart of the post-socialist transition.

The initial focus of the transformation after the collapse of the Communist Party in 1989 was the creation of institutions where individuals could make choices—the market and the polling booth, among others. But the focus soon shifted from removing the coercive hand of the state and creating domains where autonomous subjects could exercise free choice to the problem of creating those subjects themselves. The idea of creating independent subjects who make choices about action by calculating in particular ways was precisely the problem lurking behind the calls for "a change in mentality" and "culture change," which were heard at least as loudly in the political arena as they were in industrial management circles.[3] The micropractices of workplace management were one of the venues in which this transformation of attitudes would take place. Diagnosing (or, more accurately, *misdiagnosing*) the problem with state socialism as the same rigidity and lack of choice produced by Fordist capitalism, management consultants and politicians offered up post-Fordist management—a set of ideas and techniques that is in fact deeply problematic in the West—as an unproblematic panacea to the ills of state socialist enterprises.[4] Through the application of "flexible" management, including the practice of making employees into part-owners of the firm, postsocialist reformers tried to introduce the notion of *economic risk* into a society that had not known it for more than forty years.

If Polish workers in postsocialist, privatized firms are subject to the same disciplinary techniques as workers in other parts of the world, though, they have a unique vantage point from which to criticize new forms of management and person-making. Socialism—of both the "ideal" and "actually existing" varieties—contained radically different notions about work, individuality, choice, production, and power. So too does Polish Catholicism, which has been deeply shaped by Pope John Paul II's attempts to build a philosophical third way between socialism and capitalism.

Examining how Polish workers respond to new ways of constituting the capitalist self, then, opens up the possibility of using ethnography as cultural critique (Marcus and Fisher 1986). How are calculating, risk-bearing subjects created in the workplace? How is the value of labor determined under post-Fordism, and what other viable ways of valuing people and their work might there be? How is "rationality" deployed in the workplace, and how do particular ways of organizing work make certain choices rational and natural? Is self-regulation "empowering," as its proponents claim, and if so, what kind of power is at stake? How is power distributed within firms, and what kinds of people are disempowered by new forms of labor discipline? How is the distribution of power at work mapped onto power relations in society at large? Although Eastern Europe's working classes have largely been marginalized and their responses to new conditions denigrated as mere socialist survivals (see Kideckel 2001), their reactions to changes in work life open up larger questions about emerging capitalist relations.

Anthropological Methodology: Fieldwork Is Work

Although I read many studies about macrolevel changes in Eastern Europe and the global economy before I went to Poland, answering questions about how the micropractices of work and the construction of the person relate to larger-scale changes required that I both see and experience everyday life in a postsocialist firm. From the beginning of the project, I was interested not just in theories of management but in managerial practices as they were implemented in context—incompletely, in modified ways, and in the face of resistance, transformation, and subversion by those who are its objects. This theoretical commitment led me to spend sixteen months spanning 1995–97 in Poland, doing participant observation. I spent the bulk of that time at the Alima-Gerber plant, where I worked in the factory alongside AG workers.

AG's director of human resources, a former journalist who considered himself both a writer and an intellectual, took an interest in my project and facilitated my entry into the plant. With his permission, I had full access to the plant and could go almost wherever I pleased.[5] AG employs 948 people, and I came into contact with many of them. I spent much of my time among AG's 315 production workers, especially those who work in Division 1, a fruit juice bottling plant. Division 1 is a huge shop that Gerber renovated. At one end of the building, huge pallets of glass bottles are loaded onto the line by forklift. As the bottles move down the line, workers shout to one another over the din of clanking glass. Most of the work on the line is not physically arduous (and so is seen as appropriate for women, which is why 70 percent of production workers are female), but it is dull. Workers sit for hours and supervise the machines that wash, fill, pasteurize, or label bottles.

While I worked in Division 1, I spent hours watching bottles pass me on the line, visually inspecting them for "waternecks," or improperly sealed caps that allowed water from the pasteurizer to seep in. Sometimes, I stood next to the women working the pasteurizer and righted bottles that had fallen over in the machine. I helped watch for labels that had gone on the bottles crookedly, peeled off the defective labels, and put the bottles back in the machine to be relabeled. I ran the capper or helped do quality assurance tests or cleaned floors. Hour after hour after hour, I hit bottles on the back with a rubber tube to determine if they had fermented, or folded packing boxes, or packed two bottles of apple, two bottles of carrot, and two bottles of tropical fruit juice into a crate. It was often mind-numbing and always exhausting work, but it allowed me to understand the production process and to observe conflicts, negotiations, and employee discipline on the shop floor.

The work had its own rhythm, though, and often the most boring tasks were opportunities to interview workers about their jobs and their lives. I talked with workers while we worked on the line, but jobs off the line, like bottle-thumping or box-packing, were better occasions for asking questions. We sat on half-packed pallets of juice while we worked and debated or gossiped or told stories. While workers often fell oddly silent when I worked with them during the first months, I later became quite popular: I didn't have a quota to meet on off-line jobs, and so whoever would talk to me could count my labor as theirs. Soon, employees were asking me to fill in for them on the line, too. While one member of a work group went out for a cigarette or sneaked across the road to buy something at the small shop, I could work and talk with the other members of the group. I rarely, if ever, talked with people in a formal interview setting. Instead, I had conversations shouted over the din of the production line, in the break room over cups of tea and hastily eaten sandwiches, and during moments when we would sneak off into the unrenovated part of the plant or to the mechanics' room for a smoke.

Over time, I built friendships with some of the workers, and our conversations continued when I was invited for dinner. Often, I became friends with their friends and went to their homes as well. These conversations were scarcely quieter or less fragmented than those on the plant floor. Because most of the shop floor workers were women, our conversations went on around children demanding to be heard, husbands demanding dinner, and pots on the stove demanding attention. Much of my research time was spent giving piggybacks, playing Barbie, peeling potatoes, and making dumplings. No matter what was going on, the television was always blaring away. The quiet conversations over cups of coffee that I had envisioned rarely took place. Instead, I built rapport with my informants and understood their daily activities by participating in their tasks. Fieldwork was *work*.

The strategy of inquiring about work by doing work, though, was valuable. It gave me insights that neither academic theory nor survey research would have. For example, early in my fieldwork, I sat down on the production line next to Krystyna, a woman in her thirties. I began to ask her about the trade unions in the plant. "What do you think about the new contract they're trying to negotiate with the company?" I asked. "Do you think they should fight the new employee evaluation system? Do you think Ula will be re-elected as president of the union?" I went on and on. Finally, Krystyna turned to me in exasperation. "I commute an hour by bus each way to work. I work an eight-and-a-half hour shift. When I get home, I've got the cows to feed and milk, dinner to make, dishes to wash, laundry to do, and vegetables to can. None of us have had a day off in months, since we have to work overtime to get the carrots in. *When do you think I have time to care about this stuff?*" Not until I spent time working both in the factory and in my friends' homes did I truly understood why the workforce was so passive. They were exhausted, and so was I.

Understanding how new managerial techniques influenced employees meant working in jobs outside the shop floor, as well. This brought me into contact with many of Alima's 633 white-collar workers, including sales representatives, merchandisers, scientists, and managers. Here, I was required to do very different sorts of work. I spent several weeks participating in training programs along with new sales representatives and then traveled to five cities in different regions of Poland, so that I could ride along with the salespeople as they went from grocery store to grocery store. With the salespeople (90 percent of whom were male), I had more time to talk. We would often visit twenty stores in a day but would have long conversations in the car as we rode from shop to shop. Salespeople are always verbal; they make their living with words. They tend to be forthcoming, willing to see talking as a kind of work, and hence more understanding about what my work was. This made fieldwork in the cars easier than on the shop floor, in a way. But it was equally draining: after twelve hours of zooming around in a car, dashing in and out of stores, and taking notes on my jiggling knees as we drove, I collapsed in my hotel room bed.

Participant-observation in middle and upper management was yet another kind of work. After my shift on the shop floor was over, I often went up to the administration building to float around the offices of middle managers or smoke with one of the secretaries. I spent most of my time in the Human Resources (HR) Department, where it seemed there was always time for a cup of coffee and a chat. I often discussed what I was learning with the managers (many of whom had university degrees in the social sciences) who were employed in that department. Our conversations were largely unstructured and unhurried. I also took on some managerial work. I was a part of the team that designed a new employee evaluation system, helped plan training courses, and taught a "Business English" course in the training division. Later, I took whole days and weeks to participate in the training and development programs that the HR department offered. In these, I had the chance to talk with middle managers, farmers who had contracted with AG for produce, and laboratory workers. I learned about cadmium testing, apple-tree grafting, pesticide usage, government regulation of the baby food industry, and how to use statistics in quality control.

There was one group with which I did formal, structured interviews: people whose work was primarily done in meetings. They included high-level managers, government officials, and journalists. I went to Gdańsk to interview the former minister of privatization and to Warsaw to interview employees of the Ministry of Property Transformation. I also interviewed journalists who had written about privatization at the national level, business consultants involved in enterprise transformation, and even the executives of other corporations, to discuss privatization and corporate change at a more general level. (In a separate trip, I also went to Fremont, Michigan, to interview Gerber managers.)

The easy ebb and flow of conversation that I had with other kinds of workers was not possible with these people. Instead, interviewing managers was a performance in which I had to carefully monitor my own demeanor as well as theirs. I did research in newspaper archives beforehand, prepared lists of questions, and fired them off in rapid sequence. It sometimes felt to me more like an interrogation than a conversation, as I was often jostling for power with my interviewees during the interview. Managers were often less forthcoming. They were sometimes trying more to block me from learning than to illuminate me, either because they felt I was encroaching on proprietary knowledge that had to be kept from competitors or because they felt I was treading too close to issues that might embarrass the company or its managers.[6] This was not "interviewing," as opposed to "working alongside the worker," however. Gathering information, strategizing, and verbally jousting are significant parts of the ubiquitous event in managerial work, the meeting.

Participant observation—living and working alongside the group one is studying—is the hallmark of the anthropological method. The propositions and insights it generates do not lend themselves to statistical verification. There are no guarantees that what is true of one small village or even one large firm is true more generally. I do not make any claims as to the overall representativeness of Alima-Gerber or its employees. The circumstances that AG faced as one of the first firms to privatize, the company's location in one of the poorest parts of Poland, and the particular business problems that Gerber faced are too distinctive for me to claim that all firms follow the same pattern. Nonetheless, AG and its employees do not exist in a vacuum. They are full participants in the enormous changes going on in Poland and in the world economy. They face many of the same problems that other firms and other workers do, and they are aware of the solutions that others have proposed or implemented.

As one of the first state-owned socialist enterprises ever to be privatized, AG's struggles and compromises have served as models for other firms, employees, and policymakers. AG's experience is not paradigmatic, but it does have much in common with what firms, employees, and governments throughout the Eastern Bloc and the rest of the world are experiencing. Studying the details of life at AG, then, can help us to understand not only the postsocialist transition and the ways Eastern European workers react to the imposition of market discipline but also the forms of selfhood new managerial techniques impose on workers in capitalist firms across the globe. From the standpoint that Alima workers provide, it is possible to evaluate these new forms of capitalist relations.

2 Accountability, Corruption,

and the Privatization of Alima

Privatization is when someone who doesn't know who the real owner is and doesn't know what it is really worth sells something to someone who doesn't have any money.

Janusz Lewandowski, Polish Minister of Privatization,

cited in Stark 1991

In 1990, soon after the fall of the Berlin Wall, a small group of American investors ventured out of the luxury of Warsaw's Marriott hotel and checked into a small, dingy, hotel overlooking the concrete monument to socialism in the center of Rzeszów. They were from the H. J. Heinz Company, the American ketchup king, and they came to Poland looking for a piece of the $7 billion per year global baby food business. Alima, one of the strongest baby food producers in the Eastern Bloc, offered a tempting takeover target. After a few weeks of negotiations, Alima's managers, workers, and farmers all came out in favor of having Heinz as Alima's new owner. Together, Heinz and Alima approached the minister of privatization, Janusz Lewandowski, and asked him to privatize Alima.

Lewandowski saw the events in Rzeszów as an opportunity to bolster public support for the privatization process. He was eager to use Alima to prove that privatization generated *accountability*, in two senses of the word. First, he wanted to reassure international investors that the process was "transparent" by using internationally accepted accounting procedures they could understand. This, he believed, would bring in more foreign investment and help improve the Polish economy. At the same time, however, he wanted to use privatization to prove that the post-Solidarity government was accountable to the wider Polish public and that state-owned assets were being distributed in a way that was socially just. As Michał Wawrzewski,[1] one of Lewandowski's deputies, pointed out, "The issue was bigger than just this one privatization, this one company. It was about creating an investment climate in Poland. The process had to be designed in such a way to convince everyone, both inside and outside Poland, that it was a fair process."[2]

Just a year later however, with Gerber winning the bid process rather than Heinz, people were screaming that privatization was deeply unfair. Headlines like "Secret Privatization!" charged that Alima's privatization was a backroom deal (Siwek 1992). *Zielony Sztandar,* the newspaper of the Polish Peasant Party, suspected trickery:

> We are a suspicious lot. When someone acquires the majority of shares in a company as good as Alima for, frankly speaking, a modest sum, we at once begin looking for a false bottom in the contract. Does this false bottom in fact exist? *Zielony Sztandar* has had its doubts from the very beginning, and these have still not been entirely dispelled. (Andrys 1992)

Inside the factory, workers were also suspicious. The two unions hung banners outside the factory to protest the sale of the company to Gerber. Gossips on the shop floor said that Gerber's bid had actually been worse than Heinz's and that the Ministry of Privatization's decision to sell Alima to Gerber was the result of pure corruption. Workers complained Lewandowski had sold off one of the crown jewels of Polish industry for far less than its true value. Władisław, a mechanic, asked, "Why on earth would anyone sell off a firm that was doing well and making a profit? It just doesn't make sense." Eugeniusz, a former employee, made the charge even clearer: "It is absolutely certain that Lewandowski took bribes from Gerber in exchange for accepting their bid for Alima. Why else does he keep coming to Rzeszów, and why else would that American from Gerber [Al Piergallini, the CEO] keep coming here? Lewandowski is coming here to accept the latest installment of the bribe!" The gossip was powerful enough—and was repeated often enough in the national media—that Lewandowski was soon summoned to a parliamentary tribunal to face charges of corruption and incompetence. Although he was cleared of the charges, he later flew to Rzeszów and, in an emotional press conference in front of Alima's workers, apologized for the way he handled the privatization.

The tension over accountability and corruption was not unique to Alima. On the one hand, there was general public sentiment that privatization and economic transformation could draw up a moral balance sheet, settle ac-

Fig. 2. Alima-Gerber headquarters in Rzeszów. This is the main entrance to the office building. Workers entered through a special gate further down the street, where they could punch time clocks and have their bags inspected on the way out.

counts, and make the postsocialist order a moral one (Verdery 1999, 38). On the other hand, though, there was bitter disappointment and cries of outrage over corruption. Lewandowski was accused of corruption so frequently that he joked, "I should be in the *Guinness Book of World Records* under the heading 'Person Hauled Up Most Frequently in Front of Parliament.'" The newspapers promoted the idea that other government officials were on the take, too. "Only the Fish Don't Take the Bait" was the headline in one Polish newspaper (*Warsaw Voice* 2000). A poll conducted by CBOS, Poland's premier public opinion research agency, showed that 84 percent of Poles surveyed were convinced that corruption permeated all walks of life and 64 percent thought corruption had increased in the last decade(RFE/RL 2000). The hysteria over corruption seemed to be only loosely connected with actual corruption, however, at least as it was legally defined. The governor of Silesia, for example, was so distressed by widespread accusations of corruption that he opened a telephone hotline for anonymous denunciations of corruption. But out of one thousand cases of corruption reported during the anticorruption campaign, only six could be confirmed by investigators (RFE/RL 2000). Corruption, of course, is notoriously difficult to prove and impossible to measure, so it is unclear how much "corruption" there actually was. But whether or not corruption was actually rampant, *talk* about corruption was endemic.

What is it that such talk expressed? Why, so soon after the Solidarity-inspired quest for a new economic and moral order in Poland began, did bitter accusations of corruption become so prevalent? Exploring stories of privatization and allegations of corruption at Alima answers some of these questions, by revealing some of the fundamental tensions of postsocialism—particularly the tensions created when property transformation is used to create accountability. The ideology of accountability, with its emphasis on transparent processes rather than equitable outcomes, conceals some of the tensions between drives for economic efficiency and a moral social order. Talk about corruption, however, lays these tensions bare.

Alima's privatization takes on larger significance because it is one of the first post-1989 applications of auditable accounting—a post-Fordist disciplinary technology—to a postsocialist firm. As it shows how politicians, investors, and managers imported ideas about property and value, it also shows how ostensibly neutral ideas like "accountability" and seemingly arcane technical processes like accounting transform persons as much as property. By focusing on the aspects of accountability ideology that emphasized economic efficiency, privatizers attempted to revalue the firm, redefine workers, and incorporate labor into a new calculus of worth. In Poland, as in other places where accounting and audit are introduced, accountability ideology radically changed employees' power inside the firm. Polish employees, however, did not become merely the passive subjects of discipline. They had their own means of disciplining managers and foreign investors: they used accusations of "corruption" to contest the ways that firms and workers would be redefined and revalued. This was not a case of simple resistance. Like managers and privatizers, employees struggled to find a delicate balance between their desire to balance the moral books and their very real concerns about the firm's economic survival.

Underlying all these struggles were fundamental epistemological and ontological questions. What kind of information counts as a "fact," and how should "facts" about companies be assembled to create pictures of firms and the way they create value? Applying Western accounting techniques and ideologies of accountability to the problem of privatization fundamentally changed the way knowledge was produced and, consequently, dramatically reorganized social relationships within the firm. It changed the sociocultural framework that determined worth. As in most other privatizing enterprises, this reorganization of property rights and of knowledge production turned the lived world topsy-turvy. It transformed subjects into objects, owners into property, and profit into debt. At Alima, as in other places in Eastern Europe, privatization was "a problem of reorganization on a cosmic scale, and involved the redefinition of virtually everything. . . . It [meant] a reordering of people's entire meaningful worlds." (Verdery 1999, 34–35)

The Goals of Privatization and the Question of the "Real Owners"

If the revolutions of 1989 had held out one promise, it was that the state would become accountable, in both the economic and moral senses of the term.[3] In Poland, the roots of this drive for accountability can be seen as far back as the Solidarity strikes of 1980–81, when workers poured into the streets demanding "rational management" of industry as a way to improve work conditions and end shortages (Kemp-Welch 1983, 56; Laba 1991, 57). But demands for accountability grew from relatively restricted requests for more and more accurate information with which to manage production and distribution to a more general call for a public view of the workings of politics and the economy. In this expanded sense, the idea of making the Communist Party accountable became conflated with calls for truth in government. Solidarity soon conflated the idea of "living in truth," in Václav Havel's (1985) sense, with visions of political and economic equality and justice. After 1989, ideas about accountability were woven into debates over everything from property transformation to the constitution of civil society. As during the Solidarity period, ideas of accountability had both economic and moral overtones. On the one hand, accountability was about creating structures that would ensure economic efficiency, but on the other hand, it was about fairness, justice, blame, purification, and compensation for the wrongs of history.

Among the first postsocialist governments in Poland, there was a broad consensus that the privatization of state property was necessary to create accountability and to transform the economy, the government, and society (Fogel and Etcheverry 1994, 5; Grosfeld 1991, 142). This overt consensus, however, concealed deep rifts among different groups who wanted privatization in order to achieve different goals and fundamental uncertainties about the nature of property, value, and personhood. Privatization opened up questions about the larger aims that property transformation should achieve, the rights of various social groups to acquire assets, the resources that should be used to obtain ownership rights, and the proper valuation of state assets (Stark 1991). Ideas about accountability and accusations of corruption were weapons in these struggles for property and power as people sought to stabilize the rippling fabric of value.

The first major issue of the privatization process arose the moment Heinz arrived in Rzeszów. The Ministry of Privatization was immediately forced to face the most central issue of property transformation: What is privatization supposed to achieve? Why endorse trade sales or the sale of a state-owned firm to another company in the same industry over other methods of privatization? Lewandowski's description of the trade-sale process showed he had multiple and conflicting goals:

Our negotiations with foreign firms for Polish enterprises had to follow well-established international standards. Really, this made trade sales much more transparent [than privatization by ex-Communist managers]. Much easier to defend. For us, competitive bidding created a clear choice of the best offer. It was transparent privatization, although with time, it started to be very much criticized. What was specifically Polish about it—the trade sale method—was that it was multifunctional. There was a whole set of criteria taken into account, not just the price for the shares. We took four factors into account: price, investment into the company, social guarantees to workers and suppliers, and environmental issues. The trade sales had to be multifunctional, because of the pressure of trade unions and especially from workers' councils. Their requests for a social package added new dimensions into our choice.

As Lewandowski alludes, trade sales like Alima's were designed first to forestall a certain kind of corruption: the ex-Communist *nomenklatura*'s massive grab for state assets. But beyond that, Lewandowski had to maximize revenues to the state treasury, find a way to inject companies like Alima with financial capital and technological know-how, and compensate workers, farmers, and citizens for their contributions during forty years of socialism. Meeting these disparate goals was no easy matter. Lewandowski tried to assert that his criteria for privatization were in accordance with international standards for tenders and that creating an accounting-like process led to a totally "transparent" form of privatization. All the ministry had to do was accept the best offer. However, different parties to the transaction had radically different ideas about what constituted "the best offer." Lewandowski's description of the process made it clear that in a society with socialist-era expectations about the state's role in caring for workers and citizens, there were multiple frameworks of value for judging offers. Companies like Alima posed a novel situation that required criteria different from those usually employed in capitalist societies.

For the post-Solidarity government that employed Lewandowski, privatization was far more than a means to achieve revenue for the state treasury. It was the primary way to spur the development of a market economy. Leszek Balcerowicz, the minister of finance and the architect of economic reform, believed that if Polish enterprises had private owners and if firms were subjected to competition from other strong firms, owners would automatically act in market-rational and self-interested ways. That, in turn, was supposed to build the kind of market economy described by classical economists like Smith, Friedman, Hayek, and von Mises.[4] Balcerowicz's neoliberal perspective on reform, like other forms of neoliberalism, depended on a curious view of personhood and human nature to achieve logical coherence and to justify the political and social inequality it implied. For example, in his book on economic reform, he argued that people are naturally self-interested and maximizing. When given a nonrestrictive environment and private property, they naturally compete for private profit:

> The decided majority of goods (money, products, important positions, etc.) are limited, and the decided majority of people prefer their own interests (and those of their families) to those of other people. They thus would prefer that limited goods fall to them rather than to others. These two facts suffice to create everyday competition in the world. (Balcerowicz 1995, 72)

Following the neoliberal idea that the sum of private greed equals the public good, Balcerowicz argued that lifting the state's restrictions on property and allowing people to act in their own self-interest would not only create markets but also introduce accountability by creating *hard budget constraints.* That is, he believed in the classical liberal proposition that if resources were limited and business owners faced the threat of bankruptcy, their natural human propensity toward maximizing profit would compel them to demand careful accounts of how their firms used investment. The resulting increase in firm efficiency was supposed to benefit everyone by growing the economy (Balcerowicz 1995, 17, and Morawski 1992, 35; for a similar declaration in the Czech case, see Klaus and Ježek 1991, 27–40).[5]

Under Balcerowicz's guidance, neoliberals in Poland created a three-part package to tear down the economic edifices of state socialism and build a market economy. On January 1, 1990, the Polish government introduced market competition by eradicating 90 percent of all price controls and opening Polish borders to import and export. Later that year, reformers created hard budget constraints by restricting government subsidies for state-owned enterprises (SOEs) and introducing bankruptcy procedures, thereby creating negative sanctions for firms that were unaccountable and hence unprofitable (Tinsanen 1996, 2; Błaszczyk and Dąbrowski 1993, 7; Balcerowicz 1995, 380–98; Berg and Blanchard 1994; Frydman et al. 1993, 149; Johnson and Loveman 1995, 29–30). The entire set of reforms, known as "shock therapy," was designed to remove any impediments to the expression of what reformers like Balcerowicz saw as the natural human instinct toward entrepreneurship while simultaneously introducing the hard budget constraints that would force economic actors to act in a supposedly "accountable" and market-rational way.

The problem with the Balcerowicz plan was that most state-owned enterprises, including Alima, simply could not compete in an environment of unconstrained international competition. Although Alima made a terrific product and enjoyed a high degree of consumer loyalty, foreign competition would soon become a major problem. Part of the dilemma was that little Alima, in comparison with gigantic international competitors like France's Groupe Danone, simply did not have enough capital. It had aging machinery that could not put out a high volume of product, and it completely lacked laboratory facilities for quality control. Maria Czartoryska, then the president of Alima, said,

> Compared to the 1990 figure, our output has risen by half to 20,000 tons of processed food. If we modernized the line, we could perhaps reach 25,000 tons, but this would be the limit of our financial capabilities. Larger investments are needed for any further growth or change to the line of products. (Cited in Sosnowska-Smogorzewska 1992, 1; see also Żuławnik 1992)

An anonymous Alima employee quoted in one of the Krakow papers used a rather unusual metaphor to sum up the problem:

Our plant cannot afford new investments. Part of the machinery is over
10 years old, which is equivalent to a 40 year old woman. It is still working, but . . .[6] (Cited in Siwek 1992)

Alima's managers lacked certain kinds of *intellectual* capital as urgently
as they lacked finance capital. This was true at almost all state-owned enterprises. SOE managers, who were accustomed to working in an economy
of shortage, had to reorient themselves to problems of demand rather than
of supply. They also had to gain new expertise in fields central to managing
in a capitalist economy. Alima, for example, lacked in-house knowledge of
how to market and distribute its product effectively in the changing economy. Socialist distribution networks were crumbling, and the firm had no
salespeople. Just around the corner, foreign baby food manufacturers—including Heinz—were waiting to launch new sales and distribution channels
and new advertising campaigns that could take Alima's customers away.
Czartoryska took some steps to address the threat: she opened both a sales
and a marketing division. A former distribution manager became the head
of sales, and two women who had also worked in distribution became the
marketing department. But the sales and marketing departments, like
Czartoryska herself, were struggling to learn complex capitalist disciplines
in time to make a difference to the firm. Armed with only an American marketing textbook and an English dictionary, the marketers began trying to
produce promotional material.

The lack of technical know-how was particularly acute in the finance department. While foreign firms were using sophisticated cost-accounting
procedures to track down waste and reduce costs, none of Alima's book-
keepers knew even the rudiments of capitalist accounting. Trained for years
in the specialized accounting used for central planning, Alima's finance department struggled to learn enough capitalist accounting to create the documents Czartoryska needed to run the company. Contrary to the assertions
of neoliberals like Balcerowicz, market pressures alone would not make
SOEs like Alima competitive. The firm needed an infusion of new technical
knowledge as well as cash. Foreign investors like Heinz or Gerber seemed to
be the only way to obtain it.

As important as the goal of economic efficiency was to Lewandowski, he
also had to respond to groups who made historical justice a priority over
economic growth and wanted ownership rights in Alima as compensation
for the suffering they endured under socialism. Alima, unlike many SOEs,
did not have prewar owners asking to have a firm seized by the Communist
Party returned to them.[7] But many citizens—and most workers—believed

that privatization initiatives should address the issue of the socially equitable distribution of wealth and that shares in the company were instruments for correcting the moral balance sheet of the Polish nation (see also Appel 1995; Verdery 1999; Borneman 1997; Kornai 1995, 83).[8] Unlike the neoliberals, those who sought social or historical justice did not want to create a textbook capitalist economy. They wanted to ensure that the economic "losers" under the old system were "winners" in the redistribution of property rights (see Major 1993, 2). People who believed the social goal of privatization should be redistributive justice were generally not in favor of selling companies like Alima to foreign investors at all. They preferred instead some form of mass privatization or employee buyout. Those in favor of mass privatization believed that since the populace at large had worked to pay for the assets contained in state-owned enterprises, and since the state was only the proxy for the people, who were the real owners of the SOEs, each Polish citizen deserved an equal share of state assets.[9] As the Ministry of Privatization explained in a brochure about mass privatization,

> Public property belongs to the whole society since it has been the fruit of its labor and effort. It would be unfair if a significant group of the people who contributed to the creation of this property did not have a chance to participate in its privatization. Privatization is an issue concerning the whole society and not only its more prosperous strata. Thus, the goal of the program is to spread the ownership of property—to give to the people what they are entitled to. (Ministry of Privatization 1991, 3–4)

Those in favor of employee ownership of privatized enterprises made similar arguments but called on socialist-era ideology more explicitly. Where mass-privatization advocates brought up the socialist idea of the state as mere proxy for true collective ownership, employee ownership advocates used the classically Marxist idea that all commodities were the congealed labor of those who produced them. As Ula Mazur, the leader of one of Alima's unions, said,

> What do they think we did all these years? We built this firm and we built Poland under socialism! What was there before here, after the war— nothing! There weren't many people here who didn't work and were in the lumpenproletariat. We all contributed.

Alima's employees—like employees at other SOEs—frequently argued it was not just the products of labor but the means of production, the firm itself, which had been "grown" through the efforts of workers. Thus, while they didn't have much cash to buy Alima from the ministry, they argued that their labor inputs, given over forty years, were an equivalent resource for obtaining ownership rights in the company. The farmers from the surrounding countryside, who had grown fruit and vegetables for Alima during the same period, believed they should be compensated in a similar way. Workers and farmers were not opposed to having a foreign firm take over the company—especially one like Heinz, which could ensure steady jobs, social benefits, and continuing reliance on local suppliers—but they expected to be given a share of the company in order to balance the moral books.

Democratic Union, the right-wing post-Solidarity party that was the first occupant of the postsocialist government, put intense pressure on Lewandowski to satisfy all these diverse claims to Alima. To legitimate Democratic Union's political rule, the ministry had to devise a plan that exemplified moral and fiscal accountability. But the government's emphasis on the "accountability" generated by the process was an attempt at elision, a sleight-of-hand trick in which observers' attention was distracted by the rhetoric of transparency. Lewandowski asserted that the criteria were in accordance with international standards for tenders and led to a totally "transparent" form of privatization in which all the ministry had to do was accept the best offer. But the question of who should be able to buy Alima and for what reasons was very complex, precisely because morality and efficiency presented two alternate frameworks by which to judge value. The ministry tried to divert attention from the necessary arbitrariness of selecting the new owner and the inequality of the outcome by focusing on a rule-bound impersonal bidding process. This nod to moral imperatives of accountability, visibility, and fairness at least partly concealed the uncertainties of the postsocialist transformation and the ways in which privatization exacerbated rather than ameliorated injustices of the socialist period.

Value, the Arbitrariness of Numbers, and an Epistemological Gap

As complicated as the issue of selecting an owner was for the Ministry of Privatization, determining an appropriate price for Alima was an even bigger headache. When Lewandowski quipped that privatization was when someone sold something without knowing what it was worth, he was not entirely joking. How does one value something that has never been on the market before, like a company built up over forty years of socialism (Błaszczyk and Dąbrowski 1993)? Do accounts kept under state socialism provide any guide at all to value? If not, on what basis should the economic worth of a company be determined? These questions soon proved to be more than technical issues. They revealed stark differences between state socialist and post-Fordist capitalist notions of value and led to charges of corruption.

In the case of Alima, the ministry initially selected KPMG, a large American auditing and consulting firm, to audit Alima's books and arrive at an "opening balance sheet," or statement of the firm's value. KPMG appeared suspiciously diligent about conducting due diligence, however. Less than forty-eight hours after receiving the commission, the auditors handed the ministry an appraisal of Alima. To people in Rzeszów, as well as to the national press, this was the first indication that privatization was corrupt. It seemed simply impossible to conduct an extensive audit in just two days. They wondered if KPMG knew it was going to win the bid to conduct the appraisal and began the work in advance. If so, the ostensibly "transparent" competitive bidding process for ministry support services was corrupt. Or, they wondered, was KPMG paid an astronomical sum to provide an inaccurate price for Alima? In that case, the whole competitive privatization process Lewandowski was touting was shot through with corruption.

With the KPMG audit in question, each company the ministries invited to bid on Alima lined up to conduct audits and make their own estimates of the firm's value. They soon began to appreciate why KPMG's numbers seemed so arbitrary. Alima's books were compiled according to state socialist accounting standards, which bore no resemblance to either U.S. Generally Accepted Accounting Principles (US GAAP) or International Accounting Standards (IAS), the frameworks used most commonly in capitalist firms (see Sochaka and Malo 1996; Pankov 1998; Borda and McLeay 1996; Tintor 1997).

John Turnock, one of the accounting experts Gerber sent to Poland, reeled off a host of technical factors that made Alima's books murky to him and led him to doubt the company was as profitable as Alima executives portrayed it. Under Polish accounting rules, there was no way to write off bad debts or obsolete inventory, which meant such debts or inventory remained on the books even though their value to Gerber was nil.

Direct subsidies from the government were booked as income rather than as contributions to investment, which significantly altered the bottom line. Indirect subsidies were concealed in the form of artificially low prices set by the government. That meant the recorded purchase price of Alima's assets didn't reflect their value in a capitalist system. And there was no way to account for Alima's technologically outdated production line. Because Polish accounting methods used straight-line depreciation rather than accelerated depreciation,[10] machines purchased in the 1980s were still recorded as valuable assets. To Gerber, though, they were virtually worthless.

Turnock also argued that Polish accounting standards had no way of accounting for risk. This issue was one of the most important that potential investors faced. As another accountant on the valuation team said,

> The Polish accounting system doesn't account for liabilities or risk. The KPMG audit tried to account for it, but still, there were risks and liabilities that were never uncovered. For instance, Jagielski tried to put a building on an unused corner of the lot, and a local priest turned up with a land claim. What would we have done if we'd spent millions on that building? The employee apartments were another unrevealed risk. Alima was responsible for 100 percent of the maintenance costs of that apartment building, although they only owned a third of the units, but that responsibility wasn't in the books. And, of course, at the time we invested, there was a strong possibility of political risk. What if the government had fallen, and Alima was renationalized? That wasn't factored in, either.

Turnock struggled to reconcile Alima's socialist-era books with the US GAAP system he was familiar with, but he found translation difficult. Creating an opening balance sheet for the firm required arbitrary numbers.

> On all fronts, the Alima deal faced tremendous uncertainties. But somehow, [Gerber's accountant] had to convert these uncertainties into numbers and plug them into his model. So, as conservatively as he could, he guessed. (Young 1993)

Not surprisingly, the estimates that Gerber, Heinz, and KPMG arrived at varied by millions of dollars. But what the accountants did not entirely perceive was that the problem was epistemological, not just technical. State socialist accounts were troublesome to American accountants because they were fundamentally *inauditable*.

To American auditors, this meant Alima's accounts failed to fulfill their primary purpose, which was to create the illusion of transparency and hence both moral and financial accountability. Under systems like IAS or US GAAP, financial records do more than simply record value or quantify the "bottom line" at the end of a budget cycle. Rather, because they record transactions inside the firm as well as between the firm and suppliers or clients outside, IAS and US GAAP accounts create a picture of how people move value-bearing objects like products or money through a company. They claim to function as a window into the company, showing how employees add to or reduce the value of these objects by transforming them.

Implicitly, accountants using IAS and US GAAP claim that their numbers have a perfect correspondence with events and objects in the material world, and so they create completely accurate and transparent representations of what people in firms do.[11]

Capitalist accounting systems achieve this effect by stripping away the social context that produced the record (Poovey 1998). The social positions of buyer and seller and their interpersonal relationship are completely effaced. Accountants, too, are purged from the account. Even though "auditing and accounting 'facts' are negotiated . . . in contexts where local discretion is often high" (Power 1997, 38–39), accountants' identities are effaced from the record. So too are the complex negotiations between accountants, firms, and auditors, and the tremendous power accountants have to decide how facts are to be labeled and recorded.

In IAS or GAAP accounting, the presentation of the books as perfectly rule-governed representations of a firm's activity is part of a larger process of disciplining companies by making their actions public and visible. Capitalist accounting systems depend on the ability to make it appear as if the rules specify the recording of objectively existing facts in order to create moral as well as financial accountability. The illusion of transparency makes it seem to investors and other auditors that they have the power of surveillance within the firm—that they can observe how the firm works and what people are doing inside it. That, in turn, engenders a sense of trust. Auditable accounts produce *comfort* for investors because they believe not only that increased surveillance makes fraud, embezzlement, or other moral/financial transgressions visible but also because they believe it forces managers to police themselves (Power 1997). Transparency thus is set up as a proxy for external governance, because it supposedly forces a firm to govern itself. By having to produce auditable accounts, the firm is supposed to become fiscally accountable, in the sense of having to show that it produces profit for investors, and morally accountable, in the sense of following rules, avoiding criminality, and behaving honestly.[12] By declaring their actions open to inspection, managers and firms make claims about their integrity.

Socialist accounting systems do not produce this kind of accountability. They were designed for the convenience of state planners, not for enterprise managers, investors, or regulators. They produced a different kind of knowledge, which was used for a different kind of corporate discipline. Because soft budget constraints made it unnecessary to control costs or worry about profits, many enterprises used "net accounting." That is, they reported only the final results of their budgetary cycles—increases or decreases in inventories, finished goods, and work in progress. Data was often reported in natural units (e.g., jars of jam) rather than in monetary value, because central planners were more concerned with allocating material resources and forecasting how many goods would be available to ease shortages than in how much profit a company was making (see Bailey 1988; Dunn 2000). State socialist books simply did not create a series of snapshots of the firm's activity, as US GAAP or IAS accounts do. Hence, they did not create the illusion of transparency.

Socialist books never created the illusion of accuracy, either. They never successfully concealed the negotiation and judgment behind the numbers or elicited auditable performance. The politicization of the economy under state socialism and the rigors of the economy of shortage meant that firm managers were constantly engaged in negotiating with central planners for lower quotas and more inputs to production. Managers negotiated with their accountants to change the books to make it appear as if the firm needed more resources to meet targets. Accounts did not function as objective records of value transformation or as surveillance tools for outside auditors but as the language in which firms and central planners "bargained the plan" (Kornai 1992; Verdery 1996). Thus, socialist-era accounts were notoriously unreliable. Virtually everyone knew they were the result of intense social negotiations, interpersonal relationships, and political pressures rather than depersonalized representations of actual transactions. Eventually, socialist accounts could not make any claims to accuracy at all. As the editor of Alima's employee gazette put it,

> Why was it that during communist times, the company was always in a strong position and the economy was always growing by leaps and bounds, but our standard of living never improved? The growth was only in the statistics. (*Aktualności* 1995a)

So, even for Polish accountants trained in socialist record-keeping, Alima's books were inauditable. Polish accountants, however, at least knew to read the books as a cipher. They knew that the numbers were the products of extensive negotiations and were indicators of a host of unwritten deals and unrecorded transfers. In this sense, the books were legible to Polish accountants in a way they were not to the Americans, because the Polish accountants saw the books as announcements of unrevealed secrets. But this meant the accounts also hinted at corruption.

Janusz Lewandowski wanted to remove these whiffs of corruption. When he tried to make privatization into a form of auditable performance, he bet on accounting's power to blur the boundaries between the technical precision of rule-governed bookkeeping and the virtues of moral accountability.

He was banking on the idea that if he could make the process *legible*, he could convince foreign investors it was safe to invest in Poland and, at the same time, convince leading Polish citizens that the process was moral and just. But it was impossible to conceal the gap between different kinds of "facts" produced by state socialist and capitalist accounting systems, and it was even harder to hide how arbitrary that gap made estimates. For Alima's workers, Rzeszów's townspeople, and newspapers like *Zielony Sztandar,* the obvious explanation for all these arbitrary numbers was just what made accounting facts dubious under socialism: personal connections, negotiation, and the exchange of favors.

As accusations of corruption sprang up, Lewandowski tried to finesse the problem the epistemological gap caused. First, he put aside the question of who the "real" owner of Alima was by declaring that the ministry, as an arm of the Polish state, was the "real" owner and could unilaterally decide how to dispose of Alima. As Wawrzewski, the ministry official, later phrased it, Lewandowski unilaterally decided he could make a decision and then tell Alima's workers, "Dear employees, here is your new owner." Lewandowski then asserted that although the ministry used KPMG to provide a rough idea of what the firm *might* be worth, in reality the company only had *relative* value. That is, Alima was only worth what someone would pay, and its value could only be determined on the market, by the competitive bid tender process the ministry had designed for trade-sale privatization. On that basis, Alima accepted what it felt was the "best" bid: Gerber Products Company's offer of $11 million for 60 percent of Alima's shares, a guarantee of a further $14 million in investment in the plant, and an eighteen-month moratorium on layoffs or changes in agricultural suppliers' contracts. Gerber also made a commitment to invest intellectual capital in Alima. Gerber representatives promised to train Alima's employees in everything from accounting to marketing to quality control. That promise, in Lewandowski's eyes, made the long-term survival of the firm much more likely.

From Owners to Accountable Assets

Although Janusz Lewandowski tried to finesse the discrepancy between the kinds of facts that state socialist accounts produced and the kinds of knowledge elicited by IAS or US GAAP accounting, Alima's workers were highly skeptical. What made workers even less willing to believe that the figures were accurate and that justice had been done—and made them even more likely to hurl accusations about corruption—is that they soon became subject to the same processes of depersonalization and revaluation that IASC and US GAAP used to create accounting facts. The announcement that Gerber would purchase Alima was met with an uproar from employees and the farmers that supplied the company. The employees and farmers were not angry that they had not been made owners of the firm. Indeed, the ministry had set aside 40 percent of the company's shares for them to purchase. Rather, they were livid that the ministry had not consulted them about the sale. As Ula Mazur, the head of OPZZ (*Ogólnopolskie Związki Zawodowe*, the union formerly sponsored by the Communist Party) explained,

> It wasn't supposed to be like this. . . . The decision to privatize in this way was made by the *wojwód* (provincial governor), not by us. We had no idea that if we agreed to be privatized, that we would become property of the state treasury, or that this would eliminate . . . our chance to decide on the fate of the company. It was a shock. They took advantage of our ignorance.

OPZZ, along with Solidarity, the other trade union at Alima, put up protest banners outside the factory and placed employees on strike alert. The national press sympathized with employees' complaints about being disenfranchised:

> In the peculiar negotiations atmosphere, the Alima employees were a mere backdrop, no more important than machinery. It may be that some woman from a village near Rzeszów, employed to sort fruits and vegetables, is not capable of correctly judging whether the best way to privatize was selected when the controlling package of stock was handed over to a rival. Nevertheless, as a company employee who worked to build the company's reputation like everyone else, [she] has the right to be informed about the company's fate on a daily basis. This is precisely what the employees complained to Minister Lewandowski about . . . and one cannot help but agree with the complaints. (Sonntag 1992)

Employees' fury thus had less to do with the financial terms of the deal than with the pervasive feeling that they were being treated as something less than competent human beings. During the Solidarity movement, employees had claimed that they, as workers in a workers' state, were the owners of the firm and hence had rights to make managerial decisions. The Workers' Council was a powerful participant in discussions about the firm's strategy under socialism, just as in other SOEs. But with the sale of Alima to Gerber, workers' status inside the firm changed dramatically. As Jurek Goździk, the leader of Alima's branch of Solidarity, put it:

Everything happened above us. Two firms were chasing after Alima, and we thought we could have the right to decide between them. We thought we could gain a share of the profits generated by this auction. It was nothing like that. To put it in a single phrase, *daliśmy się ubezwłasnowolnić.*

Goździk's single phrase is not easily translatable into English, but it expresses one of the sentiments that led directly to charges of corruption. It refers to a fundamental change in a person's status, in which the capacity to make basic decisions about one's own life is stripped away. (*Bez* means "without," *własno* is "one's own," and *woli* means "will.") People committed to mental institutions are *ubezwłasnowolnić,* as are children and the enslaved. Other employees summed up the same feeling by complaining that they had been treated as objects rather than owners and as property rather than persons with the power to decide their own fate. "We were sold like a flock of geese!" screamed one employee to the press (Siwek 1992). Other employees used even harsher metaphors, insisting that the ministry had treated them as mail-order brides or even as slaves (Zuławnik 1992; Warzocha 1992; Andrys 1992; see also chap. 5).

It was becoming increasingly clear to the employees that they had concrete reasons to fear they were becoming "assets" who could, at a moment's notice, become liabilities on the company's balance sheet. Originally, when the employees thought of themselves as persons who were owners rather as than "human capital," they had selected Heinz, not Gerber, to run the company. One reason they chose Heinz was because persistent rumors circulated that Gerber wanted to buy Alima simply to close it down. Employees believed that since Alima's low-cost labor and raw materials could have been very strong competition for Gerber on the domestic market, Gerber was seeking to open the Polish market by eliminating its most powerful rival. Employees had other reasons to dislike Gerber. Unlike Heinz, which had a wide product line, Gerber specialized in infant food. This meant that the jam, ketchup, and canned goods lines at Alima would probably be shut down, reducing the need for both labor and raw materials. Farmers had additional reasons to be concerned. If Gerber changed Alima's product line to use fewer home-grown products, such as sour cherries and black currants, and more imported products, such as citrus fruits, the farmers would lose their livelihoods and the money invested in their fields and orchards. The eighteen-month guarantee provided some time to prepare for the future, but no one was entirely certain that once the moratorium expired, Gerber wouldn't junk its "human capital" as fast as it was getting rid of Alima's old machinery.[13]

Sensing employees' fear, frustration, and anger, Gerber immediately tried to calm the situation and foster optimism among employees by assuring them that they were not mere assets or forms of capital but part owners of the firm. Gerber managers encouraged employees and farmers to acquire the 40 percent of shares they were offered under the terms of the contract. When employees protested that they simply did not have the money to purchase the shares, Gerber offered each employee an additional month's salary. In this way, it hoped to give employees a sense of security and a personal stake in the firm's success. To combat negative press and employees' fears, Gerber's Piergallini said that since Alima workers were now part owners in the firm, they would be called "associates" and not "employees."

Yet, just a few short months after Gerber helped employees and farmers buy shares, Gerber's idea of the roles these new stockholders would play in the company diverged radically from employees' ideas. For Alima's workers and farmers, stock ownership was supposed to give them the same powerful consultative role that "ownership" via the state had given them. They wanted to be consulted on major management decisions like what products the firm would make, to ensure that the firm would meet their needs for markets and jobs. For example, when Gerber announced that it would begin making a tropical fruit version of Bobo Frut, growers wanted to insist that the firm continue producing black currant juice, which used their produce.

Once again, the conflict was between two systems of accounting for value. To employees and farmers, the firm was more than an engine to make profit or even to make products. It was the heart of a social community that extended not only to them but to their families as well. Under socialism, it was the vehicle through which the state carried out its moral obligation to care for its citizens (Verdery 1996). Socialist Alima provided its workers with apartments and dormitory beds, opera tickets and hot meals, soap and boots. It bought farmers' produce no matter what was produced or what its quality was, because the farmers needed the income. As Krystyna Leśniak-Moczuk, a sociologist at the Rzeszów Polytechnic Institute explained, under socialism, *"Ludzie byli dla Alimy, ale Alima także była dla ludzi"* (People existed for Alima, but Alima also existed for people). Like other SOEs, socialist Alima existed not only to meet the needs of consumers or investors but also to meet the needs of employees and suppliers. Having been made into "owners" during the privatization process, workers and farmers sought to use power they saw as rightfully theirs to ensure the firm continued to meet their needs.

Gerber saw things much differently. For Gerber's managers, the firm was not a community, and it did not exist for any purpose other than to make a profit. Farmers' produce was nothing more than an input to production. If the company's balance sheet was to go into the black, the cost of that input would have to be reduced. In an interview in the employee gazette, John Turnock (by then the acting director of the firm) said:

> If Alima-Gerber wants to have a stable situation and some kind of confidence in the future, we have to obey an iron-clad rule: We can only buy the kind and quantity of fruit we can make into products we can sell at a profit. That's the basic rule of the market economy, whether we like it or not.

The hard logic of capitalism was being introduced into the firm. Gerber soon came to see the constant demands from farmers and employees to have the firm meet their needs as an impediment to profit. The company had never intended employee stock ownership to confer managerial powers on employees. Rather, Gerber's managers believed that the stock would encourage employees to "take ownership" in their work. Gerber was thus banking on the neoliberal equation between private property and personal accountability, hoping that even partial ownership in a productive enterprise would be enough to transform employees' behavior and eradicate laziness and irresponsibility (which, however erroneously, figured large in the Americans' stereotypes of socialist workers). Because the stocks were not publicly traded, Gerber assumed that the share offer was a way for the firm to instill discipline in the employees rather than the reverse.

When Gerber realized that workers felt that their stock holdings made them active agents with the power to decide and strategize, it quickly offered to buy back the shares that it had just helped employees purchase, for several times the original sale price. For Gerber, the money given to employees was a way to clear the moral balance sheet and to shed the social context of labor. To make labor and produce into hard accounting numbers, rather than the artifacts of enduring social relationships, Gerber had to strip away the entangling threads of obligation between workers and the firm. By buying the shares and providing workers with cash compensation for their moral rights to ownership in the firm, Gerber tried to make labor into nothing more than a commodity that could be completely compensated for by a wage.

For most employees, the money Gerber offered was an unheard-of sum. Like workers in other privatized enterprises, they quickly accepted the offer so as to have cash for apartment renovations and satellite television. Most employees did not realize, however, that in accepting the offer they were trading away their rights of ownership and a potential basis of real power for the unions. Employees and growers were new to the whole idea of stocks, and they had little experience with the rights or possibilities conferred upon shareholders. But the general effect rapidly became clear: soon after the stock sale, the employees' and growers' unions became almost totally disempowered (Wilczak 1992). By selling the shares, the employees had traded away their claims on the firm, helped strip away their own agentive and decision-making capacities, and given themselves up to be *ubezwłasnowolnić*. Where once they were parts of a community and could demand moral accountability from the firm, their labor was now a commodity, which could be fully compensated for by a wage and entailed no further obligation. It was a new calculus of value and a new form of discipline.

Gerber did not wait long to use its new powers. As the eighteen-month moratorium on layoffs expired, John Turnock began to warn the employees that layoffs were in store. In the employee newsletter, he announced:

> It seems to me that each and every one of us is aware of the facts. The employment structure of this firm is not as it should be. Everyone also knows that our costs are too high. We've known this for a long time. If we want to be competitive, we have to change this state of affairs. (*Aktualności* 1995a)

Unlike many other foreign investors, who quite often used a rule of thumb that said that Polish enterprises were overstaffed by 33 percent and consequently began mandatory and uncompensated layoffs, AG pursued a more humane strategy. The company offered all employees a one-time-only opportunity: in exchange for leaving the firm, AG would give them a lump-sum payment equal to eighteen months' salary.[14] This was a difficult decision for most workers, because of their uncertainty about the company's future. On the one hand, there were good reasons to forgo severance pay and keep the job. The unemployment rate in the Rzeszów area was 17 percent, the other major plants in the area were also laying off workers, and the likelihood of finding another job was slim. Bogdan, a mechanic, explained why he rejected the offer:

> Look, there is so much unemployment here, that if you have work at all, you're satisfied. You can't really dream of changing professions. Under communism, there was more chance of changing jobs. If you were a mechanic at Alima, and you wanted to, you could go and get a job at WSK [the nearby airplane engine factory]. But now, it's just impossible. If you have a job, you keep it.

For employees who stayed with the company, the message was clear. Those who resisted or opposed the firm's new policies and practices could be dismissed, without a tidy severance package. The threat of unemployment was an omnipresent motivation to accept Gerber's changes, and some employees thus exchanged compliance for a modicum of economic security in turbulent economic times.

Many workers, though, chose not to trade compliance for security. Eighteen months' wages all at once was an unheard-of sum of money for most of them. It meant money to buy apartments or renovate their homes, pay for training in a new profession, or open a new business. Because those who accepted the layoff could also draw state unemployment insurance benefits for a year, they felt they would have time to find other jobs. For workers who believed that AG would not succeed, this was a chance to gain time to make the transition to another job before the firm had involuntary uncompensated layoffs. In the end, response to the offer was overwhelming. The firm planned on laying off about 250 of the firm's 1,150 workers, mostly office workers nearing retirement age. Instead, more than 470 employees, mostly young people from production, applied to be laid off. Paradoxically, AG suddenly found itself with a labor shortage where it once had a labor surplus.[15]

The problem was that no one in the firm knew how long this labor shortage would last. Sales of Bobo Frut were falling and sales of Gerber baby food were not increasing as quickly as had been hoped, primarily because Gerber was not exporting as much to France as it had planned to. The company was therefore reluctant to hire more permanent workers, who would be protected by their contracts and given a great deal of job security by the Polish Labor Code. Instead, AG hired manual laborers through a newly formed temporary agency, the *Spółka "Usługi Różni"* (Agency of Various Services, commonly referred to as the *"spółka"*). The *spółka*, a private firm founded by the son of a longtime Alima employee, had only one client: Alima-Gerber. It was originally founded to supply the extra seasonal labor needed during harvest season. However, AG quickly discovered that hiring long-term "temporary" workers through the *spółka* allowed the firm to avoid signing permanent labor contracts with new hires while, in fact, keeping them semipermanently.

Spółka workers had no job security, since they were only given contracts for thirty days. Often, the *spółka* employees were notified only two or three days before the end of the month that they would not be reporting for work on the first of the next month. They were the ideal labor force: ostensibly devoid of personal connections with other workers and without any claim to "care" from the firm, their labor was completely commodified. It was an asset, pure and simple, that could be recorded on the books and judged only by how profitable it was.[16]

Most important, *spółka* workers were not unionized. This gave the unions significantly less bargaining power, since a cheaper source of labor was easily available. Union representatives, however, did not seem to see this as a threat. Rather, they assumed the *spółka* workers were in the same genre as seasonal laborers had been under communism and hence not competing with their constituencies for jobs. The two unions, Solidarity and OPZZ, made no effort to limit the use of outsourced labor or to include outsourced workers in the union's activities. In essence, the unions accepted the weakening of their social networks among long-term workers and did not attempt to replace them with ties to the temporary workers.

Gerber also worked to improve the bottom line by removing the social connections and obligations between farmers and the company. At the end of the eighteen-month moratorium on changes in agricultural contracts, Gerber began a wholesale restructuring of AG's purchasing patterns. Whereas before, the firm had purchased small amounts of produce from farmers with small holdings, now it refused to buy produce grown by farmers who had less than one continuous hectare in production, with another hectare held in reserve for crop rotation. This limit excluded many of the smallholders who had contracts, many of whom were also current or former Alima employees. Gerber showed a strong preference for farmers with more than twenty hectares, given the costs of implementing the agricultural audit system it used in Fremont among its Polish suppliers. The agricultural audit system, which was part of Gerber's quality assurance system, demanded that soil from each farm be tested for heavy metals and pesticides. Increasing the size of holdings while reducing the number of suppliers sharply reduced the costs of this increased monitoring.[17] The result of this rationalization was devastating for the villages around Rzeszów: where once there had been forty-five hundred suppliers, now there were fewer than five hundred.

Using Accountability to Discipline Management

Alima's Polish managers were, by and large, supportive of Gerber's attempts to institute discipline on the shop floor and break up the webs of connection that bound workers, farmers, and the company. Managers were shocked, however, when Gerber began to apply similar discipline in order to make *management* more "accountable" to the firm's new owners. When Gerber first came to Alima, the Americans planned to simply transplant their technical "know-how" about production methods and management practices and then leave the Poles behind to run the plant. But they soon came to believe that Polish managers' "mindsets," not just their technical expertise, had to be changed if Alima were to succeed as a capitalist enterprise.

Gerber began by sending over a team of executives from its Fremont headquarters to "live in" during the period of transformation and to teach Alima managers new capitalist disciplines. For example, the small sales and marketing departments Alima's president founded were immediately enlarged and moved from Rzeszów to Warsaw, where American managers assumed responsibility. In the marketing department, the American manager was so convinced of the importance of transforming the way Polish employees thought about business that he staffed his department with a group of young Poles and then lived in the same house with them for several months, so he could train them night and day in the habits and values of American managers as well as in the technical aspects of marketing. Other American managers came to the firm to teach newly hired Polish employees about sales and finance. Gerber also sent managers from all over Alima to Gerber's headquarters in Fremont, Michigan, where they could observe the workings of a capitalist firm firsthand and learn more about the lifestyles and values of the firm's American employees. Shopping trips, restaurant dinners, and visits to the homes of Gerber's managers and workers were as much a part of the curriculum as factory tours and technical training. The atmosphere was clearly one of proselytism, with strong pressure on Alima employees to convert to Gerber's way of thinking, working, and consuming.[18]

Despite this pressure to transform themselves as persons, Alima's managers resisted. John Jones, who worked for Gerber, says Alima managers were completely unwilling to conform to Gerber's management style. Suggesting that Gerber should have done better "due diligence" (preliminary research) on its "management assets," Jones said that Alima managers misled Gerber by listening to Gerber's directives, nodding and acquiescing, and then doing whatever they had originally planned on:

> The Poles were outstanding hosts to the Gerber people in the beginning. Every meeting was a coffee break, a tea party. They were really nice. So we thought, "Yeah, I can work with these people" and left it at that. The Poles made us feel comfortable. Meanwhile, they were giving out as little information as was possible. [Two of the Alima directors] used to leave board meetings and go behind their office door and giggle, because [another executive] was piling it on so thick and the Americans were just nodding along. It was either laugh or vomit.

Gerber soon came to believe that the real obstacle to change was not merely "mindsets" but a form of personhood based on the enduring networks of personal connections among managers and between managers and workers. John Jones said that trying to work with the old Alima managers was a mistake from the very beginning, because they were enmeshed in personal relationships with suppliers and clients and consistently involved in side deals for their own benefit. According to Jones, Gerber should have followed the pattern set by other foreign investors and immediately fired existing management. This, he says, would have enforced Western-style management practices and broken up old networks:

> Maybe we shouldn't have played along, been so eager to work with them. Maybe we should have done what Philip Morris did when they took over the tobacco factory in Kraków. Boom, the top 25 people, gone, all at once. In this way, you break up the old management, and you break up their old deals. Like, when I first came, we were importing bananas from Amsterdam. I said, "Why are we importing bananas from Holland? I thought they grew in Latin America or the Philippines, someplace like that, not Holland." Turns out that they had always imported bananas from Amsterdam, because the guy there was "really nice." He paid for a trip to Amsterdam for them every year. They couldn't get the firm to pay for a taxi ride across town or a ticket to Warsaw, much less a trip to Costa Rica to source bananas, even though it might have saved the firm a million dollars a year. So they bought bananas from Amsterdam, because the importer was a nice guy. They had no business logic. They didn't make the decisions based on what was best for the firm, but based on what was best for them.

Networks like the one featuring the nice banana man were, of course, an artifact of the socialist economy of shortage. People built networks by giving one another gifts and favors of various sorts, then used those networks to obtain access to goods in shortage. The banana importer was therefore only entering into long-established socialist practice. But instead of seeing these kinds of personal networks as arising from the socialist economic system, Gerber managers instead chose to label them as "corrupt" and to turn talk about corruption to their own advantage.

In arguing that Alima's managers had to learn "business logic" as well as technical skills like finance and logistics, Gerber was echoing management gurus like Andrzej Koźminski, one of Poland's leading management theorists. Koźminski argues that in Eastern Europe, the key to creating a successful market economy lay in changing managers' "Communist mentalities," which lead them to assume they have the right to force others to follow the "one best way" and to offer "ordinary people" total protection and services in exchange for their compliance (1993, 2). He further argues that managers must change the "organizational cultures" of their enterprises in order to "implement successful strategies enabling survival in the new environment." Otherwise, macroeconomic change will not be translated into corresponding firm behavior and the "transformation to a market economy will not happen" (Koźminski 1992, 145; see also Tadikamalla et al. 1994, 218; Pearce and Čakrt 1994, 90; McDonald 1993; Amsden et al. 1994, 55–56).

Polish sociologist Piotr Sztompka states bluntly that changing managers' "mindsets" is the essential element in economic transformation and that the "socialist mentality is at odds with the Spirit of Capitalism" (1992, 20). He explains that

> the terms "socialist mentality," "socialist spirit," and "homo sovieticus" refer to a specific personality syndrome which is highly resistant to change, even under the new post-communist conditions. The components of this syndrome include passivity, avoidance of responsibility, prolonged infantilism, parasitic innovativeness, disinterested envy, and primitive egalitarianism. . . . It is obvious that the market and democracy require the direct opposite: activity and constructive innovativeness, self-reliance and responsibility, appreciation for achievement, acceptances of income differences, and so on. (Sztompka 1992, 19–20)

Referring to Weber's thesis about the relationship between values and economic structures, Sztompka characterizes Eastern Europe's problem in creating market economies as "the dilemma of the missing 'Protestant Ethic'" (1992, 20). What he means, of course, is that Eastern European managers have to be taught accountability as well as accounting. Just like Benjamin Franklin, the example cited by Weber (1958, 47–54), Eastern European managers were supposed to monitor their own behavior and to "take responsibility" for that behavior by recording it in auditable records and making them visible to others.

Gerber's characterization of social networks like the one involving the banana man as "corrupt" was an attempt to apply the rhetoric of accounting and to link inauditability with both immorality and inefficiency. This made Alima's managers look bad on Gerber's books, both moral and financial. Speaking of the firm's president, Maria Czartoryska, John Jones said, "The thing is, Maria was becoming more of a liability than an asset. And when that happens, you're out."

Czartoryska was not alone. Because Alima's managers were resisting becoming accountable *subjects,* Gerber quickly recast them as accountable *objects,* just like the shop floor workers and the farmers who were "sold like a flock of geese" (Siwek 1992). Gerber decided that Alima managers' corrupted personhood and corrupting networks made it impossible to reform, retrain, or "coach" existing management. Gerber's CEO, Al Piergallini, told the *New York Times,* "After bringing in American employees to train Polish management, we realized that system hadn't worked. We tried the cheap way first, but it was totally unsuccessful" (Perlez 1993). Gerber fired all but two of Alima's executives and hired new young executives to occupy the firm's highest ranks. The new managers were from outside Rzeszów, and many of them had experience in Western firms.[19]

Replacing the "old" managers with younger people who were not from Rzeszów had several apparent benefits. As "outsiders" to the factory and to Rzeszów, they were supposedly not entangled by the corrupting influences of the old networks and were therefore free to act according to the logic of capitalism and in the firm's best interests. Experience with Western business was supposed to have shown them what "real" business looked like; their youth supposedly gave them greater capacity to change and adapt to new demands for auditable performance.

Alima's old managers did not leave without a struggle, however. While John Jones was lobbying to fire Czartoryska, she responded by trying to shift the framework of accountability to purely moral issues. Jones, a married man, was involved in a personal relationship with another American employee. As Jones tells the story, Czartoryska used this as ammunition. She wrote furious letters to Piergallini, arguing that Jones's "immorality" and flagrant violation of Catholic moral standards made him an affront to the community and therefore unfit to lead the firm. According to Jones, Gerber swiftly turned the idea that employees were objects with positive or negative value against him:

> It was not about morality, it was politics and it was revenge. . . . But the truth is, they [Gerber] did not care about the truth. They thought I had become a liability. The truth did not really matter, just the perception. They did not care about my career or my personal life, just the stock price.[20]

Jones's talk about managers as "assets" and "liabilities" and employees' talk about being made into "geese" and "slaves" makes it clear that privatization marked a major shift in the ontology of labor in the company. In any capitalist system, as Polanyi (1944) pointed out, labor must become a fictive commodity. In postsocialist Eastern Europe, labor was commodified by both objectifying workers and cutting them off from their social networks, or individualizing them.[21] Just as privatization transformed SOEs from work communities and social institutions into a commodity, so too did the privatization of persons isolate them from social context and turn them into labor power, a kind of property and a fictive commodity. That labor power was then accounted for just as all the other commodities entering the firm were: it was assigned a value that could be positive or negative and entered into a balance sheet amenable to calculations of profit and loss. Employees were turned into "assets" or "liabilities" and defined in terms of their value to the firm. Objectifying workers through enterprise privatization was thus a key moment in the transformation of socialism and the creation of a capitalist economy. For the new capitalist system to function, the privatization of property had also to lead to the *privatization of persons* (see also chap. 3 and Verdery 2000).

In an ironic twist, other Gerber managers soon got a taste of what it meant to be privatized persons with monetary value. In 1994, just two years after it acquired Alima, Gerber announced that it would be sold to Sandoz, a Swiss pharmaceutical firm. This plan did not have any direct connection to the transformation underway at Alima. However, Gerber had purchased Alima as a last-ditch effort to enter European markets, and by 1994, that strategy had failed. Gerber had hoped to use AG as a manufacturing base from which it could export baby food to France, as well as to the Czech Republic and Hungary. Yet, through no fault of AG's, Gerber had failed in all three of those markets. Sandoz promised to open European markets to Gerber and to provide other new avenues for growth. Gerber's employees, some of whom owned substantial amounts of stock in the company, received a great deal of money when Sandoz bought Gerber. But for them, just like Alima's employees, it soon became clear they were now assets or liabilities rather than stockholders with managerial authority or even persons in a community. Sandoz managers quickly took over much of the strategic and operational decision-making at Gerber, and they made it clear that anyone who did not comply with its directives would be let go.

The privatization of Alima and the accusations of corruption that surrounded it bring up many of the key issues in Eastern European property transformation. Uncertainties about the "real" owners of enterprises, the problem of translating value from one form of political economy to another, and the formation of new social hierarchies around new forms of property were all issues that plagued national governments and privatizing firms throughout the Eastern Bloc. When Alima's employees accused Minister

Lewandowski of corruption, they sought to make the complexities of privatization into matters of public debate. By using the concept of "the bribe," they altered the concept of "value" and signaled the difference between two distinct measures of it: the supposedly "objective" measure set by Western accounting systems, on the one hand, and, on the other, their subjective opinions of their lives and work under socialism, which were crystallized in the firm.

It is impossible to determine whether the price set for Alima was correct or even whether Lewandowski was corrupt. (A parliamentary tribunal cleared him of any charges of wrongdoing in his handling of privatization.) But these are not the most interesting aspects of the Alima controversy. Rather, what is notable are these two very different schemata for determining the value of the firm: accounting and audit on the one hand, and corruption on the other. Both accounting as a practice and accountability as an ideology have global pretensions: seemingly objective, impersonal, and universal frameworks for valuation, they supposedly can be applied anywhere to elicit and then evaluate proper performance. They allow value to be assessed in similar terms by people in places far removed from the location of the object or institution in question, and they allow value to be converted and moved to distant places. But we also have corruption—practices like bribery, which depend on the formation and cultivation of local, personal relations. A bribe establishes value not through the mechanism of the market but through intimate negotiations, especially through knowledge of local practices. (Giving a bribe is a delicate matter that requires knowing not only whom to bribe but how to deploy cultural values, social status, and the etiquette of corruption.) Corruption is the embodiment of what Granovetter (1992) has called "embeddedness," or transactions carried on through networks of social relations.

The Alima case is an instance of a more generalized transformation of the practices and beliefs that fix value and set the rules for its movement and transformation. Breaking down the economic barriers that isolated Poland from the West promoted more than the influx of foreign products and foreign capital. It opened the door to powerful new ways of thinking about persons and things, the ways they act, and the ways they are regulated. Accountability, as a pre-existing set of ideas and practices imported from the West, requires that people act in ways that can be recorded in universally understandable terms. Auditable performance is a thus not only a way of reconceptualizing ledgers and financial reports, or of reconfiguring the economy, but of organizing persons, the ways they work, and their relations to the things they make. As I show in the following chapters, audit is not just applied to financial reports; it is applied to products, production systems, and producers. Because auditing systems as defined by IAS or US GAAP are required for entry into global markets, Poland had little choice but to comply, regardless of the political and economic costs incurred by its people.

Discourses like the one on corruption are a way for the people that audit turns into "objects" to try to steer the changes threatening to disempower them. Rather than acquiesce to the dictates of the global market, they draw on local ideas about interpersonal political-economic relations. These ideas stem in particular from social networks necessitated by the socialist economy of shortage and particular, personal knowledge about the embeddedness of economic relations. Talk about corruption makes no pretense of universality. It insists that concrete, specific persons in local contexts are responsible for decisions, not abstract impersonal forces like the hidden hand of the market. Alima employees who cried foul about corruption were therefore demanding accountability in the moral sense of the term—in the sense that Solidarity had once called for accountability—not in the narrow, technical sense that Western auditors demanded.

3 Niche Marketing and the Production
of Flexible Bodies

It was a beautiful spring day in 1996, nearly four years after Gerber had bought Alima. I stood in line outside the factory along with a crowd of Alima-Gerber employees and distributors, waiting to board the bus that would take us to an elegant theater in downtown Rzeszów. The AG employees—all white-collar workers from the office building—and I fidgeted and whispered to one another nervously. This was show time: we were about to launch the product that would make or break Alima-Gerber.

Once seated in the auditorium, we listened to the Polish head of the marketing division as he proudly displayed the firm's new line of fruit juices. Surprisingly, the bright, colorful drinks in large glass bottles with a jazzy black label were not for babies. "Frugo!" announced the marketer, who showed us that the brand came in four colors, not flavors. He explained that red, orange, green, and yellow Frugo juices were destined to be the hit product of the year: they were developed on the basis of _niche marketing,_ a form of marketing that had never been used in Poland before. "A product for everybody is a product for nobody. Nobody identifies with it," he said. "That's why Frugo is aimed especially at youth. Frugo will be a part of the young world like no other brand. It will be a fragment of their culture."

The lights dimmed, and we sat anxiously as a giant movie screen dropped from the ceiling. All at once, there was an explosion of noise and color. "_Frugo!_" intoned a disembodied voice speaking Polish. Then, set against a dynamic background of color and noise, a young kid dressed like a Los Angeles gang member appeared, wearing fashionably baggy clothes and spray painting graffiti. In the background, a voice whispered the Frugo slogan, "Frugo without boundaries" (_Frugo bez ograniczeń_). Suddenly, there was a rupture: the commercial became quiet, and the scene jump-cut to a monotonous, drab setting. In each of the four versions of the commercial, the ad presented a stereotypical adult, fat and unmoving, who began to speak. In the commercial for red Frugo, for example, the hated adult was a fat woman in black clothes and a beret, sitting against a red background. She said, aggressively, "Fruit? They want fruit? When I was young, we often lacked *beets!* And they're asking for fruit!" In the orange ad, a dumpy older woman with dyed orange hair and long orange fingernails sat at a table decorated with fussy lace doilies. She said, tremulously, "Fruit? Fruit is good for decorating tables. But of course, plastic fruit can be aesthetic, too."

In all of the ads, as soon as the repellent adult finished speaking, the scene began to expand like a bubble. As it became wider and shorter, the audience saw a Frugo bottle, with a hand on it, pushing down on the scene until it exploded. The hand belonged to the main character, the cool kid, who was using the bottle to squash and rupture the hated adults and their whole settings. The loud drum music resumed, the bright colors began wheeling around, and the audience saw the cool kid spray painting out of view of the camera. The ads ended with a recitation of the product's punnish slogan, "So, drink up!"—or, as it was in Polish, "*No, to Frugo!*"

The audience roared with delight, and the employees grinned with a mixture of enthusiasm and relief. The commercials were a hit with the distributors, which boded well for their reception by a wider Polish audience. I had a difficult time participating in the festivity, though. What did these ads mean? Why did everyone squeal with laughter when the dumpy adults appeared? What was so funny about these commercials, anyway? After employees explained to me the symbolism of the ads, I soon began to notice similar images in other places: in the sartorial habits of Polish managers, in the talk of American managers, and, accompanied by biting commentary, in discussions on the shop floor. These images of movement and stasis, flexibility and rigidity, age and youth, resonated strongly with employees as well as consumers.

What I came to discover was while niche marketing is ostensibly about structuring consumer markets by identifying and proposing new social identities, it also helps commodify labor and segment labor markets by constituting new social identities and reconfiguring old ones. The images deployed so brilliantly and humorously in the Frugo ads were part of a larger process in which some people were categorized as "flexible," "rational," and "individualist," while others were being labeled "passive," "collectivist," and "rigid," hence a priori incapable of playing a leading role in the economic "transition." Niche marketing linked marketization and personhood not only to transform the economy from one constrained by supply to one constrained by demand but also to reconstruct desire, identity, class, and occupation.

Making Postsocialist Niche Markets: The Birth of a Strategy

The general atmosphere of nervousness and tension among employees at the Frugo launch was easily understandable. Gerber executives assuaged employees' fears during privatization in 1992 by painting a picture of a prosperous future. They promised that the new Alima-Gerber would be the center of Gerber's expansion efforts in European markets. They said Alima's employees would all be making good salaries while making food for Russian, Czech, Hungarian, French, and maybe even Middle Eastern babies. But by 1996, it was clear that the situation was not as rosy as both Alima and Gerber had hoped. With the collapse of the Soviet Union and the economic downturn across the Eastern Bloc, exports had dropped dramatically. The Polish baby food market was not expanding as quickly as AG hoped, and the machines that Gerber had paid so dearly to move into AG's baby food division sat idle roughly half of the time, not even counting nights and weekends.[1]

The factory was covering costs by selling Bobo Frut domestically, but sales were dropping. The firm had no other products to take up capacity on the line. People were being laid off, jobs were being outsourced, and salaries were not keeping pace with rampant inflation. People on the production floor and in the office building were worried; the threat of unemployment hung over their heads. Employees waited and watched to find out how Sandoz would respond to AG's travails, fearful that the pharmaceutical giant might decide simply to shut the company down.

In response to this dilemma, AG devised another strategy. While growth in the baby food market was slow, growth in the beverage market was skyrocketing. Poles consumed 197 percent more juice in 1995 than in 1992. Although 1995 per capita consumption had reached 7.9 liters, AG officials believed that as Poles obtained more disposable income, their consumption could reach average Western European levels (15 liters per capita per year) or even German levels (38 liters per capita).[2] AG had long experience in making juices for children. The juice market for small children, however, had low growth potential because AG already controlled about 80 percent of the market. The beverage market for adults was crowded and highly competitive. So, instead of focusing on either young children or adults, AG decided to attempt to resegment the domestic market in order to sell a new product. Frugo, the new juice drink, was aimed at thirteen- to eighteen-year-olds—the age group with the lowest per capita consumption of juices.

The Frugo strategy was a classic use of niche marketing. Marketers define a specific group or "target market," list the qualities of the group's members and outline their particular needs, and then develop and advertise a product that meets those specific needs. Often, this group is carved out of an existing market. In this way, a new social group—perhaps one that heretofore had not recognized itself or had not been recognized as having special "needs"—is created through advertising and marketing strategies. As anthropologist Sidney Mintz points out in reference to American advertising strategies,

> TV treatment of foods is intended to encourage consumption. As such, it is differentiated in order to reach many different (and segmented, but sometimes overlapping) populations, such as little boys and girls, adolescent males and females, adult singles, both male and female, families eating out, couples eating out . . . and so on. This design aims at reaching the widest possible variety of audiences, each on its own terms, but also leaving room for continuous redifferentiation by subdivision (for instance black male basketball players and white male basketball players) . . . in order to perpetuate the sensation of innovation and of participatory membership upon which heightened consumption battens.
>
> Making the product "right" for the consumer requires continuous redefinition and division of the groups in which he, as an individual consumer, defines himself. The deliberate postulation of new groups—often divisions between already familiar categories, as "pre-teens," were created between "teenagers" and younger children—helps to impart reality to what are supposedly new needs (Mintz 1982, 158; see also Schrum 1998).

In essence, marketers deliberately fragment the market into smaller segments by using two techniques: contrived product differentiation and contrived social differentiation (Samuelson 1976; Dickson and Ginter 1987). Niche marketing is a strategy commonly pursued by post-Fordist capitalist industries throughout the world. Flexible production systems rest on the idea of small-batch production for quickly changing niche markets (Harvey 1989, 156). In contrast to the Fordist era, when stable product lines were designed for mass markets, competition in the post-Fordist era depends on specialized and differentiated products and a rapid rate of change in production design and product mix (Schoenberger 1988, 252; Piore and Sabel 1984).

As common as these techniques have become in the capitalist world, the niche marketing strategies that AG pursued were almost completely new in Poland. Socialism was based on the Fordist idea of mass consumption: economies of scale could be obtained by consolidating producers and product lines. Because of socialism's focus on mass production, because of the chronic shortages that plagued the economy, and because of the underground exchanges of gifts and favors, there were no niche markets. Everyone wanted everything. Even if one did not have a child, for example, Bobo Frut was a valuable commodity because it could be traded for something else through the extensive networks of personal connections that typified state socialism.

True, the socialist state went to great lengths to differentiate groups of people (mothers, children, pensioners, and so on) and to give them access to valued goods. Socialist states created different documents (e.g., the "child health book," which proved one had a child) and different purchase points (e.g., stores for party members) to classify groups of people by age, gender, occupation, class status, ethnicity, and party membership. These classifications gave some people access to particular kinds or quantities of goods that others could not get. Anderson (1996) calls these differentiations "citizenship regimes." The regimes determined not only what goods one could get, but by reifying differences with documents and privileges, they also determined *what kind of citizen one was.* Citizenship regimes are not the same as niche markets, however. Citizenship regimes are necessary only when desire is generalized—when everybody wants everything, and a product for everybody is a product for anybody:

> Socialism . . . which rested not on devising infinite kinds of things to sell people but on claiming to meet people's basic needs, had a very unadorned definition of them—in keeping with socialist egalitarianism. . . . As long as the food offered was edible or the clothes available covered you and kept you warm, that should be sufficient. If you had trouble finding even these, that just meant you weren't looking hard enough. No planner presumed to investigate what kinds of goods people wanted, or worked to name new needs for newly created products and newly developed markets. (Verdery 1996, 28)

Niche markets, in contrast, are about creating groups with specialized desire and products that precisely match the minute differences in those groups' wants. In this system, products that don't meet specialized wants don't sell—and that means a product for everybody is a product for nobody. Niche marketing therefore contributes to the transformation of the supply-constrained economy into a demand-constrained one. More important, it is part of the restructuring of desire and social personhood. Now a consumer has to be a particular sort to want a certain product—or, perhaps, finds that wanting a certain product is enough to become a particular kind of person.

The introduction of niche marketing meant that AG was not only discovering "the market," it was learning to create and make use of multiple *markets* that could be resegmented and redefined in order to boost consumption via the practice of *marketing*. It was precisely socialism's inattention to consumption and the dearth of technologies, habits, and traditions in that domain that made it so possible and so fruitful to import Western marketing techniques. Alima-Gerber was one of the first companies in Poland to aim a product at a narrowly defined target market. This marked a major change in the way Polish enterprises approached markets. Rather than being fixed entities that passively absorbed product, markets and consumers became objects that could be subjected to technologies of government; they could be studied, classified, created, destroyed, and manipulated.

Both AG's Polish advertising and marketing staff and the staff of Grey and Associates, the New York-based advertising agency hired for the Frugo campaign, described the genesis of the Frugo strategy as if there were a well-defined group with an unfulfilled need. However, it was not at all clear that either the group or the need existed prior to the product. That was why the advertisements had to define the "teen" target group as a distinct social entity in order to sell the product (see also Schrum 1998, 158).[3] Making teens distinct from babies and toddlers was easily done. AG removed all traces of the Gerber name from the product, with the exception of the company name and address, in small type on the back of the label. When the product was put in stores, AG ensured that it was placed on shelves next to soft drinks and juices for adults rather than on the Gerber racks.

Making teens distinct from adults was a more difficult problem. The Frugo advertisements did this by contrasting not only socialist and capitalist lifeworlds but also socialist and capitalist persons. On the one hand, the adult lifeworld was a stereotype of the socialist era. The first adult in the commercials—the woman set against a red background who complained that youngsters didn't know about beet shortages—represented the Party, with its emphasis on the nobility of sacrifice and struggle. The second woman represented a person trying to create elegance in the face of a shortage of material goods. In both cases, the stereotypes were tongue-in-cheek. While the orange woman clearly believed plastic fruit has aesthetic value, for example, the audience was expected to realize it is horrible and ugly.

Table 1. Ideas of socialism and capitalism

Socialism	Capitalism
Backwardness	Modernity, civilization
Stasis	Dynamism, movement
Rigidity	Flexibility
Age	Youth
Drabness	Colorfulness
Deprivation	Satisfaction of desire
Obedience	Critical self-reflection
Collectivism	Individualism
Personalized "connections"	Impersonal relations based on rational calculation
Gifts	Sales
Isolation within boundaries	Transcendence of boundaries

On the other hand, the ads showed the teenager rejecting the entire socialist lifeworld—not just the Communist Party, but the entire experience of the socialist era—in favor of another, new form of being. These adults, the ad implies, just could not change with the times. Such images indexed and mocked socialist ideas of noble suffering and sacrifices for the radiant future.[4] They also indexed qualities such as drabness, passivity, immobility, and unresponsiveness to needs and desires, all of which are imputed to the socialist system. In contrast, the teenaged boy (and Frugo) was associated with dynamism, foreignness, color, noise, and the gratification of desire. This strategy, of course, rested on the creation of difference: if both the product and the targeted consumer were not somehow "different" from others, there would be no need for this specialized product.

The idea of creating new differences in personal identity using socialism as a foil was not unique to Alima. A similar process was going on across the Eastern Bloc. Ads often sorted images and personal characteristics into categories of "socialist" and "capitalist" and associated their products with one or the other. "Businessman" cigarettes and "Business Centre Club" beer were blatant examples of domestically produced products that marketed themselves by conjuring an image of capitalist personhood.[5] In an analysis of Czechoslovak political imagery, Holy (1992) found that the planned economy was associated with highly negative characteristics, whereas the market economy was associated with a wealth of positive qualities. Table 1 illustrates some of these dichotomies.

Part of the drive to create new social identities through consumption may have been a reaction to socialism's demand that people be the same and to its dislike of social differentiation. As the Czech president and former dissident Václav Havel explained,

The fall of communism destroyed this shroud of sameness, and the world was caught napping by an outburst of the many unanticipated differences concealed beneath it, each of which—after such a long time in the shadows—felt a natural need to draw attention to itself, to emphasize its uniqueness, and its difference from others. (1993, 8)

The accusation that people under state socialism were all alike is, of course, exaggerated. Ethnographic work conducted during the late 1980s showed that people set themselves apart from others and marked themselves as participants in subcultures by doing everything from adopting particular fashions, to becoming deeply involved in reenactments of American Indian powwows (Rayport 1995), to struggling to preserve regional identities. But socialist mass production gave people reason to feel that the socialist state was pushing for sameness and discouraging people from differentiating themselves through consumption. For many Poles, consumption became a way of rejecting socialist egalitarianism. Producing black market goods, making one's own (more stylish) clothing, and acquiring Western goods on the black market was a way for socialist citizens to show they could have things the regime said they didn't need. As Verdery notes, it was a way to "differentiate yourself as an individual in the face of relentless pressures to homogenize everyone's capacities and tastes into an undifferentiated collectivity. Acquiring objects became a way of constituting your selfhood against a deeply unpopular regime" (1996, 29).

It is no wonder, then, that in the immediate aftermath of socialism, Eastern Europeans reacted with a flurry of pent-up consumerist desire. Socialism had engendered the desire to create oneself as a different kind of person through consumption, but the economy of shortage had by and large denied people the means to do so. While the pump was primed for niche marketing, then, the social differences that niche marketing depends on were not necessarily "naturally" present and waiting to leap out once the lid of Communist oppression was lifted. Rather, new and different kinds of personhood were actively created through a variety of means: advertisements and fashion magazines, identity politics, redefined occupational hierarchies, and leisure-time activities (Sampson 1996, 92). Companies like AG were primed to step in to meet the desire for differentiation and to help create new identities—including the identity of the flip, hip, rebellious teen. With the aid of Western advertising agencies like Grey and Associates, AG was ready to help school Poles in the art of assembling themselves as they assembled products to consume.

Postsocialism, Postfordism, and Flexibility

By gambling so heavily on Frugo, AG bet the company's survival on its ability to differentiate consumers and to elicit in them the "need" for new products to define their own identities. But why did AG choose these particular images to differentiate groups? Why portray socialism as dumpy, drab, immobile, and rigid, and why portray the hip capitalist teen as hyper-mobile, agile, and colorful? Oddly enough, the Frugo images of mobility, agility, and flexibility echoed a wave of similar advertising in the United States. In her study of American popular culture, Emily Martin found ads for baby shoes with "flexible soles" that promised to make children more "agile." She also found ads for bank cards that billed themselves as "your flexible friend" and offered consumers flexible payment schedules. Advertisements for management seminars promised to help executives gain "flexibility—the most important leadership tool of this decade," while an ad for a temporary services agency used Gumby, the iconic rubber cartoon character, to demonstrate how much flexibility temporary workers could give a firm (Martin 1994, 150–54). Martin argues that by vaunting flexibility and nimbleness, the ads rejected the "rigidity" that was the hallmark of Fordist production (Harvey 1989, 142) and instead embraced post-Fordist flexible accumulation, an aesthetic style associated with a particular kind of capitalism (Piore and Sabel 1984; Schoenberger 1997; Jameson 1991).

By using similar images of "flexibility" to reject socialism, AG's simple commercial made a strong statement about socialism's ills and postsocialist people. By portraying socialism as "rigid," the commercial presented a broader narrative that portrayed the centrally planned economy as "stagnant" (Sachs 1993, 3), "ossified" (Csaba 1995, 35,) and incapable of changing without collapsing (Kornai 1992, 383). This echoed the fundamental critique of Fordism:

> More generally, the period from 1965 to 1973 was one in which the inability of Fordism . . . to contain the inherent contradictions of capitalism became more and more apparent. On the surface, these difficulties could best be captured by one word: rigidity. There were problems with the rigidity of long-term and large-scale fixed capital investments in mass-production systems that precluded much flexibility of design and assumed stable growth in invariant consumer markets. There were problems of rigidity in labor markets, labor allocation and in labor contracts. . . . Behind all these specific rigidities lay a rather unwieldy and seemingly fixed configuration of political power and reciprocal relations

that bound big labor, big capital, and big government into what increasingly appeared as a dysfunctional embrace. (Harvey 1989, 142)

Others have made the equivalence between Fordism and state socialism more explicit, portraying socialism as a *kind* of Fordism, complete with heavy industry and mass production. Zygmunt Bauman argues that socialism failed because it was too rigid to give up the modernist dream, even when the West had moved on to a more flexible, postmodern economy:

> The communist state, in its own admittedly unprepossessing way, seemed to serve the same ideals of the modern era which even its capitalist haters readily recognized as their own. In these now uncannily distant times the audacious communist project seemed to make a lot of sense and was taken quite seriously by its friends and foes alike. Communism promised . . . to do what everyone else was doing, only . . . the real doubts appeared when the others stopped doing it, while communism went on chasing now abandoned targets; partly through inertia, but mostly because of the fact that—being communism in action—it could not do anything else.
>
> In its practical implementation, communism was a system one-sidedly adapted to the task of mobilizing social and natural resources in the name of modernization—the nineteenth-century, steam-and-iron ideal of modern plenty. It could—at least in its own conviction—compete with capitalists but solely with capitalists engaged in the same pursuits. What it could not do and did not brace itself to do was to match the performance of the capitalist, market-centered society once that society abandoned its steel mills and coal mines and moved into the postmodern age. (Bauman 1992, 169)

Of course, making state socialism into a kind of Fordism meant ignoring that, in practice, socialism diverged significantly from the Fordist ideal. The advantage of making Fordism and socialism into equivalents, though, was that it gave economists and managers—Americans as well as Polish "converts"—a set of ready-made tools with which to change the planned economy. At the macroeconomic level, that meant using neoliberal techniques for undoing the Keynesian welfare state to dismantle the socialist welfare state. At the level of the firm, it meant engaging in massive processes of "reengineering," which changed the organization of the firm and the daily practices of its inhabitants.

The fad for "reengineering" Fordist companies' internal organizations came from the idea that they were "inefficient in the face of a turbulent environment" and "unable to accommodate the need for rapid and continual change by virtue of their structure" (Schoenberger 1997, 84). Fordist firms were organized with a central authority—the CEO—who made multiyear plans, aggregated the firm's resources, and then distributed them to subordinate divisions. Each division then disaggregated the budget and the production quota, handing down production targets and money to buy raw materials to their subordinate divisions. This division of labor inside the company made design, manufacturing, and marketing into separate departments with little communication among them, supposedly delayed the pace of innovation, and hampered the firm's ability to respond to the market:

> The extreme compartmentalization of the information characteristic of an advanced division of labor undermines the organization's ability to recognize and respond to significant disruptions that do not present themselves in the established categories. Often the left hand truly does not know what the right hand is doing, so the organization can end up working at cross-purposes with itself. (Schoenberger 1987, 84)

When American managers came to Poland and began to hear about how the central planning system was supposed to work, they immediately found it familiar. Because socialist firms were *supposed* to work like Fordist firms (although, thanks to shortages, they rarely did), and their formal organizational structures *looked like* those of Fordist firms (although, because of labor shortages, power was distributed quite differently inside the company). Thus, American managers saw state-owned enterprises as analogues of the Fordist companies they had been working to transform for more than a decade. At AG, Gerber managers immediately focused on the command-and-control organization of management, which was organized as a pyramid with Maria Czartoryska at the top. John Jones was aghast at the vertically organized bureaucracy in the firm:

> Maria Czartoryska had this little pad on her desk stamped "REGULATION," and anything she wrote on it was assigned a number and became law in the company, just like that, without consulting with any of the other managers.

Although neither of them used terms like "Fordism," both Jones and his colleague John Turnock immediately identified Alima's internal organization as a source of "rigidity" that would keep the firm from responding "flexibly" to market demand. In keeping with post-Fordist management practices used in the United States, they rushed to break down what they saw as the compartmentalization of knowledge in the firm. John Jones was absolutely floored by what he saw as barriers to the free flow of information inside the company. "Can you believe the fax, the telephones, and the Xerox machine were all under lock and key when I arrived?" asked Jones. "You had to fill out a form in triplicate just to make a photocopy." Unlocking the Xerox machine took on great symbolism for Jones, who saw it as a way to "empower" employees and to encourage them to communicate with one another across departmental lines.[6]

Applying post-Fordist remedies to make the firm more flexible didn't stop at unlocking the Xerox or reorganizing the chain of command (although Gerber did both those things). One of the great innovations of post-Fordist management was a set of techniques to make individual workers, not just firms, more flexible and adaptable. In the United States, firms sent individual workers through Outward Bound-type programs, to stand on teetering poles and jump off cliffs with only a climbing rope to prevent them from plummeting to the ground. The programs were supposed to instill agility and an appreciation for risk into workers' psyches via their bodies:

> The bodily experiences of fear and excitement deliberately aroused on the zip line and the pole are meant to serve as models for what workers will feel in unpredictable work situations. (Martin 1994, 213)

In Poland, few people rushed out to dangle off belay ropes. Nonetheless, Poles rushed to incorporate metaphors of flexibility into their physical selves. In the postsocialist atmosphere of intense consumer demand, it is not surprising they chose to redefine themselves as "flexible bodies" by consuming products like Frugo. Products that conferred flexibility did more than create niche consumer markets, however. They contributed to making niche labor markets. Like the American employees who went on Outward Bound courses, many of the Poles who consumed "flexible" products were employees who sought to keep their jobs by exhibiting their "flexible capitalist dispositions" on their bodies and through their presentation of self. In so doing, they were to prove that their labor was a valuable asset to the corporation and that they were inherently suited to positions of power in the new economic order. But the opportunity to become "flexible" and to gain status in the new economic order was not open to everyone. Other groups of people were remade into the embodiment of socialism, which naturalized their increasing powerlessness and impoverishment.

From *Kierownik* to *Menadżer:* Managing the Self

As foreign investment rushed into Poland in the 1990s, white-collar Poles came under enormous pressure to transform themselves and to differentiate themselves as a class. Much of this pressure came from the way foreign investments were structured. Whether foreign investors were purchasing state-owned enterprises (e.g., using the trade sale method of privatization) or setting up new subsidiaries, most of them came to Eastern Europe with a strategy to transform themselves from foreign to local entities. Although they initially staffed management positions with expatriates, they had strong incentives to train local executives to run the company. This was not only because expatriate managers are costly—a two-year tour of duty can cost more than $1 million—but because rapid turnover in management jobs as expatriates come and go creates unwanted turnover in the firm. Rather than rotate expatriates through jobs, it made more sense to attempt to transfer knowledge of capitalist business practices to local Eastern European executives (McDonald 1993). Having received this knowledge, Eastern European managers were supposed to diffuse it to other firms, thereby making the economy as a whole more flexible.

Gerber employed this strategy from the time it took control of Alima. Gerber wanted personnel from Fremont to retrain existing management at Alima. However, when Alima's managers proved recalcitrant, Gerber fired them and hired new managers who, it hoped, would be more able to adapt and to adopt Western management practices. Gerber was not alone in this strategy. In many other companies whose managers I interviewed, foreign management made decisions about which employees were capable of adapting to new conditions and which were not.

On what basis did foreign managers decide who received the all-important knowledge of foreign business practices and who would be fired? Most American managers I interviewed told me that the most important criterion they used was "attitude." Sam Kendall, an American manager for Transco, told me that some experienced managers in the Polish SOE that his firm acquired would soon be fired.[7] "These people want an eight-to-five job, but those are the people who won't be joining us," he said. Instead, he planned to evaluate each of the firm's managers, looking for people who "had the ability to adapt and change" and who were "willing to take responsibility." He said that Polish managers who gained experience under socialism "may not have the same attitude toward career advancement" as he would like and therefore "might not have the right attitude."

We might summarize the difference between the "right attitude" and the "wrong" one with the distinction between two Polish words for enterprise managers: the Polish word *kierownik,* and the newly popular polonization of the English term "manager," *menadżer.*[8] *Kierownik* refers to a stereotypical socialist manager, an inflexible paper-pushing bureaucrat. This kind of manager, as American consultant Bob Murphy told me, is always trying to build his own power while escaping responsibility. *Kierownicy* were also portrayed as relying too much on personal or social ties with employees in order to manage them. Because the *kierownicy* are supposedly enmeshed in these ties, they are said to be ineffective. In the words of another American manager, "They can't swing the ax."

In contrast, people used the term *menadżer* to refer to the stereotype of a manager who is highly flexible and eager to change. He might not have much experience. In fact, inexperience is an asset rather than a liability, since he is therefore autonomous and not enmeshed in messy social ties with ministries and workers.[9] However, he has the inner qualities that allow him to learn new managerial techniques, to apply them rationally and impersonally, and therefore to succeed. These qualities would get him a job in privatizing companies. As an article in the *Harvard Business Review* put it,

> In seeking [Eastern European] general managers, Western partners look for self-confidence, initiative, and sophistication as well as work experience. They pay attention to their own first impressions and instinctive likes and dislikes. . . . They tease out underlying beliefs about business ethics, profits, labor relations and political institutions. (Lawrence and Vlachoutsicos 1993, 49)

To attract the attention of a Western manager, land a managerial job, and gain access to Western business knowledge, Polish managers had to demonstrate the right personality characteristics: attitude, beliefs, flexibility, receptivity, and initiative. But how did they go about demonstrating these very personal, "inner" characteristics? Unlike their Western counterparts, Polish managers could not rely heavily on resumés listing their past achievements. For many Poles, job histories and track records were of little value because of their ties to the socialist past.[10] Instead, they had to rely on the idea that the outer self signals changes in the inner self. They used changes in dress, personal possessions, and personal space to display their supposed transformations from a socialist being—a *kierownik*—to a capitalist being—a *menadżer*. By signaling this inner transformation from socialism, managers hoped to demonstrate that they had the "right attitude" and were ready and willing to learn new Western management ideas.

A look at some of the glossy Polish-language business magazines showed that Polish businessmen saw this recreation of self—of both the interior, knowing self and the exterior façade—as a crucial part of doing business. The first half of the July 1993 issue of *Businessman* magazine, for example, had articles on interpreting economic indicators, buying computers for a more efficient office, and motivating employees. In the second half of the magazine, however, were articles seemingly not about business: an article on the history and rules of tennis, a piece on how to buy and drink fine port wine, and a photo essay on the new men's fashions from Milan. The magazines presumed little prior familiarity with either business or tennis or port. But what was interesting about them was not just their primer-like quality but their emphasis on acquiring knowledge about Western business culture, including leisure habits, dress, and consumption practices, as a means to self-transformation. Like a Western business journal, the magazines showed the equation between knowledge, power, and money. Like a Western women's magazine, however, they stressed changing one's inner and outer being to become pleasing to another. These magazines were how-to guides for Poles who wished to acquire the selves that they imagine Western executives possess by acquiring the habitus of the Western businessman.[11]

I saw one striking example of this one Saturday night in Warsaw in 1993, at a restaurant across from the new IKEA and the second Warsaw McDonald's. Billed as "an American restaurant," the Falcon Inn offered high prices, foods fried in no-cholesterol vegetable oil, and tall blond waitresses in t-shirts and short, cut-off jeans. It was rumored to be where the American businessmen went to eat. But on the Saturday night I was there, no American businessmen were to be seen. It was about eleven-thirty at night, certainly outside of regular business hours. As I sat on the sidewalk terrace, waiting for my drink, a group of Polish men arrived. They seated themselves at a café table. Then each one bent over, rummaged in his briefcase, and took out a cellular telephone. Carefully—almost reverently—each man placed his phone upright against the umbrella pole in the center of the table, so that the phones made a circle. None of the phones rang while the men were at the table, and none of the men made any calls.

The point of having the cell phones went far beyond making calls. By adopting the dress, leisure habits, and consumption practices of Western businessmen, Polish managers signal their desire for membership in the imagined community of the transnational market economy. The men at the Falcon Inn carried their cellular phones at midnight on a Saturday night because cell phones have potent symbolic value: they represent membership in a network of people who are important enough that they must be able to be reached at any time. Because the cellular networks bypass the antiquated and often impossible-to-use Polish telephone system, they also represent membership in a community that transcends both national borders and the national infrastructure. The men at the Falcon Inn wished to signal that they were new, modern, and European. They attempted to show that they possessed advanced technology and instantaneous links to the rest of the world, that they were ready to do business in a capitalist economy. In many ways, they and their cell phones symbolized the same thing as the Frugo advertisements: an existence without borders and without limits, based on instant adaptability and moved by continuous change.

One of the top-level managers at AG was a negative example of the same phenomenon. He was one of the only executives at AG who had neither lived abroad nor had much previous experience with foreign firms. He was a painful example of the importance of symbolism in becoming a *menadżer*. He struggled mightily to acquire all the prestige goods (a Ford Taurus, two cellular telephones, imported skis, a Franklin Planner, and so on) that would legitimize his fragile status. Yet his lack of knowledge often tripped him up. His symbolic errors, like hiring a stripper to entertain at the company party, wearing striped ties with checked jackets, and making off-color remarks, were the subject of endless gossip. He often appeared ignorant or uncouth, and he knew it. Finally, he hired an elegant assistant who had lived in New York. A large part of her job was managing his personal appearance and arranging for him to acquire the necessary prestige goods. Regardless of how much this man knew about industrial management, he had to "manage" his own social personhood as well, and he knew his rise to the top was blocked by his ignorance of these matters.

The experiences of the cellular-phone-toting, Ford-driving Polish middle manager might be dismissed as simple cultural imperialism. There is nothing particularly unique about an influx of American (or French or German) cultural, commercial, and technological forms following American (or French or German) corporations abroad. Nor is it unique for foreign business and governmental organizations to create a local élite partly assimilated to foreign culture. But it appears that in this case, more was at work than simple cultural imperialism. When Polish managers acquired the habitus of the Western businessman, thereby making the leap from *kierownik* to *menadżer*, they literally embodied the idea of the transition from socialism to capitalism. The way magazines and my corporate informants portrayed *kierownicy* and *menadżerowie* illuminates the manner in which Poles, Western Europeans, and North Americans conceived of what socialism was and what capitalism would be. Just as in Frugo advertisements, images of flexible, dynamic capitalist people were juxtaposed with caricatures of people from the socialist era in order to highlight the novelty and implied superiority of the new system.

The transition from *kierownik* to *menadżer* is an important aspect of the privatization of persons. In turn, this aspect is a critical element in the transformation of the socialist economy into a capitalist one, because it promotes an ideology of individualism. The corporate managers I spoke with labeled *kierownicy* inflexible because they see *kierownicy* as tied down by extensive personalized social relations with both subordinates and superiors. This fits well with their critique of socialism, which they also see as inflexible and inefficient (Wedel 1986; Kornai 1992; Bauman 1992). The *kierownik* becomes an icon of this entire system and its problems: he represents both the person to blame for socialism and the person shaped by it. The *menadżer,* as an ideal image from the pages of *Businessman* magazine, represents the other side of the coin. He is supposed to be flexible precisely because he has no experiences of socialism and was not shaped by that system. He represents a free-floating and autonomous person who can shape and reshape himself. In the view of both the foreign and Polish managers I interviewed, the *menadżer* is the representation of the system to come: a system in which the impersonal logic of the market rather than personal ties dictates the rational and efficient allocation of goods.

The transition from *kierownik* to *menadżer* represents not just a transition from socialism to capitalism but also a transition from an orderly, bounded, and rigid system to a fluid, flexible, and global one. The foreign managers' conflation of socialism and Fordism, on the one hand, and postsocialism and flexible accumulation, on the other, determined the kind of managers they sought to hire or retain. Polish managers were therefore forced to demonstrate certain attributes. This was certainly the case at AG, where the managers Gerber hired were almost all English-speaking Poles highly familiar with the world of international business.

In essence, then, a particular niche within the labor market was quickly built in the years after 1989. There was a labor surplus in the Polish economy, but the kinds of managerial jobs that required a symbolic presentation of self as a *menadżer* were initially quite hard to fill. As the economic transformation continued, more and more Poles became trained and qualified for these jobs. By 1995, the only jobs that were hard to fill were in specialties like finance and strategic planning. Marketing, sales, and human resource management—three disciplines that did not exist under socialism—were all suddenly booming job markets.[12]

Although they don't say so explicitly, executives who aspire to become *menadżerowie* are pursuing essentially the same strategy that Frugo marketers did: they seek to segment the market by associating "capitalist" or "post-Fordist" values with their products. Private or privatizing companies become their market niche, as they caricature "socialist" persons in order to show the distinction between the lifestyle they wish to have associated with their products and the habits and values of the past. The difference between *menadżerowie* and Frugo marketers, of course, is that the product the *menadżerowie* market is themselves. Because their experience is of little value (unless it was acquired outside Poland), the quality of their labor can only be specified in reference to their internal qualities. To commodify their labor and to portray themselves as desirable assets, they must learn to manipulate images and to change their own habitus (cf. Schoenberger 1998).

Slick Salesmen and Simple People

The new breed of manager could contrast himself to a stereotype of an old-style *kierownik* in order to show his rejection of socialism and to appropriate the qualities of flexible capitalism. He could do that precisely because there were managers before 1989, ready-made "others" against whom he could define himself. People in occupations that did not exist under socialism were not the same type of "other" and therefore had to seek to define themselves and their niche in the labor market. This was particularly true for sales representatives, who worked in a department that did not exist before 1993. Like managers, they gained value by associating themselves and their labor with flexible capitalism. To highlight their flexibility (and all the related qualities of flexible capitalism), they had to constitute an "other" against which to contrast themselves. At AG, the "other" opposed to the sales force was the workforce in the production halls. This opposition between sales representatives and shop floor workers was constantly repeated throughout the plant, even though the sales representatives were rarely there and the two groups almost never met.

The redefinition and division of groups within the firm began from the moment sales representatives were hired. Sales representatives were believed to have special qualities that made them different from other employees (especially shop floor workers) and similar to the product they sold: they were supposedly dynamic, agile, and assertive. These qualities were also supposed to make them fit for a new department and a new kind of firm.

I saw how this "sales representative" identity was created when I sat in on a full day of job interviews for a vacancy in Lublin. All of the nine candidates for the position were men and, with one exception, all under thirty years of age. The interviewing team, which included the district manager and the director of sales, was led by Iwona, a psychologist in her late twenties who worked as the firm's recruitment specialist.[13]

Iwona began by asking the candidates what they were looking for in a job and what they imagined a day's work might be like. Without exception, all nine candidates responded that they wanted to be sales representatives because they liked "*ruch*," movement or circulation, and abhorred the idea of sitting behind a desk. Then, Iwona asked them about their job experience. Most of them had already been in four or five jobs, even though they had only been out of university for four or five years. Short job tenure didn't bother Iwona, however. She told me later that people typically worked six months here and five months there, and she really never expected sales representatives to stay long, anyway. Keeping the one hundred sales-rep jobs filled was a full-time job for her. After the last candidate left, the four of us discussed, analyzed, and compared the job seekers. Iwona was partial to a man she called "the rugby player." In her opinion, his athleticism made him a desirable candidate, since he had the strength, aggression, and dynamism needed in a sales representative. She dismissed another candidate because he was too quiet and still; she said he was "hiding something." The interview process was designed to allow Iwona to make these kinds of judgments about the personality and predisposition of the candidates. According to her, experience in this type of work was less important than predisposition. "You can train someone to sell," she said, "but you can't train them to have more energy, to move faster, or to be extroverted."

The key theme in all of these discussions was movement. Movement, rather than being a sign of instability, failure, or flightiness, was seen as bold and innovative. Most important, the images in our conversation after the job interview transformed the idea of movement from an *activity* into a *personality trait*. The same qualities of movement that managers like Iwona believed were desirable in an economic system (flexibility, circulation, change) became aspects of people's personalities. The interview process was designed to allow the hiring committee to see these personality traits as they were manifest on the surface of applicants' bodies—through their dress, gestures, voices, and mannerisms. Just as the physical persons and possessions of *menadżerowie* were icons of the new economic system, so too were these salespeople. By rushing around, actively moving products from the factory to the stores (rather than passively taking orders, as company representatives did under socialism), these salespeople were to contribute to the transformation of the company and of the macroeconomy.

The manner in which new hires were trained reinforced the idea that internal dispositions were a critical element of being a sales representative. Iwona and her colleagues showed each salesperson a video on self-presentation. The video demonstrated how to make internal dispositions such as vitality, friendliness, and self-confidence manifest through dress, speech, and body language. The aim was to convert these internal qualities into bodily activity that would elicit another form of activity—purchase—from wholesalers and grocery store managers. Later, all the salespeople in Poland, including the new hires, were invited to the annual two-day sales training seminar. At this meeting, AG's human resource department lectured on topics such as "negotiation skills," "creative thinking," and "business ethics." The point of this training was not to transfer a certain body of facts. Instead, through a set of simulations, games, exercises, and explanations of human psychology, the trainers asked sales representatives to examine their own "mentalities." They were asked to search within their own characters and to transform their own thinking. In this way, they were to become more *intensely* energetic, mobile, and outgoing, and they were to externalize these qualities and display them to potential customers more effectively.

The sales reps and the company together engaged in a form of image or niche marketing similar to the one used by the Frugo advertising campaign. First, in the hiring game, the salespeople sold themselves: like the product, which was supposed to transfer its qualities to the consumer, the candidates billed themselves as employees who could transfer their qualities to both firm and product. As they began working for the company, the firm used them to transfer qualities among firm, product, employee, and consumer. A sales manager told his salespeople: "A sales representative is a calling card from our firm." Jarek and Mietek, two sales representatives from Warsaw, assured me that they quite literally "represent" the firm. So their look, demeanor, and actions create images of the company and its products in the eyes of clients. Even the formal job description said that sales reps' duties included "developing and maintaining the trust and faith of clients through pleasant and friendly relations and an elegant look." As the assistant director of sales told a group of new sales reps, *"Wygląd i opinią o was będzie reprezentowała nasze produkty."* This phrase literally means "Your look and others' opinions of you represent our product," implying that the salespeople, rather than the product itself, elicited trust and goodwill from consumers.

The goal of all of this image marketing was to create another sort of identity between the sales representatives and the product. If the sales reps moved quickly, circulated among clients, and elicited good feelings in them, the product would also circulate quickly through the store. It would come in from the firm, pass through the store, and go out the door in customers' bags, while money would trace the path backward from customer to firm, thus hastening the circulation of capital.

Just as in Frugo commercials and among cell-phone carrying managers, the niche for dynamic people was created in opposition to an image of static, rigid, ignorant people. In this case, the foil was shop floor workers, who are constructed as the antithesis of the sales reps. In one of the job interviews I attended, the candidate mentioned that in another firm he had worked for, production workers were given the option of interviewing for sales representative jobs. AG's director of sales and the Lublin area manager were clearly horrified by this idea. They quickly vetoed it, saying that because the two jobs have such different characters, the people who do them must also have different characters. Hence switching between the two jobs was clearly impossible.[14]

When I asked Alima employees in sales, marketing, and operations why shop floor workers could not be moved to other jobs within the corporation, or why they could not be organized in such a way that they took greater responsibility for production, the response inevitably was *"Oni są proste ludzi"* (They are simple people). *Proste* carries a variety of meanings: literally, it means "uncomplicated" or "straightforward" but often is a euphemism for "unintelligent."

This view of the workers as unthinking—or incapable of thought—permeated the production process, particularly in the field of quality assurance protocols. Shop floor workers conducted some of the tests at various stages of the production process. However, they were required to follow instructions and record results, rather than make judgments about which tests to perform and when to perform them. There were strict written protocols for how the tests should be conducted. As a quality control manager told sales representatives, "People can forget how to do the tests, or they can forget to do them. They might feel bad, or have a quarrel or something and forget the tests or do them wrong. That's why we have directions on the report pages, and why there are directions in the binders at each station." Shop floor workers quickly pointed out that there were no similar directions written out for either salespeople or the president of the company, although presumably they also might have bad days or quarrels, and interpreted these protocols as a slight by management.[15]

Shop floor workers were equally irritated that even the people who did the tests were not permitted or required to analyze the data they collected or to make changes in the production process. Instead, changes to the product or the production process had to be made after samples had been sent to the quality control laboratories for confirmation and a manager decided to make adjustments.

The training procedures for shop floor workers also presented a view of workers as merely physical labor, not thinking beings. Unlike the sales representatives, who were trained in thinking skills and interpersonal relations, shop floor workers only attended two types of training: an occupational health and safety class mandated by the Polish government, and classes on the operation of different machines. The courses were superficial and aimed at delivering a specific body of data. For example, the in-class exercises for sales representatives asked them to rate their "reactions to conflict and disagreement." In contrast, the examination for the occupational health and safety course asked, "After working four hours, how many minutes is a break?" and provided multiple choice answers. Workers who took the course (and who had to pass the examination in order to keep their jobs) were allowed to cheat on the exam.

When I took the exam, the members of my brigade circulated a list of the question numbers and the letter of the correct answer during the test. The health and safety inspector saw this and even encouraged it. When one of us lost track of the number-letter correspondences and marked down the wrong answer, he came and corrected it before the paper was handed in. In this way, the whole training process not only deemed production workers incapable of critical thinking, self-reflection, and making decisions, it (and the health and safety inspector) also constructed them as incapable of understanding even simple concepts and memorizing facts.

The lack of self-reflection and thinking that employees outside the shop floor attribute to shop floor workers also led them to categorize production workers as people who could not understand the changes in the economy and therefore in business practice. This assumption disqualified them for other jobs in the company. Shop floor workers were not just subsumed under a Fordist separation of mental and manual laborers. They were also construed as products of the socialist system who could not adapt to changing economic conditions, precisely *because* they did not have the ability to think. A member of the marketing department, for example, told me:

> These old people, who worked here before, they don't understand the need for the existence of marketing. Marketing only started in 1993, and it was never in Poland before then. These people on production used to only have to produce as much as they could; they never had to worry about selling it. They didn't understand then why marketing was needed, and they don't understand now.

The marketer drew a parallel between work experience, being in production rather than distribution, lack of understanding, and the socialist system.

No one actually called the shop floor workers "socialist" in the sense of accusing them of having been members of the Communist Party. That would have been ridiculous, since many of them were affiliated with Solidarity. However, managers and salespeople clearly associated them with "the way things were before" and the inefficiencies of the socialist system. One way nonproduction employees made that connection was by asserting that shop floor workers were older than other employees—even though a survey I conducted showed that the average worker on the line was only about thirty-three, or *younger* than the thirty-five-year-old cutoff for newly hired sales representatives. One manager told me shop floor workers can only take orders because they spent too long submerged in the strongly hierarchical socialist system. The image of shop floor workers as "older" reflected not their chronological ages but the fact that because they began work at a younger age rather than continuing in the educational system, even thirty-five- year-olds had fifteen years of experience working under the socialist system. By assuming that shop floor workers were "older" and therefore "more experienced under socialism," other employees implied that these workers were passive, dependent, and incapable of the independence higher-ranking positions now required.

By assigning particular qualities (or the lack thereof) to different kinds of persons that reflected the differences between images of "socialism" and "capitalism," people in the firm were soon classed not just as "privatized persons" or "objects" but as "assets" or "liabilities" with distinct values. The Frugo advertisements and management ideologies contrasted images of immobile, backwards, old socialist persons with young, dynamic, mobile ones. Descriptions of shop floor workers and sales representatives also contrasted socialism and capitalism. On the one hand were persons associated with production, backwardness, lack of critical or analytic thought, collectivity, and an inability to innovate. On the other were highly mobile, active, modern individualists associated with sales, who continually learn because of their self-awareness. In the process, the managers and sales representatives who used these images mapped a set of ideas about socialism onto shop floor workers, so that they came to embody the socialist past. Just as advocates of market economy believed that socialism was unreformable, shop floor workers were seen as untrainable and unchangeable, and hence liabilities (Kornai 1992, xxv; cf. Martin 1992). In management's view, the only flexibility on the shop floor was in the size of the labor force—and the only way to reduce the "liability" that labor force represented was to reduce the number of workers.[16]

A view of shop floor workers as untrainable, whether due to disposition or lack of native intelligence, is an integral part of flexible production in multinational firms. As Wright (1996) points out in her study of the Mexican maquiladoras owned by U.S. firms, for some workers to be constituted as "trainable," others must be made "untrainable." In the post-Fordist organization of production within multinational corporations, "unskilled" workers are "the uniform constant for reading everyone else as comparatively more skilled and legitimately more powerful" (1996, 200). Similarly, for some employees in Eastern Europe to have "dispositions" that make them more amenable to sales or management, some other group of workers has to be classified as lacking those traits.

> The general idea of organization learning in FDI [foreign direct investment] situations is that an imported "top management" becomes the font of wisdom for a managerial elite of local employees. The latter group is immediately signalled out for special attention—although indoctrination might be the more appropriate term. At the same time, the local labor force as a whole is daubed with the brush of commercial ignorance as a result of the bogey of Marxism [in the East European case]. (Czeglédy 1996, 328)

By "othering" shop floor workers and portraying them as "inflexible," "socialist," and "incapable of thought," sales representatives and managers carry out another key element of the privatization of persons: the commodification of labor. As Polanyi (1944, 73) pointed out, the idea that labor is a commodity—the personal possession of the laborer—is essentially a fiction. Segmented labor markets, in which different kinds of labor are sold at disparate prices, depend on that fiction. But to have segmented labor markets, which depend on qualitative differences in *labor*, first *laborers themselves* must be differentiated and commodified.

Niche marketing of consumer goods helps that process. As the Frugo advertisements demonstrated, newly reconstructed relationships of personhood and possession mean that *who one is* and *what one has* are becoming overlapping categories in Eastern Europe. At the same time, the distinction between *who one is* and *what one does*—the distinction between the labor and the laborer—is becoming blurred as well, through disciplinary techniques like Iwona's job interviews and employee training programs like those the sales representatives went through.

The result is not just that workers are changed from acting subjects to labor power, a generalized commodity. They are transformed into different kinds of labor power that are qualitatively different kinds of commodities and become assets in distinct niche markets. Because personal identity and one's position in niche labor markets melt into one another, the disparate value of different people's labor comes to be seen as a natural emanation of the kinds of people they are rather than as the artifact of a socially constructed division of labor or as the product of a class system.

This creation of difference leads to increased inequality, both of condition and of opportunity. The construction of shop floor workers as "inflexible" excludes them from arenas where they might gain more knowledge about Western business practices and the habits and values of Western businesspeople. Since this kind of knowledge is a prerequisite for social mobility in postsocialist Poland, people from the working class are handicapped in the race to acquire power and wealth. However, at AG, shop floor workers did not accept these differences or the attempts to naturalize them. Instead, they challenged the definitions of themselves as *proste* and inflexible and looked for other bases on which to determine the allocation of resources within the firm. They reinterpreted socialism to break up the associations that put them at a disadvantage while appropriating parts of the powerful new ideology of Western business. To do so, they challenged the bases on which laborers were commodified. They denied that they were privatized individuals and put forth an alternate form of personhood.

Alternate Interpretations of Socialism

Because the new management techniques at AG were filtered through the culturally constructed categories of socialism and capitalism, shop floor workers could dispute them by arguing about the meaning and interpretation of the terms. That is, the dichotomy did not go unchallenged: the terms within it were often recategorized and used to resist management practices. Shop floor workers did this intentionally. They argued that their experience under socialism made them *better* workers for a capitalist firm because they could adjust to batch production more quickly and create better quality products. In this way, they reinterpreted "socialism" as a symbol and recontextualized it so that arguments about the character of socialist production became disputes about the organization of production in the present. Such reconfigurations and negotiations went on constantly, disrupting the company's attempts to institute American management techniques.

During my first few days at AG, I asked Ula, one of the union representatives, if she believed that what I had heard in Warsaw was true: workers who worked under socialism cannot adapt to the new requirements of capitalist enterprises. She responded,

We all worked hard to build this factory, to build Poland after the war. So they can't tell us we don't know what we are doing, that we have nothing to contribute. You can't say that everything was bad under socialism. What was bad under socialism will be bad under capitalism, and it has to go. What was good under socialism will be good now, and it has to stay. [ECD: What things were good here under socialism?] Well, everything. This was a really good firm. It's not like there wasn't an economy under socialism, you know. We made profits, and that has to stay. Frankly, we don't have to make very many changes here, because this was the best firm in Poland.

Ula's lecture significantly complicated the idea that what was socialist was inefficient and bad, and what is capitalist is necessarily better. She, like many other workers, believed that aspects of the socialist organization of work were suited to the new constraints of the capitalist enterprise. Workers with long experience, she asserted, are not merely repositories of "bad habits" but also have expertise that can make the firm successful as a capitalist enterprise.

This idea recurred during my stints as carrot peeler, time-stamp inspector, and bottle-cap cleaner in AG's Division 4. The Division 4 line could produce either baby foods or Frugo. Baby foods for Russia, Saudi Arabia, Israel, and Kuwait as well as Poland came off the line on days when we made baby food. In the course of one shift on a baby food day, we often made four or five different kinds of baby food, each destined for a different market. Even if we made only one flavor of baby food all day, the recipe and the packaging had to be changed between batches, since, as everyone assured me, each nationality has "different taste," and Polish babies won't eat food made for American babies.[17] Often, we had to do more than change recipes for the same thing all day. We had to shut down the line after a small batch of forty or fifty thousand jars, wash everything, reset all the machinery, and begin production of a completely new product. Depending on the degree of change, we could have the line down and back up again in under thirty minutes.[18] In all, the Division 4 brigades could produce more than forty-one different kinds of baby food and four kinds of Frugo, not including different recipes for the same product.

Small-batch production with extremely quick changeover times is a hallmark of post-Fordist flexible specialization and is the production component of a niche marketing strategy (Piore and Sabel 1984). At AG, just after the last bottle of a batch passed each station, the workers in my brigade would quickly clean their machines, reset, and move to the stations the next batch called for without being directed by supervisors. Workers moved quickly from sterilizer to pasteurizer, for example, when we switched from meats to fruit. Brigade leaders quickly dispatched those no longer needed at their stations to the vegetable processing area to peel carrots or potatoes, or to another division to begin fermentation testing on finished juice products. When I commented to Marysia, my brigade supervisor, on how smoothly the changeovers went, she replied, "Oh yes! These are universal people—our brigade workers can do any job in this factory."

This very "universalism" was a means for production workers to defend their jobs, both against layoffs and against being replaced at prestigious stations by lower-paid temporary workers. Permanent employees constantly asserted that although unskilled workers from the *spółka* (temporary labor firm) might be able to replace workers with years of experience at certain tasks, there was no way temporary workers could ever replace them at the full range of the various tasks they are called on to perform. In making this kind of assertion, the permanent workers adopted much of the language of flexibility and mobility that management and the sales representatives called upon as their ideological justification. Shop floor workers stressed that they, like other kinds of workers, had the ability to move quickly between tasks and adapt to changing conditions without wasting time. Yet, they reversed the assertion made by niche marketers, that a product for everybody is a product for nobody. Shop floor workers argued that their labor, as a product for everybody, was a product for anybody and any job.

The production workers, however, did not ground their assertions of flexibility in their individual characters or in terms of Western management jargon, as the sales representatives did. Instead, they called on their histories as production workers under socialism. Marysia explained that before Gerber bought Alima, Alima used to make literally hundreds of different products—not only juices for babies but also ketchups, jams, canned dinners, and frozen vegetables. This wide variety in products was necessitated both by seasonal variations in the fruits and vegetables available and by the socialist economy of shortage. When Alima lacked some of the ingredients for one product, it simply shifted to another that could be produced with the materials on hand. Even when shortages caused such extensive delays in production that fruit rotted in wagons by the factory gates, Alima had a product that could be made: fruit-based alcohols were in the repertoire of the company and its employees.

Marysia asserted that these constant shifts in the production array made workers highly flexible: since they had to shift jobs all the time, they learned a wide variety of skills and could move quickly between tasks. She presented a set of traits in the language of "flexibility," which is an ideology with a lot of power in the firm. Yet, it was a different kind of flexibility from that of the sales representatives. The salespeople based their assertions of flexibility on their *specialization*, especially on the specialization of their characters and personalities. The production workers, however, used historical experience to assert that their *generalism* makes them flexible.

The salespeople, whose claims to special efficacy were based on personality characteristics, also based their claims on their *individuality*—their uniqueness, competitiveness, and ability (or need) to work alone. This was a stark contrast to the shop floor workers' claims to flexibility based on their *universality*, or the interchangeability of experienced workers within and among brigades. Sales representatives based their prestige on a particular niche in the labor market; shop floor workers based their "flexibility" on eradicating niches altogether.[19]

Shop floor workers based their claims to flexibility and interchangeability not on the attributes of their individual characters but on their work community's continuity. Permanent workers argued that since they had worked together for so many years, they could coordinate their labor and hence were uniquely suited to smooth over the difficulties and irregularities of production. That is, they asserted that their interpersonal connections were an asset, not a liability. This ideology often set them in conflict with the firm's managers, almost all of whom came to AG after privatization and who had no roots in the community. These managers tried to use merit bonuses and individual quotas to increase workers' productivity and flexibility by setting up competition between individuals. Permanent, full-time shop floor workers saw this as divisive and counterproductive, since it would make it impossible or impractical for them to help one another, break the community apart, limit interchangeability, and impede the smooth flow of work. Danka, a worker with fifteen years of experience, told me that once individual merit bonuses were put into effect, mutual aid among workers would end. "Then nothing will get done around here," she snorted.

It is debatable whether the historical experience of socialism makes workers somehow more flexible. Certainly, the kind of flexibility required by socialism was different from that required by capitalist production, since socialist production required adaptation to uneven quality and supply of inputs, not to consumer demand.[20] It is significant, however, that shop floor workers reconstituted "socialism" as a contemporary symbol, as both a social and an economic system. They refitted specific aspects of state socialism and historical experience into a new context in order to challenge the niche labor-market system that devalued them and their labor. After all, workers did not argue that socialism or the socialist organization of production was wonderful. Rather, they insisted that the experience of socialist constraints made them better workers for a capitalist enterprise. Rather than accept the assertion that their ties to others made them inflexible, they asserted that the interpersonal connections they generated in response to shortage constituted a flexible response to an inflexible situation (cf. Burawoy and Lukacs 1992).

In this way, workers constructed a kind of expertise that allowed them to take control of the production process to some degree. In Division 1, for example, bottles went from the filler to the capper, clattered down the line to the pasteurizer, then moved down to the labeler and finally to the packer, which put the bottles into boxes. As in most production lines, all the machines did not produce at the same rate; workers had to rely on their experience and sense of community to control the line speed. For example, the capper at the beginning of the line could cap more bottles per hour than the packer could put into boxes at the tail end of the line.

This unevenness was a serious problem. If the packer at the end of the line slowed down and backed the line up to the pasteurizer, hundreds of bottles that were capped but not pasteurized could sit too long in the machine or sit on the line waiting to be pasteurized. These bottles became microbiologically contaminated and had to be thrown away. Hence the workers running the packer, the labeler, the pasteurizer, the capper, and the filler all had to be attentive to the speed at which the others were producing, watch for production problems, and adjust the running speed of their machines. Moreover, not all the workers at these stations could actually see one another, especially if pallets of juice were stored in the production hall. To solve this problem, the workers at these key stations devised a system to notify one another. If the packer backed up, the lead worker at the packer "hooted" over the deafening din to notify the pasteurizer operator, who signaled the person running the capper to slow down.

Likewise, although they were supposed to wait for reports from the laboratories, workers often notified one another about defects in the product and worked out their own solutions. When the capper was making microscopic cracks in the glass bottles one day, the pasteurizer operator, who could detect the flaws when the cracked bottles filled up with water from the pasteurizing bath, informed the capper operator, who changed how tightly her machine screwed on caps. This kind of coordination and adjustment, workers told me, was a direct result of the experience of socialism: workers learned how to coordinate among themselves to compensate for defects in raw materials and machinery (see also Burawoy and Lukacs 1992). In effect, it gave workers power to resist their deskilling. As long as the line speed varied and production problems occurred that could immediately be fixed, the "experts" who worked in the labs or wrote protocols could not completely control workers.

"People look on you differently when you give them presents"

Shop floor workers used ideas of interpersonal connection and social embeddedness to challenge the objectifying and individualizing effects of niche marketing. In doing so, they indexed a completely different form of personhood. This form of personhood is based on social interconnectedness, rather than individualism. In this "embedded" form of personhood, people are defined less by their internal qualities and more by their places in networks of social relations. More than just symbolism was at the heart of this revision of personhood: just as the creation of the "privatized individual" centered on practices like niche marketing, "embedded personhood" centered on the practice of gift exchange.

These two contrasting forms of personhood are discussed in greater depth in subsequent chapters. The important point here is that expectations of gift giving often made the division between "socialist" and "capitalist" persons, which I have presented in clear-cut fashion in this chapter, much more ambiguous. Although managers and sales representatives had incentives to appropriate qualities associated with "capitalism," they often had to confront or even make use of practices associated with "socialist" personhood. In short, they could not completely reject the socialist habitus, including the practices, symbols, or rationales of socialism. Rather, they had to confront and manipulate them, often in the course of conflicts with other groups of employees. At Alima-Gerber, this was never as clear as during battles over the marketing budget.

Problems surrounding the marketing budget centered on the small promotional items the company gave to salespeople. While sales staff were highly encouraged to create "professional" rather than "personal" relationships with clients, the clients often expected salespeople to engage in the personal networking that was typical of socialism. In the socialist economy, people often gained access to goods in shortage by forging personal relationships with people—like store clerks—who had the power to allocate resources. Those relationships were often created and maintained through the exchange of small gifts. Once marketization had changed the economy from a supply-constrained one to a demand-constrained one, grocery-store workers began to rely on their power to buy goods from suppliers rather than on their abilities to allocate goods to consumers.[21]

Since relationships with suppliers were created and maintained by exchanging gifts, clients often refused to deal with salespeople who did not offer them. This forced AG's salespeople to struggle with the company in order to get the resources they needed to meet their clients' demands. Salespeople had to confront the discrepancy between a construction that made them out to be the representatives of capitalism and the "socialist" practices that they had to use to get sales.[22] They entered a domain where one of the most important practices mandated by Gerber—the creation of a separate budget line for sales and marketing—went up for negotiation. These negotiations were complex. Since the marketing budget battles were about the transformation of socialist reciprocity, they formed a spectrum of values and interpretations that led to conflict. Yet, the lines of conflict were not always clear. People in different positions within the firm had to contend both with the structures and values of the socialist system as well as with the imperatives of a profit-making business and the rhetoric of Western management.

The first conflict was between the salespeople and the marketing department. The marketing department had a fixed sum of money, which had to cover advertising, promotions, and "freebie" giveaway items, such as t-shirts and pens with the company's logo on them. Marketing decided to focus its attention on television advertising, with a secondary focus on print advertising. Marketers saw ads as more effective, since they reached a broad spectrum of the population and covered the dispersed members of a targeted niche market.

The sales representatives disagreed strongly with this use of advertising funds. Mostly, they bemoaned the loss of pens and t-shirts and plastic bags to give to their clients, the grocery store managers. The salespeople were caught in a problematic situation. While AG marketers and many clients (mostly owners or managers of large private stores) wanted to create relationships based on mutual profit, impersonal relations between businesses, and a constellation of business practices they labeled "professionalism," other store managers ran formerly state-owned shops as if they were still state-owned. Selling to these managers entailed using the repertoire of practices developed under state socialism, including the building of personal relationships through gift-giving. The use of both these tactics—and the different systems of relationships and value they implied—was often difficult for sales representatives to negotiate.

A salesman named Jarek showed the contradictions in his approach to gift giving when we were in a shop in Lublin. The store manager refused to buy any more creamed turkey (a bestseller) until she had sold the jars of lamb she still had. Jarek, fuming, tried patiently to explain that if people wanted turkey, they weren't going to buy lamb any more than they would buy apricots. They would just go to another store and get turkey. She held firm. Outside the shop, Jarek exploded: "If people want coffee, they won't buy tea! They'll go to another shop! Doesn't she know there are other shops around the corner? Stupid Communist, that's what she is!" More quietly, he muttered, "I bet she would have ordered that turkey if I had given her a present. She bought a lot of stuff when I gave her some pens." "Why don't you give her a present?" I asked. "Because I don't have any, that's why!" he crowed. He seemed happy that he could refuse to use the old system of creating personalized business relationships through gift giving. Yet, when he had gifts with the AG logo on them, he did give them away in exchange for purchases or concessions from shop owners. "After all," he reflected, "people do look on you differently when you have given them a present, don't they?" Other sales reps said they could not get permission to hold promotions, to place their products on advantageous shelf space, or to write orders without these promotional items, if the store manager was experienced under socialism.

Salespeople were therefore in an ambiguous position. They had to rely on different strategies depending on the relationship they felt the client wanted: either old-style "arranging" with managers of formerly state-owned shops or an emphasis on quality, customer service, and other tenets of nouveau management theory when dealing with managers of new, privately owned, or foreign-owned grocery stores. They were caught in the middle of shifting forms of economic relations and had to have the tools to deal with different groups of customers with very different beliefs about how business is done.

Shop floor workers were appalled by the outflow of gifts from the firm to the salespeople. They tended to see the marketing budget as a part of the firm's overall budget rather than as a discrete budget line and therefore argued that money spent on ballpoint pens or sales reps' cars was money not spent on wages. Yet, production workers' complaints were not simply about the use of company resources. Rather, they were disputes about the way various kinds of personhood were constructed in the firm. Production workers did not see the pens and t-shirts and so on as tools that salespeople used to build relationships with clients in order to sell more product. Instead, they saw them as gifts from the firm to the salespeople, which were for the salespeoples' personal use and were meant to create personal relationships between them and the company. Shop floor workers did not object to the fact that salespeople received these gifts, Rather, they were angry that the company did not offer the same presents to production workers. The workers often implied that by excluding them from gift exchange, the company was treating them as objects rather than persons.

The issue was contentious and burst out at odd times. When I was given a small pocket calendar with the firm's logo on it, a shop floor worker named Arlena commented, sourly, "They have those for everyone but us. But of course, we're not people, we're just negroes (*murzyny*)." My jaw dropped when Arlena said this. But she continued on, unaware how shocking such racist terminology was to a North American listener. In Poland, where there has never been a substantial black population and where the society is not polarized around black-white relations, the term "negro" is not considered to be particularly venomous or even socially gauche. Assumptions about race and ethnicity are completely naturalized. Racist remarks that would offend Americans pass by in Poland without comment.[23] In using the term, then, Arlena did not mean to be as pejorative as the English term suggests. Rather, she meant that she felt the firm considered line workers to be "slaves" or "unpersons" in an abstract sense. By using the term *murzyn*, she asserted her belief that the gift of pocket calendars expressed a kind of human relationship between the firm and its employees and clients that production workers, considered as machines or slaves, were excluded from.

The issue of the cars (which bore the firm's logo and also came out of the sales and marketing budget) was even more contentious. During contract negotiations between the unions and AG, the sales reps (who were non-unionized) had to send in their car registrations to prove the firm still owned the automobiles and had not presented them as gifts to the sales reps. Sales and marketing, in the eyes of most production workers, diverted company funds to nonproductive and unnecessary activities or directly into the sales reps' pockets, thereby depriving production workers both of the money and of their rightful status as human persons.

The same marketer who dismissed shop floor workers as "those old people" and insinuated that they were relics of socialism told me that workers

> don't understand why all this money should be spent on marketing, or why sales reps should get cars and good salaries. They look at the money that we spend, and see it as money that could be given to them. They think they work hard, and they don't understand why they don't get that money. They see it as coming out of their pockets.

What the marketer failed to appreciate was the likeness production workers saw between the firm and a family: the resources of one member were the resources of all and should be shared equally. Moreover, most production workers continued to believe the firm had the same quasi-parental role toward its employees that it had under socialism and should be "caring" for them both materially and symbolically, in exchange for their labor(Verdery 1996, 61–82).

The idea underlying the shop floor workers' complaints was that persons are connected to one another and therefore have obligations to one another. From this viewpoint, persons express their connection and their obligation through the exchange of goods. Ula, the union representative, expressed this notion cogently when writing about the employee social fund in the company gazette. The social fund, one of the most significant ways that the firm "cared" for employees, was teetering on the brink of insolvency:

> It is hard for me to agree with the thesis that in capitalism everyone must look out for himself. We live together, we work together, and we must help one another. Sometimes people who earn a lot must sacrifice and give a morsel of cake to those who find themselves in difficult circumstances.

In essence, by arguing that people are not individuals but are (and must be) socially connected, Ula argues for completely different forms of personhood and person-object relations than the ones expressed by niche marketing. Niche marketing emphasizes the relationship of persons to things. It implies that persons are defined by possession—that is, the objects persons incorporate into themselves through the relation of ownership become defining elements in their social identities. At the same time, niche marketing in segmented labor markets supposes that persons are objects whose qualities can be transferred to other objects via the activity of work. The relational personhood that Ula indexes, however, emphasizes the relation of persons to persons. For Ula, persons are connected to one another in social groupings. They create, maintain, and express that connectedness through the exchange of objects. For Ula, redistribution is not necessarily the defining feature of socialism. It is the defining feature of human personhood.

Socialism, Capitalism, and Forms of Personhood

As the management gurus expected, the transformation of state-owned enterprises did indeed lead to substantial changes in employees' "mentalities." As the property regime changed and as firms developed needs for new kinds of labor, the labor market was segmented in new ways. Employees were forced to reinvent themselves to enter these new labor market niches. The result was a giant dance in which people not only evaluated themselves but also evaluated one another using particular tropes, stereotypes, and practices and sought to forge new (or at least refurbished) identities out of material imported from American capitalist disciplines and distinctions. At the heart of this drive for flexibility was the reorganized firm's demand that its employees become privatized individuals—people cut away from entangling social connections who could sell their labor as a commodity. Just like the products coming out of a flexibly specialized factory, which had specific characteristics to meet the needs of minutely defined consumer groups, employees were supposed to create specialized forms of labor to sell to the firm. They did so by changing themselves as human beings. The marketization of Poland therefore depends to a large extent on precisely the sorts of processes occurring at AG, whereby persons come to be perceived and to perceive themselves as internally and essentially different from others.

Given the tremendous amount of pressure on Polish state-owned enterprises to transform themselves into post-Fordist firms (and at Alima, the particular pressure that came from Gerber to do so), it was no wonder the firm sought to reconstruct its workers by applying disciplinary techniques like the job interviews and the training courses. Given the ever-present threat of unemployment, it was also understandable that employees worked so hard to transform themselves and participated eagerly in the firm's attempts to change them as persons. What was surprising was the role that images of socialism played in that process. State socialism was continually invoked as the antithesis of new flexible capitalism. Managers and sales representatives struggled to define themselves as flexible bodies by defining themselves in opposition to the blue-collar workers they portrayed as socialist. This is postsocialist Eastern Europe's own variant of Orientalism: for the flexible capitalist self to be naturalized and unmarked, certain people, practices, and aesthetics have to be made into the marked and denigrated other.

That the creation or attenuation of difference leads to increasing inequality should come as no surprise. In her study of concepts of flexibility in the United States, Martin (1994) discovered that both the medical establishment and corporate human resource departments portrayed members of groups traditionally excluded from power—blacks, women, homosexuals, the working class, the elderly—as physically and mentally less flexible. Discrimination was legitimized on a new basis. A similar process is going on in Poland. Ideologically, at least, the eradication of inequality and difference was at the heart of the socialist project. The famous slogan "we all have the same stomachs" was not only about treating all members of society as equals but also about treating them as fundamentally the same. Because this notion was such a fundamental part of the socialist ideal, and because opposition to socialism tended to be based on socialism's antithesis rather than on a different concrete program, the creation and naturalization of inequality and difference is a major social project in the post-1989 era.

Most advocates emphasize that income inequality in particular should be based on "merit," on achievement rather than on ascription. Images of flexibility play into this in a peculiar way: while they are ostensibly about achievement (e.g., successful adaptation to changing circumstances), they in fact conceal ascribed characteristics based on age and class. One is deemed more flexible because one can display the attributes of upper-middle class standing, not the reverse. Ideas surrounding socialism and capitalism or rigidity and flexibility therefore naturalize the exclusion of some groups from the sources of knowledge, wealth, and power.

As much as managers, marketers, and sales representatives might like to make socialism and capitalism into polar opposites, however, in practice they are forced to become hybrids who rely on socialist ideology and socialist practices—like the formation of social networks through gift exchange—as much as they rely on capitalist competition and individualism. If shop floor workers are forced to define themselves in terms of flexible capitalism, then managers and sales representatives are also forced to continually confront enduring social practices and institutions of state socialism. Although the sales representatives might like to make socialism "the past," it is continually reactivated as "the past in the present."

Constant ambiguity and the lingering presence of the socialist past in the post-Fordist present provide employees disadvantaged by "flexibility" with grounds for objecting to the commodification of laborers and to growing inequality. While new forms of employee discipline constitute persons as individuals and premise social interaction on sale or purchase, some employees constitute themselves as persons embedded in social context. They do so not by stressing ownership but by focusing on the gift. In chapter 4, I examine these two forms of personhood in more depth. I look at another form of employee discipline: quality control, as it is applied to both persons and things. Quality control elaborates the private individual by creating persons *qua* individuals, as objects with interior spaces that can be measured and changed. Quality control, however, does not go unchallenged. Some employees use practices of gift exchange, like the ones discussed in this chapter, to cultivate networks of social relations known as *znajomości*. With these networks, they blunt the effects of capitalist discipline and create alternate forms of personhood.

4 Quality Control, Discipline, and the Remaking of Persons

In social systems mediated by technology, coercion is enforced not only through labor relations but also through corporate discursive regulation of work performance, comportment within and without the factory premises, and the workers' sense of self.

Ong 1987, 142–43

When Gerber agreed to bring new forms of management to Alima, niche marketing was not the only (or even the most important) technology it had in mind. At the center of Gerber's post-Fordist revision of business practice was a single idea: quality. Gerber managers believed that by teaching Alima the practices of Total Quality Management (TQM), they could build AG into one of the main contenders in both Western and Eastern European markets. In essence, Gerber managers were hoping to contribute to the economic transformation of Poland by expanding their own firm's foreign markets, particularly in Western Europe. They believed they could do this by changing the way employees worked, thought about the products they made, and conceived of their own capacities for action.

As with niche marketing, AG applies quality control practices to both persons and products. Just as niche marketing objictifies workers by applying the same techniques to fruit juice and human beings, quality control creates a fundamental likeness between workers and raw materials by conceiving of both persons and products as *processes*. Quality control takes the reconstruction of personhood begun by niche marketing even further. The symbolic creation of difference funnels labor into different niches, but quality control disciplines labor within these niches. More significantly, by constituting the person as an individual with interior qualities that can be worked upon, processes of quality control treat workers as objects and blur the boundary between persons and things. By using similar technologies for both quality control of products and employee evaluation, American managers and the techniques they import are creating a world that is vastly different than the world created by the socialist gift economy, in which persons and things were contrasted (see Dumont 1985, 109). In the context of socialist gift exchange, objects create relationships among persons rather than serving as a model for how persons should be treated.[1]

Like the kinds of persons created by niche marketing, the elaborated form of personhood put forth by TQM techniques is an artifact of power. In this case, the "power" is not amorphous or unidentifiable but is clearly the power of the corporation as applied via technologies of audit such as quality control. In applying these techniques, AG asserts that it has "scientific" and "objective" methods of determining value and quality, that both workers and finished goods are amenable to conscious strategies of "continuous improvement" through the application of managerial techniques, and that it has the authority to apply those techniques. It gains this authority by virtue of its association with Gerber in Fremont as well as through the technical expertise of its human resource managers. However, employees can modify and dispute the likeness that TQM draws between persons and things and challenge the company's authority to determine personhood. In this case, employees subvert quality control processes when they rely on social relationships among themselves and their ties to the wider community.

Bringing Quality from Michigan

When Gerber employees first came to Alima, they assumed that state socialist enterprises were similar to the Fordist firms they knew at home. Not surprisingly, they diagnosed Alima's problem as the same one that had plagued American industry: deficient systems of quality control.[2] Gerber managers argued that these problems stemmed from Alima's role in the socialist economy. Alima was obliged, by virtue of its role as part of an association, to accept all the fruits and vegetables local farmers produced, regardless of quality or type. The hundreds of recipes that Alima workers produced (and which, according to some on the shop floor, proved the workers' "flexibility") were a response to the uneven supply and quality of agricultural produce.

Gerber officials found Alima's wide product array not only unacceptable but also contrary to the imperatives of a capitalist business. Rather than being supply-oriented, Gerber believed that AG had to become focused on what people would buy, rather than on what it could make. One company official who spent several months in Rzeszów told the story of how the employees' union representatives and the representative of the farmers' association approached him with the idea to make apple juice concentrate:

> There was an apple juice concentrator out in the plant. [Union representatives approached me and said,] "Well, to get more sales and more revenue, why don't we make apple juice concentrate?" But in that region, the apples are too sour to make apple juice concentrate that customers want. [I told them] "I'll make it, but I'll lose money, so I'm not going to do it." Now, that type of question often came from the farmers' union or the employees' union, because [they wanted us to buy their] sour apples. What I saw was us using up sour apples to lose money, because my end product, nobody wanted. Consumers don't want to add sugar to their apple juice, they want us to use sweet apples. And we have problems getting enough sweet apples over there for our own product. [The unions] weren't looking at us selling those products, they were hoping we would have more people working and we'd buy up more product from the farmers. But we'd lose money . . . and that was where I'd say, "Sorry, but this doesn't make sense to me!"

More than one Gerber official told me that the nature of Alima's business had to be completely transformed. The firm had to be changed from an entity designed to support workers and agriculturists and to provide food for children into one whose sole function was to make money. The same Gerber official continued,

> It gets down to what the purpose of a business is. If the purpose of a business is to act like a government-supported cooperative that is there to put the yields from the farmers to use, even if it means that the government has to subsidize it, then a farmer who wants to grow something can grow it even if it is not something that he can sell for a profit because there is a glut in supply. He can say, "Alima has to buy this because I grew it," and Alima has to buy it even if they don't know what to do with it. Alima made farmers' produce into something even if they couldn't sell what they made or make a profit. And the government subsidized it to make that happen. There was a point in time when that is exactly what Alima was viewed as being there for, to use up the agricultural supply from that region. The trouble [came when the government] started privatizing industry. What is that business there for? Now we're going to take the business—recognizing that [the way the socialist government viewed

business created] a huge amount of inefficiency, and we're going to turn it into a for-profit enterprise. This economy is going to evolve into a capitalist economy, and in a capitalist economy, you've got a profit motive. It's a different world.[3]

In short, Gerber officials argued that because Alima was a socialist state-owned enterprise, it had social functions above and beyond making a profit. Because it had to produce jobs as well as (or even instead of) profit, it was obliged to accept produce of widely varying quality. This meant that it did not—and could not—have the same tight quality control parameters for its products as Gerber did. Gerber managers also argued that Alima's position in a central planning system affected the quality of its products. Alima was strongly oriented to meeting its plan, which specified the amounts but not the qualities of the products it was to deliver. According to Gerber managers, it was to Alima's advantage to control quality as loosely as possible (cf. Haraszti 1977).

These pressures are part of the story that Gerber officials tell about the way Alima was under socialism. But there are aspects of Alima's approach to quality control that they do not tell. They do not mention the very strict regulation of Alima's products by the government's Institute for Mothers and Children, and they do not mention Alima's own quality control procedures, which had been in place for decades. Rather, they emphasize that because Alima was a socialist enterprise, Alima's products were of inferior quality—at least by Gerber's standards. As another Gerber employee says, "Their view of acceptable quality and our view are not the same. [With the new quality standards, the product is] just worlds apart from what might have been considered acceptable before."

To bring AG products up to Gerber's quality standards, Gerber gutted the workers' hostel and installed a sophisticated laboratory. Alongside the new machinery, Gerber instituted a highly detailed and routinized set of quality control protocols that demanded product testing at every stage. These protocols are extremely involved and demanding. The soil is tested prior to planting, to ensure there is no contamination by heavy metals or by unacceptable levels of nitrates. The crop is tested in the fields as it grows. Then, when it reaches the factory, it is tested yet again. The carrots are not just tested for nitrates or cadmium but are also graded according to a host of other categories, including sugar content, color, and consistency. They are assigned a number that not only specifies which of the many categories of carrots they belong to but also identifies the grower and the field in which they were grown.

Under this system, carrots are no longer just carrots, a vegetable that can produce useful food for people. Instead, the vegetables are broken down into a multitude of qualities, each of which can be measured and recorded. A given batch of carrots is defined as an object with a given range of values making it suitable for specific sorts of products: some carrots are good for baby food and others for carrot-based juices. Some carrots meet the Polish government's standards and so can be turned into products for the domestic market. Other carrots meet only the looser French standards and so are suitable only for export. A class 5B carrot, then, is an entirely different object than a class 7 carrot: they cannot be used in the same kinds of manufacturing operations, made into the same products, or sent to the same consumers.

The idea of constantly breaking apart a commodity into various qualities, measuring those qualities, and making it into a unique object is carried on even further during the production process. The number of tests is bewildering. The temperature of the product is tested at multiple points in the cooking and filling process. The number of microbes is counted at several points, to make sure the product is not bacterially contaminated. The consistency of the baby food is tested by taking samples, placing them in a special device with a closed container that snaps open, and then recording the time it takes for the product to flow a given number of centimeters. The flavor, aroma, and color are tested both by electromechanical means and by human taste testers. The mixture is tested again for metals, including cadmium and magnesium. Empty jars are scanned both manually and by machine to ensure that their bottoms and rims have no defects. Filled jars of baby food are x-rayed to ensure no foreign matter has inadvertently gotten into the jar. Samples are taken every few minutes and sent to the laboratory, both for further testing and to be placed in the "library," which keeps samples on hand in case of complaints about the product. Crates of packed product are held in the warehouses for up to a month to be "incubated" and are tested at ten-day intervals to ensure they have no bacteria. At each testing station, the specific qualities of the product are carefully recorded and manually graphed.

All in all, there are dozens of samples taken and tests performed at regular intervals—some as often as every ten minutes—to ensure that the baby food and juices coming off the line are of the highest purity and quality. The forms used to record the results of tests on one batch of product can total more than ninety-seven pages.[4] This process also ensures that every jar of a given Gerber product is identical, regardless of the variations in the fruits and vegetables used. A jar of applesauce made in Poland is identical in taste, color, consistency, and purity to a jar of applesauce produced in Fremont or in Costa Rica.

AG's approach to quality control is consistent with the tenets of Total Quality Management and one of its management tools, statistical process control. These two approaches to rethinking production came into vogue in the United States in the 1980s. The primary difference that TQM brought to manufacturing was an emphasis on the idea that products are not just *products*—manufactured things that must be inspected after production to ensure their quality. Rather, products are the results of an ongoing *process* that can be broken down into repeatable, measurable steps, contained within statistical parameters, analyzed further in order to explain and correct defects, and tinkered with to produce improvement. This emphasis on process is the conceptual foundation of TQM.

Contained within TQM's shift in emphasis from product to process is the idea that the process itself, not merely the qualities of the finished product, must be analyzed to make the relationships between the steps of the process and the qualities of the product explicit (Easton 1993, 5). Gerber's quality control process is designed to do this by measuring the qualities of the inputs as well as the conditions of production. To this end, the quality control process measures factors such as how tightly the cap is screwed on, the temperature of the product at multiple stages of production, and the consistency of the product at various stages.

Using statistical methods to analyze the measurements reveals the relationships between product and process at varying stages of production. This act is supposed to make the product amenable to change: changing the process supposedly changes the product. Quality control works on the same principle of audit as the reorganized, "accountable" IAS and US GAAP financial statements described in chapter 2. By constantly measuring the product along standardized scales and recording its values, quality control creates a picture of the flow of product through the factory, just as IAS accounting created a flow of money through the factory. By making the production process both visible and auditable, quality control makes it possible for managers to "control" the product. Revealing the relationship between process and product allows managers to ensure the product falls within predefined statistical standards of acceptability. Because both products and processes are broken down into minute qualities, a defect in the product should be logically traceable to its root cause in the process. AG is especially proud of this statistical control feature: if there is a complaint about any particular jar of baby food, AG laboratories can use the code stamped on the jar lid to identify the batch it was a part of, any peculiarities in any of the steps of the production process, and even the particular piece of ground it was grown on and the farmer who grew it.

One of the most important promises of Total Quality Management is that it provides a rational, scientific, and objective basis for management decisions—"management by fact"—that replaces irrational methods of management by "gut feel" or "instinct," which are inherently subjective (Easton 1993, 7). Scientized, rationalized management provides a firm's leaders with a basis for "controlling" production processes. George Easton, a TQM theorist, proposes a very specific definition of control. A process is in control when it is functioning in a stable manner, according to the well-defined sequence of steps it is composed of, and is out of control if it is functioning erratically or is disrupted. He believes that this definition of control is necessary in order to apply the concept to management or staff processes outside of manufacturing. By positing a process as its object, the definition is designed to exclude the power relationships that are inherently a part of management.

Yet, despite the scientization and apparent objectivity that statistical process control and "management by fact" provide, TQM—as a kind of quality control procedure—is very much about controlling persons as well as processes. Rather than accept the exclusion of the human and social element that Easton proposes, we should take the idea of control in its full and vernacular sense, which encompasses notions of mastery and power. The Polish equivalent of this verb, *kontrolować*, attempts to do exactly what Easton's definition of control does. *Kontrolować* can be used in the sense of "monitor" or "check." Saying that Alima Gerber *kontroluje* the carrots in the fields, then, does not imply any sense that AG is "reigning" over the carrots in the fields; it is merely monitoring them.

Yet a sense of power and mastery can occasionally sneak into the verb, too. *Kontrolować* can imply surveillance by the authorities, which ensures compliance with the law (as when inspectors on buses *kontrolują* the passengers, demanding to see each person's ticket and assigning penalties to those who are riding for free). By having employees carry out these tests at regular and frequent intervals (sometimes as often as every minute), record the results on a form that can be scanned by managers, and sign the tests with their initials, AG *kontroluje* the employees as well as the products and processes.

The production logs are a paper panopticon. Just as the prisoners in the hexagonal prison described by Foucault (1979) never knew if the guard in the tower in the center was watching them but knew he could be at any moment, Alima employees knew that the entry of the temperature (or any of the other values) of the baby food revealed a great deal about where they were and what they were doing. Just by looking at the logs, a manager could tell if a worker was at her station taking time-stamped samples every five minutes, if she had been constantly attending her machine to prevent large variations in cooking and bottling temperatures, and if the brigade was keeping the line moving at a steady speed. Managers' disciplinary "gaze" was mediated by the paper logs, but this mediation made the gaze more powerful, not less.

The logs made workers accountable for being constantly at their station working by the simple expedient of making them compile an account of the products they made. Where they could once dodge off the shop floor to go to the bathroom or sneak a smoke whenever Mr. Jagielski or the brigade supervisor wasn't looking, now the workers had to discipline themselves to stay at their machines and fill out the quality control logs. This is a far cry from the direct surveillance and often brutal physical discipline that managers used on workers in the Fordist semiconductor factory in Malaysia described by Ong (1987). At Alima, managers didn't need to watch the workers constantly to ensure the speed and quality of their work or use piece rates as a disciplinary tool, as they did in the Fordist maquiladora in Mexico where Fernandez-Kelly (1983) worked. The production logs took care of that for Alima's managers. Just as the introduction of IAS made firms into self-regulating entities by demanding they produce auditable accounts of themselves, quality control protocols attempted to make Alima's workers into self-disciplining subjects by demanding they produce auditable records of their production. Quality control may appear to be objective and scientific, but it is also a form of power and discipline on the shop floor (see also Shore and Wright 2000; Miller and Rose 1990).

Quality control protocols also create a kind of power and mastery over the consumer. The idea that Gerber products must meet demanding standards along a wide spectrum of qualities is not only about reorienting the firm to make safe, healthy products that meet minimum criteria for salability. It is also an important part of a marketing strategy aimed at increasing the number of mothers who feed their babies with Gerber and the number of jars per baby per year that they buy. As both Gerber and Alima officials pointed out to me, "growing" the baby food business is a long process that requires fundamentally changing the eating habits of the population. Part of this change involves gaining mothers' trust that Gerber products are, in fact, good for babies. In Poland, most mothers[5] still prefer to make their own baby food, reasoning that if they make it, they can be assured of the quality and purity. Gerber's marketing strategy is to convince them that only Gerber, not mothers, can really know that baby food is nutritious.

The "We See a Difference" advertising campaign used AG's new quality control methods as a selling point. The advertisements featured pictures of two ostensibly identical carrots, one on the left side of the ad and one on the right. The caption read, "We see a difference" *(My widzimy różnice).* Alongside the carrot on the left, the text read,

> This good looking carrot was grown on just any farm. Nobody controlled/monitored the way it was grown. Nobody checked if it grew in a good environment. If this carrot were given to a research specialist, he might discover, that despite its attractive look, it is not safe for a child's health. If you make your baby's food yourself, you might be endangering your child with food made from exactly this vegetable.

Next to the carrot on the right, the text read,

> This beautiful carrot is delicious and healthy. The farm where it was grown was carefully selected and tested. A specially planned system of agriculture was precisely monitored. This carrot underwent laboratory research to show it was rich in nutritious substances, and its healthful qualities were measured against the highest norms. This is exactly why these fruits and vegetables are the ones that Gerber uses for the production of its products.

In the center of the advertisement, the text continued,

> For almost sixty years, we've carried out research on the correct nutrition for infants and children. We profit from our entire knowledge and experience, from the initial selection through successive steps, to make products which are healthy, full-of-value, and delicious meals for the youngest children. Our work goes to ensuring a healthy start in life for every child which enjoys Gerber products. A rich choice of our products, which are an ideal means of fulfilling the needs of children at each stage of their development, is the best aid for the everyday care of the health of your child. Gerber. The expert in children's nutrition. [And in small type: "Every Gerber product is certified by the Head Sanitary Inspector and the Institute for Mothers and Children."]

Through these advertisements, Gerber constitutes itself as an entity that knows most about what to feed and how to feed children. It has sixty years of experience, where the average mother only has a few months or, at most, years of experience in feeding children. The ads also assert that because Gerber has extensive technological means at its disposal, it can see things in the composition of the food that mothers cannot. It can differentiate between carrots, by breaking them down into minute qualities in order to categorize them, in a way that the average mother, without training or an in-home laboratory, cannot. The ads imply that because Gerber is all-knowing and has the means to penetrate beyond the visual differences perceptible by the untrained eye, it is better at feeding children than mothers are. A graffito in a grocery store in Płock suggested that consumers were well aware that Gerber's ads implied it had more power and knowledge than the average mother: under the "We See a Difference" slogan on a Gerber flyer, someone had written in "But we do, too!" This may have just been flippant, but it also may be a way of recuperating the knowledge and expertise about one's children and how to feed them that the Gerber advertisements attempt to appropriate.

Part of Gerber's strategy for appropriating the qualities of knowledge and safety is to assert explicitly that mothers who rely on their own judgment, production methods, and labor may be endangering their children's lives. This approach reverses the whole meaning of feeding in Polish culture. Rather than the mother's work of selecting, cooking, grinding, and feeding baby food to her infant being an expression of maternal love and nurture, it is presented as a form of ignorance that may poison the child. In a parallel fashion, Gerber's insistence that its standards are better than Alima's—whether because they are new standards or because they are higher—constitutes Gerber as better at feeding children than Alima. Gerber has the money to build expensive scientific laboratories. By this, it implies it has the scientific protocols, expertise, and technology to see differences in carrots that tiny, undercapitalized, socialist Alima did not have.

The quality control protocols Gerber brought in from Fremont do two things to carrots. First, they make carrots "divisible," by breaking them down into a wide range of qualities. Then, they "differentiate" them into categories that are fundamentally different. Carrots are no longer just carrots, interchangeable and useful for the same sorts of products. They are individual classes of vegetables made up of divisible and measurable qualities. As a logical consequence of this ability to differentiate and divide carrots, Gerber can allocate to itself a scientific authority that allows it to *kontrolować* processes, products, and employees. Scientific authority also displaces maternal authority and expertise, to engender mothers' trust and encourage them to buy more products.

Gerber implementing special "knowledge"

Valuing Labor

Having learned principles of quality control, AG set about revamping its human resource management techniques as well as its production processes. Since it had learned to "see a difference" in the vegetables, the company now sought a way to see a difference in another of its raw materials: labor. In 1995, AG convened a committee to evaluate and describe the work carried out in each of the firm's jobs. The committee comprised the personnel manager, a psychologist acting as the firm's recruitment specialist, and the occupational health and safety inspector. A member of the firm's training department who had a background in sociology, the firm's directors of production and human resources, the chief engineer, and the company lawyer were occasional guests, as well as consultants from the Western consulting firm that had designed the evaluation process. (Significantly, the commission did not contain either Solidarity or OPZZ representatives, even though the job evaluations would substantially affect their constituencies.) With help from managers in each division, concrete and detailed job descriptions were written for 111 jobs. (AG employs only nine hundred people.) A specific number of points was assigned to indicate the value of each job to the firm.

The idea of job evaluation is not a new idea in Poland, but it is an increasingly trendy one. One of its primary advocates has been the newly founded Lublin School of Business, which launched the only advanced certification program in human resource management in Poland. (Not coincidentally, AG's personnel manager pursued a degree there.) According to a flyer prepared by the school and handed out at a meeting of the Lublin Human Resource Management Association by AG's personnel manager, work station evaluations are "methods of appraising [*ocenić,* which also means to set a value on] the difficulty of work." This evaluation can then be linked to pay, to promotion, and to hiring decisions.

AG also developed new methods of evaluating individual employees' performances of their jobs and linked the new methods to merit-pay bonuses. Why did AG managers suddenly feel the need for this kind of a system? What are the effects of such a system? Although the stated purpose of these evaluation systems is to provide an apolitical and objective means of determining salaries, there are several more covert uses. First, like niche marketing, employee evaluations not only allow the firm to "see a difference," but also allow it to create differences among groups of employees. However, as a managerial technology, employee evaluation does more than niche marketing can. Just as the quality control system does for carrots, the evaluation systems create boundaries between categories of employees and make them amenable to managerial control.

Many methods of work station evaluation, some of which originate with American management practice of the 1920s and 1950s, have come into fashion in Poland. Alima's system was based on the idea of "compensable factors," first developed by Merrill Lott in 1926. "Compensable factors" were abstract elements not just of *a* job but of *all* jobs in an organization. He asserted that all jobs in an organization could be broken apart and compared on the basis of the relative amounts of compensable factors in each job—hence the generic name for these kinds of systems, "factor analysis." Then, pay could be accurately and objectively linked to the amount of each compensable factor in the work, which was precisely quantified as a number of points (Henderson and Clarke 1981, 17). Another variation, the Hay Method, became the most widely used method of determining pay grades and salary scales in the 1950s; it is still used to classify U.S. federal government jobs. The Hay Method asserts that some compensable factors are not just applicable to every job within a given organization, but that there are also "universal" compensable factors—like know-how, problem solving, and accountability—that are applicable to *every* job, period.

The system that was put in place at AG was unique to it, though a variation on the general method of factor evaluation (see table 2). First, universal compensable factors were delineated and weighted. The committee agreed that the number of points assigned to "professional expertise" would comprise 46.3 percent of the total; "responsibility," 30.4 percent; "strength," 17 percent; and "conditions of work," 6.3 percent. Within each category, a wide number of subfactors and sub-subfactors were isolated and described. For example, the criterion "professional expertise" *(fachowość)* had five major categories. Professional education was granted a maximum of 75 points, professional experience was granted 60 points, innovation and creativity were granted 40 points, cleverness and skill *(zręczność)* was given 25 points, and cooperation was given a maximum of 20 points. The same breakdowns were given for "responsibility," "strength," and "conditions of work."

Once the system was developed, a set of criteria was written to evaluate each job and assign it points based on this scale. At the same time, a set of highly detailed job descriptions was written. Supervisors, in concert with the work station valuation team, were given the responsibility for writing the job descriptions for their subordinates. With the job descriptions and the "analytic keys" in hand, the commission set about assigning points to each job. For example, the subfactor "innovation and creativity" under the "professional expertise" category came with the "analytic key" reproduced in

Table 2. Major factors and subfactors in work station analysis*

Expertise (46.3%)	Responsibility (30.4%)	Strength (17%)	Conditions of Work (6.3%)
Professional education	Progress and effect of work	Physical strength	Danger
Professional experience	Decision making	Psycho-nervous	Monotony
Innovation and creativity	Means and subjects of work	Mental strength	Strength
Cleverness and skill	Responsibility for the safety of others		
Cooperation	Supervision		
	Outside contacts		

*Categories (points as percent of total)

table 3. Using a set of similar "analytic keys" for each subfactor, each job was assigned a given number of points for each subfactor. The points were then added, weighted, combined to form a total number of points, and then rank ordered. Needless to say, shop floor workers were on the bottom of the scale. Other jobs received varying numbers of points, up to a maximum of 475.[6] The different point totals assigned to each job were supposed to express the value of each job to the firm in precise terms (Barlik 1996).

Table 3. Analytic key for the criteria "innovation and creativity"

Level	Qualities of the level	Number of points
1	Routine thought. Job does not require initiative or reflection (*pomysł-owości*).	0
2	Semi-routine thought. Job requires normal initiative and reflection.	5
3	Diagnostic thought. Job requires greater initiative and reflection.	15
4	Conceptual thought. Job requires great initiative and reflection.	25
5	Creative thought. Job requires very great initiative and reflection.	40

Clarifications:

Level 1: Routine thought enters into those jobs where the conditions of executing actions are tightly regulated by instructions, such as jobs on the assembly line, cashier, or messenger.

Level 2: Semi-routine thought has a place in situations in which there is a safe choice between selected alternatives of action and simultaneous predefined tasks. This type of thought dominates jobs such as production foreman, driver, traffic inspector.

Level 3: Diagnostic thought enters into situations in which solutions demand reflection or diagnostic research. Characteristic jobs are quality controller, repair workshop manager, instructor, foreman in a craft workshop.

Level 4: Conceptual thought has a place in situations that demand deep analyses, interpretation of facts or events, or synthetic thought. Jobs include independent designer in a construction or technology firm, economic analysis specialist.

Level 5: Creative thought is needed in new situations, where current knowledge and experience do not provide any ready-made solutions, and new conceptions are required. Jobs include head of an advertising firm, scientific worker, fashion designer.

Table 4. Categories for job performance evaluation

Knowledge of own duties
Execution of duties
Know-how (including ability to solve problems and execute multiple tasks simultaneously)
Initiative
Responsibility (especially for property)
Flexibility (readiness to accept new ideas)
Creativity (managing to think constructively and untraditionally)
Communication (ability to express yourself clearly and logically)
Working with others (working effectively and loyally in all spheres; ability to keep good relations
    with others)
Relations with persons outside the firm
Leadership qualities
Information (does the worker know how to find information quickly and accurately)
Training and development

As a second component of the job valuation process, a new system of performance evaluations was developed. A form meant to be used for every employee in the firm (but with supplementary written comments for those above the level of "production worker") was based on the universal compensable factors. On a one-to-five scale, it asked managers to evaluate each employee on the basis of the thirteen categories in table 4. Scores on these evaluations were directly linked to a merit pay bonus, which was supposed to equal 1–2 percent of salary.

The committee carried out the work station evaluation to provide an ostensibly objective and scientific way of determining salary differences. AG's director of human resources said in a national newspaper, "The goal, as we come to decisions about how to determine the value and also the qualifications for work, is to make the different levels of jobs objective and to make the differences in pay rational" (cited in Barlik 1996). This is critical in a firm in which the differences between the highest earners and the lowest are rapidly widening (as is the case in Poland on the whole). As the personnel director told me,

The way the firm was, it had a different organization and a whole other relationship between pay and work. There just was another context for work. So these job evaluations are a real revolution in the way we value work. Alima has changed a lot. We have whole new divisions which never existed before, like sales and marketing and quality control. So now there are new questions about the relation between work and pay. We have to determine how much these new jobs give to the firm and how we should pay for them. Before, everything depended mostly on ideology. But this was not effective. So now we have to determine the value of what some-body actually does. We have to do this in an objective manner, so as to eliminate the jealousy and rivalry.

Nonetheless, while the work station evaluation process provides the aura of scientific objectivity and rationality, it is in fact a highly subjective system that instantiates a particular set of power relationships and then masks them. The subjectivity of the system is not "personal," in the sense that it is not directed either for or against particular named individuals. It is, how-ever, about defining and creating particular sorts of persons in concrete so-cial relationships (see also Quaid 1993, 4–5).

From the very beginning, the system has been designed to reproduce and concretize the occupational hierarchies that have emerged in the firm since privatization. Since 1992, the sales and marketing divisions, and, to a lesser extent, the quality control laboratories, have risen in the corporate power structure through a series of pitched battles. In the new job evaluations, the qualities assigned to people in those jobs were, a priori, valued more highly. To begin with, the evaluation team designed categories such as "professional expertise" and "responsibility" to reflect the qualities of white-collar jobs, and they used shop floor workers as a baseline or antithesis for those qual-ities. Then, the team gave the qualities obviously meant to describe the "pro-fessional" jobs a significantly higher weight than the qualities intended to reflect "nonprofessional" jobs. Thus, a high score in areas where production workers would obviously outscore administrators, such as "danger," was less valuable than a high score in another area. A full score in the "dangerous work conditions" category was only worth 10 points, which, when combined with its weighting of 6.3 percent (from the "conditions of work" factor), pro-vided only 6.3 points. Placement in the level three (out of four) category of "responsibility for decisions"—where one might assume that marketers or laboratory technicians fall—gave 10 points, which were multiplied by the 30 percent weighting of the "responsibility" category to yield 30 points.

Moreover, while the job titles were supposed to be evaluated by the cri-teria, quite often the number of points assigned under a criterion were de-termined by the job title. This is evident in the analytic key to "innovation and creativity," reproduced in table 4.2. The "clarifications" provide job ti-tles in order to illuminate which point values should be applied. A shop floor worker gets a score of zero on "innovation and creativity" *by definition*, not by an empirical analysis of the tasks of a production worker.

An empirical analysis might have highlighted how the point system failed to name many of the value-producing activities and skills that shop floor workers did have and thus failed to give those skills any value at all. Despite the image of shop floor work as mindless and repetitive, keeping the line running smoothly and thus profitably required a whole host of knowledges about how to make fine adjustments to machines and about coordinating the work at various stations. Adjusting the capper to ensure that it didn't make microscopic cracks in the bottles, for example, required a constant flow of information to the capper operator from the pasteurizer operator and the visual inspectors, who could see when water had seeped into the bottles during pasteurization. The capping machine operator, in turn, had to have a "feel" for which minute adjustments to make to her machine and how they interacted with the varying qualities of bottles produced in different lots at the glass factory. She had to know how changes in the temperature of the hot juice filling those bottles, which were necessitated by the varying qualities of the fruits and vegetables that went into the juice, affected the glass and hence cap torque.

Scott (1998, 313) calls this kind of practical know-how "mētis" and says it is a "wide array of practical skills and acquired intelligence used in responding to a constantly changing environment." The shortage economy of state socialism, in which inputs to production were always of variable quality and supply, required workers to develop a strong capabilities of mētis and to exercise it relatively autonomously (Burawoy and Lukács 1992). The "flexibility" that shop floor workers insist they have is largely related to the application of mētis, which allows them to adapt to changing production conditions. Yet the work station evaluation has no framework for including this form of knowledge or compensating workers for it, even though it is one of the key factors in amortizing fixed production costs and therefore of ensuring profitability. This effacement occurs not just because mētis resists codification and generalization (cf. Scott 1998, 316). Acknowledging its existence—and the firm's continuing reliance on it—would highlight the failure of the quality control system's project of standardization, codification, and control.

The effect of the work station evaluation and its effacement of mētis was to rationalize and depersonalize the firm's internal power relations. By displacing authority onto a supposedly "objective" and "scientific" system, the evaluation masked the essentially *social* nature of power within the firm. When the director of personnel said that the goal of the system was "to avoid jealousy and rivalry," he was referring to the political battles over the firm's allocation of resources such as high salaries, company cars, and company-subsidized housing to employees in sales, marketing, and the executive offices. The firm wanted the production workers and the unions to stop objecting to widening differences in pay and benefits. For this reason, it was not enough simply to institute this system. Careful thought had to be put into educating workers about the "need" for the system and convincing them of its objectivity. "We carried out the process of work station evaluation in several steps," the director of human resources told *Rzeczpospolita*. "First, we wanted to persuade employees of the need for change, which we carried out thanks to our information policies."

Persuasion took the form of articles in the employee gazette, a "sociological" survey in which employees could anonymously record their complaints about the current salary structure, meetings in which the work station evaluation was explained, and the involvement of key managers in the process of work station evaluation. The articles were particularly telling, as the firm's management attempted to explain why such a system was to employees' advantage. Some of the justifications cited a chance for AG to set policies rather than just react to legislative changes in the Employment Code made in Warsaw and the contribution to the firm's effectiveness and profitability. More important, however, management stressed the advantages in having each employee know the responsibilities and entitlements associated with his or her job. In an open letter to employees published in the company gazette, the director of human resources stated,

> The ambitious goal to which we aspire is not just that each employee at Alima know precisely what he is entitled to under the contract [which was based on the evaluation system] and national labor laws, but that he can, whenever possible, actively understand how what he receives is related to his particular sphere of competence. (*Aktualności* 1995a)

In another article, the director of human resources put the problem even more bluntly:

> An employer can't ignore the situation of the labor markets if he wants his firm to remain attractive to competent specialists and if he wants to maintain a relatively stable workforce and prevent a high rate of turnover among employees. This proves that a change in the structure and proportion of pay has to evolve over time on the basis of principles and differences specified in advance. . . . What we can say to those who are crying "unfair!" is that this simply has to happen at this stage of the firm's—and the market's—growth. (*Aktualności* 1995b)

In the early months of the process, union leaders agreed. Jurek Goździk, the head of the firm's branch of Solidarity, noted:

The most important part of the upcoming contract is going to be that we [the unions and management] work together on an agreement about wages, which should reflect a tight relationship between knowledge, competence, responsibilities and salaries. (*Aktualności* March 1995)

Constant discussions and explanations of the process were an integral part of obtaining employees' consent. As a member of the evaluation committee commented, "The most important part of this process is public relations. We have to explain why we are doing this; employees have to know. We need their opinions and their reactions."

Another means of "persuasion" was through the composition of the commission. The members of the committee that carried out the evaluation were all "professionals," with degrees in various aspects of personnel management or in social studies. The director of personnel, for example, was completing an advanced certification in human resource management, the recruitment specialist has a degree in psychology, the training specialist has a degree in sociology, and so on. The qualifications of these people were intended to lend a greater sense of scientism and objectivity to the proceedings and to further mask the operation of power. As the personnel manager said, "The point of building the team this way is that the work stations evaluation does not come down from on high, by fiat. Rather, it has to come from people who have *moral authority* to do it." The commission's level of education and prestige within the firm were supposed to ensure not only that the evaluation was carried out "scientifically" but that employees would accept both the existence of such a system and the number of points or ranking assigned to their jobs by virtue of the experts' right or authority to construct such a ranking.

The degree to which this was a successful strategy is questionable. Both union representatives asserted that by excluding them, the commission excluded expertise based on experience rather than on education. Both Ula Mazur, the OPZZ union representative, and Jurek Goździk, the Solidarity representative, objected to the fact that the commission was almost entirely made up of employees hired in the last few years, who had little experience with the wide range of work carried out in the firm. As Goździk said, "It was bad that the commission on work station evaluation didn't take advantage of the experience that the unions have. We've had a first glance at the material they prepared, and already we see certain complications." Mazur added that without the input of employees who had been at the firm for years and who had worked at a variety of different jobs, the commission would have no way of knowing precisely what each job required.

Yet, the administrators on the committee refused to admit the unions into the process. The personnel manager said that the reason the unions were excluded is that "we're not negotiating on this." The public disputes between the committee and the union representatives no doubt compromised the "moral authority" of the commission, as the union representatives redefined the kind of expertise that granted legitimate authority for this undertaking.

However, the firm did negotiate in the end, and the points assigned to each job were not defined purely by the criteria contained in the formal evaluation process. After the commission had done its work, the representatives of the two employees' unions were invited to negotiate with the commission before the document was finalized. They had several complaints about the number of points assigned to specific jobs. Was it fair that employees in exports division got more points than workers in the imports and supply division (where, not coincidentally, both union representatives work)? The unions did not think so. Was it fair that the manager of a warehouse in Gdańsk got more points than the manager of a warehouse in Rzeszów? The unions did not think so. They argued and quibbled over the evaluation of different factors for particular jobs. This, however, had a rather paradoxical effect. Although the unions argued and negotiated over the details of who would be on the commission or the number of points that were assigned to particular workers, they also tacitly accepted the existence of such a commission, the idea of rank ordering workers by the amount of value they provided to the firm (rather than seeing the value of different jobs as incommensurable or unquantifiable), and the idea that such a rank ordering could be established "scientifically" by breaking particular jobs down into lists of the personal qualities of the employees who did them.

By entering into the argument on these terms, the unions lost the right even to object to the widening differentials in salary and benefits between workers in different parts of the firm and the rapidly vanishing salary gap between new hires and employees with considerable seniority.[7] This system thus effectively codified emergent hierarchies and legitimated the fact that some members of the corporation made salaries comparable to those of managers in the West,[8] drove Toyotas and Fords provided by the company, and lived in houses that the firm paid for, while others made less than two dollars an hour.

Motivation and the Construction of the Person

The idea of having a factor comparison system for valuing work created kinds of power relations that went beyond merely setting up new hierarchies and legitimating differences in pay and prestige. Rather, it reinforced the idea of the "privatized individual" and reconstructed employees as asocial monads who were the unique sums of qualities measured on the common scales provided by compensable factors. Although applying the audit technologies of quality control to employees was a disciplinary technique, it did not produce the "docile bodies" described by Foucault (1979). Instead, it transformed some (but not all) of the firm's workers into self-activating and self-regulating persons. It "empowered" them, but it empowered them to constantly observe and improve themselves in accordance with norms set by the company, much as the quality control process "empowered" workers on the baby food line to ensure that the product complied with the company's standards.

To unravel just how the work evaluation process "makes" privatized individuals, we can begin with what AG managers see as the second function of work evaluation. In newspaper articles, letters to the employee newsletter, and interviews with visiting anthropologists, AG human resource managers assert that once the point system is in place and is tied to salary, it will have a "motivating" effect. They believe that prior to the changes in work station evaluation, the salary system strongly linked both pay and rank to seniority; workers had no ability to control their work, no financial incentive to improve, and no way to control the outcome of salary decisions. Under this new system, they say, workers will be able to look at their evaluations, pinpoint their weak spots and improve them, and gain the qualifications for promotion. As they do so, their salaries and benefits will improve.

There are two keys to understanding this assertion. First, the idea of motivation is linked to the idea that people are methodological individualists. Like the financial accounting systems, which stripped transactions of their social contexts in order to make them into quantifiable accounting "facts," the job valuation system examined the person almost completely in isolation from the work community and the work process. The job valuation system asked managers and employees themselves to look at the person in the job as a bundle of internal knowledge and predispositions. Even the category of "cooperation" focused attention inward to an individual, rather than outward to his or her relations with others in the firm. "Cooperation" focused on an individual's "knowing how" (umiejętność) to work with others, how to understand and motivate them, rather than on the quality or type of specific relations with others. Like carrots, which were treated as objects devoid of social context, people were also treated as if they had no relation to one another.

This kind of methodological individualism is an important part of "motivation," as AG managers defined it. The director of personnel asked me, "Do you love individualism, as an American? People here don't. They fear it, fear being alone. For them, being part of the mass is strength." He links this to the idea of motivation, because he believes that without the idea of monadic individualism, people are afraid to work hard, to excel, or to make more money than others. The tropes of "envy" and "jealousy" are significant here: both managers and workers complain that whenever one person has more than others, they become the subjects of jealousy and gossip and are ostracized by the group. AG managers believe that to avoid becoming the target of this "jealousy," people avoid performing excellent work so as not to stand out from the crowd. The salary system in which those judged "better" or "more valuable" to the firm receive more cannot be "motivating"—unless people reject the socialist idea of equality of condition, accept differences among individuals as a matter of course, and are willing to strive to be different, in the sense of better than the rest. Said the personnel manager,

> People have to understand the disproportions in pay now. Salary has to be an individual secret, but I can't be ashamed of earning more than another person, if I'm good. People have to understand, simply, why some people earn more than others. They have to understand that others get more, because they have more education, experience, and merit.

Like niche marketing, quality control and personnel audit systems construct people as the aggregate of many different qualities and categories, each of which can be concretely measured and assigned a value. The quality control system transformed Alima's workers into analogues of post-Fordist workers in the United States—no longer just acting subjects, but the bearers of a portfolio of assets and liabilities that have to be managed (see Maurer 1999). This opens up aspects of the person to the actions of managers, trainers, and even the conscious self. By knowing which quality needs to be "improved," some employees can take classes, read books, or change their habits to receive a higher score on their individual job performance evaluations and make themselves and their labor into more valuable commodities.

Managers assume this disaggregation is motivating. If employees know the areas in which they are weak and know that their salaries are linked to improving their evaluation scores, they will work hard to improve them. If the point values for "innovation and creativity" make up a large part of the total score for the job of sales representative, for example, but an individual sales rep gets low scores in that area on his or her performance evaluation,

managers assume he will be "motivated" to find a way to become more innovative and creative. This idea is fundamentally the same as the entire quality assurance protocol. If the production process is broken down into finite
and measurable steps, the product as a whole can be improved by the application of rational thought to the individual steps.

This idea is the force behind employee training programs, which assume
that what employees do to the product, they can do to themselves or to other
employees. As part of my field research, I attended two different sets of employee training programs. The first was a three-day seminar prepared by
AG's training division for its sales representatives. Sales representatives were
brought to Rzeszów from all over Poland. The sessions were broken down
into a course on business ethics, a course on creative thinking, and a course
on negotiation.

The three sessions used a set of common techniques. First, the participants were asked to fill out a questionnaire, in which they judged their own
responses and personal qualities. For example, during the session on negotiation, they began by indicating on a scale from one to ten their responses
to conflict and disagreement. Statements included "conflicts are a part of life
and I try to solve them," and "conflict is something positive because it helps
me to specify and verify my thoughts." Once the participants filled out the
questionnaire, an overhead indicating how "good negotiators" feel about
these topics was displayed. Afterward, participants engaged in a role-play-
ing game in which they negotiated for the privatization of a city building.
The trainer, Elżbieta, circulated around the room and made observations
and comments about different individuals' negotiating styles. Handouts
specified the qualities of different types of negotiation situations. In "soft"
negotiations, for example, both negotiators were friends; in "hard" negotiations, the participants were opponents. A "meritorious" situation was one in
which both participants understood the problem and worked together to re-
solve it. Other handouts described a plethora of ways to change the self in
accordance with a given model. The active listening skills section, for example, not only counseled mental dispositions such as "willingness to understand" but also mandated particular bodily postures ("sit in a comfortable
position, keep your expression 'open,' hold eye contact and be relaxed and
have a respectful expression") and speech events ("Use phrases such as, 'Is
that so?' and 'What would you like to say on that topic?'"). Similar techniques were used during the creative thinking training. Participants were
asked to rate their own qualities, presented with models to emulate, and required to reflect on how they might change themselves.

This kind of training "opens up" the person even further, as an individual with divisible qualities. By asking participants to reveal their thoughts and responses, it makes them amenable not only to measurement but also to teaching. Having received the teaching, participants are expected to act upon themselves to transform their deepest thoughts, attitudes, and actions. This is a curious construction of the person: one that, although it exists in social contexts such as negotiation can achieve the desired results simply by acting upon private aspects of itself, rather than upon external situations or persons.

The second training program I attended reached even deeper into the recesses of the person. This was a course entitled "Assertiveness as a Condition of Managerial Work," given by an outside consulting firm in Kraków. Maria, a psychologist, led the course, and participants were middle managers from large companies in the Kraków region.[9] Maria first asked participants why they came to the course. Basia, a manager at the Polfa pharmaceuticals firm, responded that she had received low marks on her last evaluation. She wailed, "It's not true that I'm just a certain number of points on an evaluation! They are six, seven, eight page evaluations, but that doesn't sum me up! It's really hard! They don't give you any means of achieving improvement, no concrete steps!" Maria replied, "It's really important, though, that employees know their limits and their possibilities, in addition to a clear description of their duties in their job. Because when they do, they can make realistic plans for their work. But without this knowledge, they make unrealistic plans." From this exchange, it was clear that the evaluation process drove Basia into a training course. Maria assured her that once she had the training and could put it into place, she would be able to improve her scores. The other participants in the course agreed that one reason they were there was to improve their evaluations. In a climate of massive layoffs, the managers were deeply afraid that failure to comply with the company's demands for personal transformation would lead to loss of livelihood.

Maria defined assertiveness in a way that stems from within the bounded self but reaches outward to act upon others:

> [Assertiveness is] knowing what we want and what our goals are. In every human contact, knowing what we want is the most important. If we know what the goal is, we can act to achieve a desired effect. If we want to act better, we have to understand and analyze what we want, in very concrete terms. In the example of reorganizing the workplace, we have to know how we want it to be, then we can reorganize, fire people, etc. Sometimes you have to make unpleasant decisions in order to achieve the goal. . . . If we don't tell others how we really feel, we are having false contact. As-

sertiveness is *honesty.* It is an appreciation of yourself as unique: "I am a unique and unrepeatable person" (*Jestem jedyną i niepowtarzalną osobą*).

To teach the participants to become assertive and to make unpleasant demands on others without either feeling guilty or arousing resistance, Maria began by having participants reveal aspects of themselves, their lives, and their personalities. We filled out forms detailing our jobs, the skills we were proudest of, and those aspects of our behavior that we did not like. Then Maria had us discuss situations in which we felt uncomfortable. She did not query us about what the other person in the interaction did but about how we felt about ourselves. She had us repeat a list of statements about "the assertive person," using the first-person voice. "I have the right to my own opinion, feelings, and emotions and the responsibility to express them," repeated Basia, tremulously. "I have the right to make mistakes."

As the exercise progressed, the participants became visibly more emotional and upset. Another woman in the group, Grażyna, exploded: "Why don't they teach us these things in school? Maybe the humanists get taught these things, like communication, but we technical people don't! And we need to know them too! People are really afraid now. There is a lot of competition for every job, so we have to struggle." Maria responded, "You have to learn to defend what is yours. You have to mark your territory. You have to defend your time, your space, your secrets, and your property." All the women in the group concurred that it is difficult to say no. Grażyna said, "I worry that if I say no, the boss will knock points off my evaluation and I will lose my job."

The irony of the course is that as Maria counseled us on how to create boundaries around ourselves and our private spaces, she did so by encouraging us to plumb our deepest feelings about ourselves and to expose those to the group. In one exercise, she had each member of the group describe a situation with his or her boss, in which the boss has asked the employee to do something the employee does not want to do. Then, with another member of the group standing in as the boss, the participants acted out the situation. When it was Basia's turn, a male participant asked her to fill out some paperwork. She responded hesitantly, "Please, *Panie Dyrektorze* [a naming form which indicates extreme deference], I really can't do it because I'm busy. I'm sorry. . . . Maria led the group in critiquing Basia's response. "Basia, this work isn't part of your job. Don't you respect yourself enough to stand up for yourself?" Basia had to describe how she felt not only about her boss but also about herself. The group commented on her words, her tone, her posture, and her gestures. Over and over, Basia was forced to act out the scenario, until, on the verge of tears, she provided a response that the group accepted.[10]

Applying audit technologies to persons and providing training courses in which people transform themselves marks the introduction of a completely new form of discipline to Poland: neoliberal governmentality. Neoliberal governmentality depends, in the first instance, on "inculcating new norms" into "organizations and individuals in their capacities as self-activating agents (Shore and Wright 2000; see also Miller and Rose 1990). By individualizing Alima's employees and dividing them into bundles of qualities, the performance and work station evaluations helped inculcate new norms. By making workers render accounts of themselves, the performance evaluations ensured their constantly "accountable" behavior. And by giving them the means for self-transformation, the training courses ensured that they would constantly discipline themselves more effectively than any external agent. This is a radical change from the power of the socialist state, premised on the very overt presence of surveillance or, at least, the omnipresent possibility of surveillance (see Burawoy and Lukács 1992, 139).

It isn't just the appearance of agentless power or the ability to elicit self-discipline that makes neoliberal governmentality a qualitatively new phenomenon in Eastern Europe. It is that by making people into analogues of the production process or into scaled-down versions of corporations that hold assets and liabilities, neoliberal governmentality brings the principles of the free market to bear on the construction and conduct of individuals. Through the quality control program, individuals are now forced to actively and "freely" regulate themselves to reduce production costs, increase profit margins, and add value to products. Post-Fordist neoliberal governmentality elicits willing participation in the work process and naturalizes inequality.

As much as scholars of audit in the European financial system (Power 1997) or in British universities (Shore and Wright 2000; Strathern 2000) might portray these concepts of personhood and rationality as inescapable elements of new work systems, there are alternatives. Interrogating the differences between the post-Fordist construction of the person and the one that preceded it in Polish factories shows other ideas about human nature and other explanations of what makes people work (and work harder). Ideas of personhood based on *znajomości*, or personal connections, show that the self-activating self created through neoliberal governmentality is contingent, even though it is a fundamental part of the kind of capitalism being built in Poland.

Znajomości

"A hundred years of communism without *znajomości!*" chuckled my landlady, Ela. "That is the worst curse that you could have imagined under socialism!" *Znajomości*, which comes from the verb *znać*, or "to know," is usually translated as "acquaintance" or "connections." These, however, are impoverished translations of a rich and multifaceted phenomenon also known as *blat* in Russia, *pile* in Romania, and *guanxi* in China (cf. Ledeneva 1998; Kharkhordin 1999; Yang 1994; Yan 1996). The Polish variant is derived both from Polish traditions of gift exchange and from the experience of a shortage economy. *Znajomości* provides a model of personhood and of social relations vastly different from the ones the evaluation and training models implied. Contrary to the expectations of social scientists (Kennedy and Bialecki 1989, among others) and even of AG managers, the end of socialism and the shift to a market economy have not ended these relationships but rather have placed them in a new context.

One way of looking at *znajomości* is as networks of horizontal exchange relationships among a circle of intimates. Wedel (1986) illustrates how members of particular social circles, or *środowiska*, use their personalized connections with one another to gain access to goods in shortage and to exchange information. Under conditions of shortage, having a *znajomy* was often the only way to get desired objects. Whether the *znajomy* was a clerk in a store who saved goods under the counter so that his exchange partners could purchase them (Verdery 1996; Wedel 1986, 47), a teacher or a bureaucrat (Szakolczai and Horvath 1993), or a civil servant who arranged visas and other documents, *znajomości* was often the only way to get things done. This process is known under the heading of *załatwić sprawy* (Wedel 1986, 104–7), which means "to arrange things." To *załatwić sprawy*, one calls on the access that one's *znajomy* have. In return, one can give gifts of equal value or merely let the debt remain outstanding so that one's partner can call in his or her chips in a time of need. *Znajomości*, then, is a kind of relationship that does not have a linguistic equivalent in English. It is not "friendship," for the relation does not necessarily imply affection, although it may well include that component. (One's friends and relatives make up an important part of the *środowisko*.) Rather, it is an exchange relationship that is kept active by small gifts and favors.

The state socialist system, as many commentators (Kornai 1992; Verdery 1996; Nagengast 1991; Wedel 1986, 81) have pointed out, depended on these informal relationships to "chink the gaps" of the socialist system by mitigating distribution problems, bringing hard currency into the economy, and obtaining necessary information. This happened not only at the level of individual consumption but also at the enterprise level. Managers of firms, for example, often inflated their requests for allocations so that they would have surplus to trade with other firms when they lacked sufficient quantities of another good. Workers and managers both often had to call on their *znajomy* outside the firm in order to produce at all. For example, a mechanic at AG tells of how he once had to trade fruit juice he "arranged" from Alima for a needed freezer part, made "on the side" by an acquaintance at a local airplane engine factory. In this way, *znajomości* blurred the lines between individual consumption and industrial production.

Another case in point was the way that relationships in the workplace facilitated theft from the plant for personal ends. At Alima, relationships that workers developed with the guards at the factory gates allowed them to smuggle out finished products, raw materials, and even objects that workers had made on company time, with company materials, for personal use.[11]

As a system of horizontal relationships, *znajomości* formed the basis for the ideological division between "us" and "them" or between "society" and "power" that was so critical for the Solidarity movement (Tymowski 1993, 192–99). The concepts of *znajomości* and *środowiska*, which were aggregated into the collective subject *społeczeństwo*, or society, presumed a fundamental equality within those groups.

However, *znajomości* is not only a horizontal relationship between equals trading favors. It can also be a form of relationship between individuals on different levels of a hierarchy. Kennedy and Bialecki (1989), in their study of political elites and lower-level functionaries, call this "vassalage." Although they assert that manual workers do not often participate in vassalage, it became clear to me that such relationships not only exist on the shop floor but are also an integral part of how the production floor works. "Vassalage is not a demeaning status but a means by which advancement is made possible," say Kennedy and Bialecki (1989, 309). Fundamentally, vassalage was a personalized patron-client relationship; "loyalty" was demonstrated by the exchange of "gifts," both tangible and intangible. At Alima, for example, the old "motivational" system comprised *bonusy* and *nagrody* (bonuses and prizes), which were gifts such as dinners in fancy restaurants and weekend trips to the nearby Bieszczady Mountains (cf. Pancer 1985). According to many workers, the gifts were given out purely on the basis of *znajomości* rather than on the basis of merit. One worker, Anna, said that managers sometimes gave the bonuses to workers who had been on "sick leave" for months and so had not even been at work. The return was sometimes a personal gift but could also be a gift that enhanced the power of the superior within the organization. Thus, when the mechanic used his *znajomości* with other workers at the airplane engine factory to get the necessary part for the freezer, the part could be presented as a gift to his superior, thus creating *znajomości* between them and obligation on the part of the superior. As Kennedy and Bialecki state, "Vassalage is a mutually advantageous relationship for notable and vassal. . . . Vassals can provide resources and information essential to a notable's success" (1989, 310).

Personal relationships with superiors were of critical importance for Alima workers under socialism. For example, many Alima workers were not urban residents but worker-peasants. In these households, often one adult worked at Alima while others ran the family farm. Through their connections at Alima, these farmers could secure valuable contracts that ensured Alima would buy their produce. Most of the planters, in fact, were relatives of Alima workers or Alima workers themselves.

The horizontal and vertical relations of *znajomości* in the firm have come under substantial attack. One goal of the work evaluation/merit pay process that AG is instituting is to eliminate "jealousy" and "rivalry" among employees. In some senses, this is also a covert reference to the aim of dismantling the *znajomości* system. Because subordinates have to vie with one another to create *znajomości* with their superiors, those who are excluded often use gossip and rumor to allege unfairness. The "objectivity" of the job evaluation and evaluation processes is supposed to eliminate the need to cultivate *znajomości,* to award pay and bonuses "fairly," and hence to eliminate jealousy and gossip.[12]

However, judging from the frequency with which gift exchange goes on, it appears that the creation of *znajomości* within the firm has in no way diminished. In AG's Division 1, where I worked as a juice bottler, I saw many different instances of the cultivation of *znajomości.* One of the most significant ways was through name-day celebrations, where people celebrated the feast day of the saint for which they were named. In the shop floor and in the offices of middle managers, people who were having a name day brought in cakes and coffee to serve to their colleagues. Sometimes these were served only to one's closest *koledzy,* or colleagues. Other workers made a studied effort to include the widest possible range of persons: one woman baked for four days and then invited her entire shift up, four at a time, for a feast of several different kinds of cakes, chocolate, coffee, and tea. The largest name-day celebration I participated in was that of Jolanta, the head of Division 1. Her name-day celebration went on for an entire day. Managers from divisions throughout the firm came bearing flowers, exotic plants, and other gifts, and they were treated to a sumptuous spread.[13]

These exchanges contribute significantly to the creation of solidarity on the shop floor. By creating and maintaining a personal relationship between the participants, they facilitate the work process, ensuring that necessary information passes among *koledzy* later on. Moreover, they often serve to limit destructive gossip: by being included in the *środowisko*, a person is expected not to damage another by backbiting. Such conduct would be tantamount to betrayal.

Vertical relationships between subordinates and superiors are also constructed through gift exchange. For example, when I brought cakes and coffee to Division 1 to say good-bye at the end of my stay, we were immediately faced with a shortage situation. Although I had brought six cakes, including a huge chocolate torte, I had not brought enough for everyone. One member of my brigade, Danusia, immediately took over the cutting of the cakes and the preparation of plates for everyone. She cut huge slabs out of the chocolate torte and substantial pieces out of the other cakes. These were arranged carefully on plates to be given to Jolanta, the shop forewomen, and the shift supervisors. Then, Danusia cut tiny, paper-thin slices of what was left of the torte and a small piece of another cake to put on paper napkins for the members of the brigade. "It doesn't matter how small it is," she told me. "It's important that everyone get some." In this manner, Danusia fulfilled two contradictory obligations. She helped me create better relations with those in power, by giving them the biggest and the best.[14] Then, she helped me create *equal* horizontal solidarity with the members of my brigade, to show that I had no favoritism for any of them.[15]

Other attempts to create *znajomości* with higher-ups went on constantly. For Jolanta's name day, Danusia and Jadzia purchased special name-day greetings. For the outrageous price of one million old złoty (a week's wages for some on the shop floor), they had a special name-day video and greetings from them played on a national television program. This, they felt, would give them preferential *znajomości* with the division head. Other workers tried to build *znajomości* with me, knowing that I had developed a close relationship with Jolanta. At one point during my stay, the rumor circulated that some of the workers who were on monthly contracts, rather than permanent ones, were about to be laid off. My close friend Gracjana begged me to discuss her case with Jolanta. "Tell her I have three children and that I am the only employed adult in the house," she pleaded. "Tell her that my husband Marek drinks and he beats me." (He did drink, but he did not beat her.) What Gracjana wanted me to do was to get Jolanta to think of her as a *person*, not just a worker. She wanted to bring Jolanta into her *środowisko* via me.[16]

The example of Gracjana reveals one of the primary reasons that employees cultivate *znajomości* with their superiors: the belief that even though hiring, firing, and promotion decisions are supposed to be made objectively on the basis of job evaluations, they are in fact governed by *znajomości*. When I commented to one worker that the firm's directors had promised that the new merit-pay bonuses would be handled without *znajomości*, she snorted. Because the new directors of the firm were not from Rzeszów and had little *znajomości* with either the shop floor supervisors or the workers themselves, they would have no way of knowing if *znajomości* had biased the evaluations or not. Moreover, Gracjana and other workers alleged that opportunities to get ahead in the job evaluation scheme were limited by *znajomości*. Chances to work on new machines, to get additional training, and thus to score more points on the "professional expertise" section of both the performance evaluations and the factor analysis were given out by managers to their *znajomy*.

Whether or not personal relations affected the performance evaluations of workers that were already there, it was clear that they did significantly affect hiring decisions for production workers. After AG laid off a large number of production workers in 1994, there was a real need for both seasonal and new full-time workers. These were hired through the *Spółka "Usługi Różne"* or Firm of Different Services, a temporary agency. The *spółka* was supposed to use objective evaluation procedures to hire new workers for the firm and to decide which workers would be laid off as the firm's labor needs declined at the end of the growing season.

Yet, *znajomości*, not "rational" or "objective" evaluation, was clearly the operating principle. The *spółka* was set up by the son of a long-time AG administrator and provided workers only for AG. With one exception,[17] all of the contract workers hired by the *spółka* had a relative or close friend who worked for the firm, usually in the middle level of the firm's hierarchy. Even the *spółka* employee who was charged with gathering information on workers from managers, so that the employees could be rationally evaluated, was the son of one of Jolanta's neighbors and close friends. He also was the twin brother of one of the laboratory technicians.

Whatever employees say about *znajomości*—and they complain bitterly about the unfairness of it all—it *works*. Just as gift exchange helps sales representatives create *znajomości* with grocery store managers and therefore to get sales, gift exchange helps shop floor workers create *znajomości* with supervisors and obtain preferential treatment. When it comes time for managers on the shop floor to do performance evaluations, for example, they are faced with a dilemma. Since so many of the categories on the new performance evaluation form (such as innovation and creativity) do not apply to the workers' jobs, in which they are supposed to accept direction rather than think for themselves, the forms are hard to fill out. Many workers believe that relations of *znajomości* lead managers to arbitrarily give their *znajomych* higher marks. One operator told me that for categories such as "know-how," managers might state that a non-*znajomy* worker knows how to run three machines and therefore gives them a lower evaluation, when in fact the worker knows how to run ten. As Gosia, a filler operator, says, "Those who kiss ass always get ahead, even now." The performance evaluation system, precisely because of its "universality," in fact makes the process arbitrary and dependent on *znajomości*.

The creation of personal relations, both horizontally and vertically, not only gets people hired or gets them bonuses, it also often keeps them from being fired. When it came time for Mr. Jagielski, the director of production and Jolanta's boss, to decide which of the contract workers would be fired, he did not use the "objective" evaluation system to make his decisions. He did not use a construction of workers as asocial monads. Rather, he collected information about each worker from shift supervisors, forewomen, and Jolanta, as well as from permanent full-time workers and from the *spółka*. He not only looked at how each contract worker performed his or her duties but also interviewed each one about his or her family situation and the difficulties that a layoff would cause them. That is, he looked at each worker as a member of a set of social relationships both inside and outside the factory. In the end, he tried to give the layoffs to those workers who could best afford it—students working part-time and people who were in households with multiple employed adults.

Znajomości was supposed to be an aspect of the "defective" relations of production and distribution under socialism. Scarcity and arbitrariness, which derived from the socialist ruling elite's control over planning, created an atmosphere with a high degree of uncertainty. "Vassalage is essential to survival in this system of uncertainty . . . [and] survival is critical for vassals. There is only one employer in centrally planned economies, and loyalty is the primary criterion by which vassals are judged" (Kennedy and Bialecki 1989, 312–13; see also Nove 1983, 71–73). Vassalage was therefore one of the compensatory mechanisms that kept the socialist system functioning. Despite the turn to a market economy, however, *znajomości* still exists, contrary to Kennedy and Bialecki's (and many other commentators') predictions. This is because, at least in situations like the one at AG, the basic conditions that Kennedy and Bialecki describe still obtain. Of course, the primary good in shortage now is money. But in an economy with 17 percent unemployment, in which industrial production workers' prospects for finding employment in other large industries is slim, mobility is limited. The uncertainty of the situation is therefore even greater, and workers' dependence on the firm and on their superiors is even more significant. Hence, even with all its drawbacks and injustices, workers still seek to create a unified front (*my*, or "us") to those at the high reaches of management while cultivating direct personal ties with immediate supervisors.

Two Systems of Personhood

Kennedy and Bialecki state that while the two official bases of socialist distribution were "to each according to his need" and "to each according to his work," the actual tendency shaping the logic of distribution was "to each according to his significance in the reproduction of power relations" (1989, 315–17). Rather surprisingly, this is true in both the "objective evaluation" and the *znajomości* systems. However, these two systems construct the person in strikingly different ways. Where factor evaluation constructs the person as an individual who can be broken down into personal qualities that are his or her constituent parts, *znajomości* views the person as embedded in a social context. An interesting comparison might be drawn with Strathern's work in Highland New Guinea. Borrowing from Marriott (1976), she asserts:

> Far from being regarded as unique entities, Melanesian persons are as dividually as they are individually conceived. They contain a generalized society within. Indeed, persons are frequently constructed as the plural and composite site of the relationships that produced them. (Strathern 1988, 13)

We might see persons, as they are conceived of in *znajomości*, as similarly the plural and composite sites of ongoing exchange relationships (although separable from them if they fail to maintain them). This conception of person shows up not only on the factory floor or in the butcher's shop but also in institutions as prominent as the Polish Catholic Church. In the Church, persons are not seen as having an individual relationship to God (as they do in Protestantism) but as parts of the body of the Church whose relationship to God can only be mediated through the totality of the Church community, via ritual gifts. Here, persons are inherently social. They are neither asocial monads nor contained microcosms of sociality but instead are loci of multiple human relations.

This view of the person as "dividual," or socially embedded, is a sharp contrast with what Strathern labels the "Western" person. The fundamental premise about persons in Western society is not just that they are individuals but that they are individuals who are the owners of their "parts," or qualities. In this sense, persons become composites not of social relations but of "properties" in a dual sense: both possessions and qualities. The "possessive individual" (MacPherson 1962) is, above all, the owner of him or herself. In this sense, "possessive" and "individual" are mutually constituting, and the self becomes a kind of private property.

The differences between the two models of personhood fundamentally change the way in which persons can become social actors. The "dividual" person acts upon the world by acting upon others. In a Melanesian context, this is done through the extension of personal "spacetime" via the exchange of gifts, which supposedly moves others' minds (Munn 1986). Under the conditions of *znajomości* or vassalage, persons attempt to "know" others and to make themselves known to them, to incorporate one another into *środowiska*, and, consequently, to move one another to exchange goods. The relations of *znajomości* are a way of "moving another's mind" and, in doing so, changing the experienced world. In contrast, the privatized individual acts upon the world by transforming the self.

Whether through education and training, quality control, psychotherapy, or the application of cosmetics, changing the self is supposed to change the qualities of either other persons or things, and hence to change the world external to the self. When one uses *znajomości* to "arrange things" *(załatwiać sprawę)*, one is using personal connections to maneuver around immobile obstacles. When becoming "more assertive," one is attempting to change the obstacles by transforming the self. The way of acting implied by *znajomości* is focused on the world outside the self, while the evaluation and training model is focused within the self.

Despite Strathern's division of personhood systems into "the West" and "the rest," it is clear that multiple forms of personhood exist in any given locale. Thus, rather than labeling Poles or shop floor workers as "primitive" by comparing them with Melanesians, I mean to show that in one Polish factory, there are multiple ways of constructing persons. The same is true of Americans in general,[18] as can be seen in any American corporate setting. Quips like "it's not what you know, it's who you know" and the whole set of practices labeled "networking" are obvious reminders that the exchange of gifts and favors and the construction of both horizontal and vertical relationships exist there, too. But why, then, in a capitalist social economy, is social embeddedness constantly swept under the rug, while the person as an "individual" in the senses I have outlined is constantly recreated, celebrated, and reproduced? Why is it important that the myth of the monadic individual who is an aggregate of personal qualities be propagated?

In their discussion of Foucault's concept of governmentality, Miller and Rose (1990) suggest that we must begin to think of both politics and economy—that is, "government"—as encompassing a realm substantially wider than the state (1990, 2). That is, for particular political economic forms to exist, persons must be "governed" or regulated by forces beyond the state (1990, 18). They see technologies that constitute the self-governing choice-making individual as key in the formation of both liberal democracy and market economy:

> Governing involves not just the ordering of activities and processes. Governing operates through subjects. . . . To the extent that authoritative norms, calculative technologies, and forms of evaluation can be translated into the values, decisions and judgments of citizens in their professional and personal capacities, they can function as part of the "self-steering" mechanisms of individuals. Hence "free" individuals and "private" spaces can be ruled without breaching their formal autonomy. To this end, many and varied programmes have placed a high value upon the capacities of subjects, and a range of technologies have sought to act on the personal capacities of subjects—as producers, consumers, parents and citizens. . . . Experts have played a key role here. They have elaborated the arguments that the personal capacities of individuals can be managed in order to achieve socially desirable goals. . . . They have acted as powerful translation devices between "authorities" and "individuals," shaping conduct not through compulsion but through the power of truth, the potency of rationality, and the alluring promises of effectivity. (Miller and Rose 1990, 18–19)

The kind of individual, partible, and "privatized" person that I have outlined is a condition of existence of at least two necessary aspects of late twentieth-century capitalism: consumerism and wage labor. First, purchasers in the Polish market are being transformed from either "hunters" seeking products through *znajomości* or the passive recipients of goods from the state into active consumers with preferences and choices.[19] This comes not only from the widening array of goods in the market but also from the fact that people are devoting increasing amounts of time and resources to reworking and elaborating their *individual differences* through the consumption of products especially for them. The language of evaluation and self-transformation is replicated here, as individuals become "entrepreneurs of themselves," maximizing their quality of life and defining themselves through the products they purchase and assemble (Miller and Rose 1990, 25).

Consumption is heightened when people are believed to be the aggregate of potentially divisible qualities that can be acted upon by the purchase of specific goods (i.e., a young woman's attractiveness can be improved by face cream, or a man's sexual attractiveness can be enhanced by the purchase of a sports car). Consumption is further heightened when specific groups of consumers believe that their aggregate qualities are unique and, hence, can only be acted on by particular products. This is the genesis of a niche marketing strategy (see chapter 3). When a firm has the authority that leads consumers to believe that it and its products can act most effectively on these qualities, it has carved a place for itself in the market. An individual who is a choice-making "entrepreneur" of him or herself and who consumes products in order to act upon his or her qualities becomes an engine of economic growth.

If consumers in a market economy are "entrepreneurs" of themselves, they must also be "owners" of themselves (see Strathern 1988, 135; 1996) and all of their properties, in the dual sense of that word. We might think of the reconstruction of wage labor in Poland along the same lines. If persons are the private owners of themselves, they are also the owners of their labor. As the private "property" of the self, labor is something that one individual is free to sell to another. A notion of the person as both partible and individual is a necessary condition of this type of wage labor. A person must be an individual if he or she is to be "free" to sell his or her labor unencumbered by others' rights to that labor. Moreover, if the sum of the relationship between employer and employee is to be contained in the exchange of labor for wage, "labor" must be detachable from the individual so that its alienation is fully compensated for by the wage without any further encumbrances on the employer. This is a sharp contrast with ideologies of labor under socialism. In socialist systems, people often believed that by investing parts of themselves in an object through labor, they created some form of enduring property right to the product and an enduring relation to coproducers (see also Verdery 1998). The privatization of firms thus entails the "privatization" of persons, so that employees may freely sell their labor.

These reconstructions of consumption and of labor through regulating technologies of the person lead to a rethinking about how power is operating in Poland. For, in the end, technologies such as the factor evaluation of jobs and performance evaluations of persons are about *control*. In a simple sense, the direct effect of individualizing employees is to break up the intractable collectivity of the workforce that was so brilliantly deployed by Solidarity (cf. Kennedy and Bialecki 1989 on the inert force of the collective bureaucracy). If employees are judged individually and must compete with other employees on an individual basis, their collective force is lessened. This is precisely what the maintenance of *znajomości* on the shop floor is designed to avoid.

In a more complex sense, the nature of power and the way that it is deployed in the enterprise and in the economy are being transformed. Burawoy and Lukács (1992, 139–40) suggest that the wide gap between what socialist ideology promised and what socialist reality delivered made power visible. The workings of socialism as a kind of "gift economy" also made power somewhat visible. If in gift economies, as Strathern asserts, "those who dominate are those who determine the connections and disconnections created by the circulation of objects," then human social relationships and power must be made at least partly visible (1988, 167).

Under capitalism, power relationships are quite different. Because visible power and authority are displaced onto technologies such as the forms of audit I have described here, power comes from the creation of an accepted version of "reality" and the internalization of discipline through self-audit rather than from exhortations, overt ideological formations, or brute force (Miller and Rose 1990, 19). It is therefore less visible and more difficult to challenge. But it is not impossible to challenge. Just as a re-emphasis on the practical skills of mētis allowed workers to challenge their deskilling and to assert their flexibility, networks of *znajomości* allowed employees to resist discipline, mitigate inequality in the firm, and assert their value in the new economy.

5 Ideas of Kin and Home on the Shop Floor

My first weeks on the shop floor, I cringed every time Mr. Jagielski, the director of production, passed my station. He is a huge man in his late fifties, dressed in the same white lab coat that all production workers (but none of the other directors) wear and a dark blue cap, which signaled his higher station. Like a huge bear, he roamed the shop floor from time to time, casting a knowing eye on the workers and their machines. He knew exactly what we were supposed to be doing, and like a grizzly sighting prey, he could detect the instant we weren't doing it. "No talking! Pay attention to what you're doing!" he would bark when he saw me talking with a line worker. "Do you have a machine operator's certificate?" he asked when he saw me running a filling machine, knowing full well I didn't. If I saw him before he saw me, I ducked behind huge pallets of filled bottles, hoping he would overlook my existence. Renata, one of the women in my brigade, laughed when she realized what I was doing. "Don't get so upset! He looks stern but he's a nice man. I told you, he's like a father around here."

On another occasion, I asked a worker named Stasia why she was chosen to keep the very delicate and touchy labeling machine going, instead of being assigned to a simpler job like packing cartons or folding boxes. She said, "I was having a really hard time when I worked in the other division. I really did not like the people there and I hated the work. I told Pani Jolanta, the supervisor here, about my troubles, and she got me this job. She really looks after us. She's the *dobrą mamą załogi* (good mother of the crew)."

These were just two examples of how line workers used kin metaphors to describe labor relations in the firm. Female employees, who made up 70 percent of AG's 315 shop floor workers, regularly depicted supervisors as parents, the firm as wife or mother, and themselves as dutiful children. At first, I thought nothing of it. As time went on, though, I found it more and more puzzling. Workers were upset about losing their voice in the production process and about being excluded from decisions about how the firm allocated resources. Many felt disheartened by the job evaluation, which quantified just how little the company valued their work. Yet, they deliberately used metaphors that not only cast them in subordinate roles but also portrayed that subordination as a positive thing.

Understanding why women workers would deliberately bring up images used to discriminate against them became, for me, a window into two more weighty questions. The first was a question about gender and unemployment. During the Communist period, Polish women (like other Eastern European women) made huge inroads in the workplace. Because of the party's ideological goal of gender equity and the socialist economy's insatiable demand for labor, almost 80 percent of working-age Polish women were employed by 1988. Women made up 45.5 percent of the total labor force (Einhorn 1993, 266).[1] When the postsocialist transformation began, Western feminist theorists predicted privatizing enterprises would solve overstaffing problems by laying off female workers rather than male ones. Feminists foresaw a new cult of domesticity that would force women back

Fig. 3. Bottles coming out of the labeling machine are individually inspected to ensure they are properly sealed.

into the home, much as gender stereotypes pushed American women out of the labor force after World War II (see Fodor 1997; Einhorn 1993, 5; Funk and Mueller 1993; Goven 1993; Hauser, Heyns, and Mansbridge 1993).

However, even as very conservative ideas about gender roles were becoming more and more widespread, Eastern European women were not affected by unemployment as severely as feminist theorists had predicted. Even in Poland, where the discrepancy between genders was more pronounced than anywhere else in the Bloc, only 17.3 percent of working-age women were unemployed in 1993, as compared with 14.3 percent of working-age men. As Fodor (1997) asserts, "Women, as a group, cannot be considered the resourceless victims of the 'velvet revolutions' that dismantled the state socialist economy." But just what resources did women—particularly working-class women—have to deploy?[2] Why wasn't unemployment worse?

Investigating that question led to more general questions about Polish labor and anthropological framings of power and resistance. The historiography of Polish labor activism generally centers on a romantic narrative of Solidarity's resistance to totalitarian communism (e.g., Kubik 1994; Laba 1991). But by the early 1990s, it seemed that Solidarity had become completely passive. Leaders like Lech Wałęsa and Leszek Balcerowicz told trade unionists that labor had to accept losses of power and benefits if the "shock therapy" reforms were to save the Polish economy. Solidarity's trade unionists therefore stood by as the government dismantled workers' councils in privatizing enterprises and weakened workers' rights under the *Kodeks Pracy* (labor code). They did not try to organize workers in new start-up businesses. There was a general sense that with the fall of the party, labor could declare victory and demobilize.[3]

The story of Solidarity was framed in two polar modes: active political conflict or passive submission. This division echoes traditional Marxian notions of class struggle, in which working people are seen as either the helpless victims of capital's machinations or—if they attain class consciousness—active subjects struggling against repression. It also echoes anthropological framings of power, which seek to overturn the view of local people as the passive objects of history by portraying them as actively resisting capitalism, colonialism, and other forms of domination (see, e.g., Sahlins 1985; Comaroff and Comaroff 1991; Scott 1985; cf. Asad 1993).

Power and resistance. Passive objects and active subjects. These dichotomies shaped conversations at Alima as much as they shaped anthropological theory. Yet, they did not fit what I saw on the shop floor. Alima's workers were not particularly active in the unions, and they were not threatening strikes. They did not participate in national politics, as they had in the 1980s. But they were not completely passive, either. As I listened to them talk and watched them quarrel with supervisors and the firm, I began to explore the idea that in using kin metaphors to talk about labor relations, Alima-Gerber's workers were attempting to recontextualize labor relations. Might working women be using the very essentialisms that discriminated against them to move away from the individualizing practices of post-Fordist management and to create a new basis for valuing work and workers? If so, that might at least partly explain why women's unemployment was not higher than men's. If that were true, though, it would mean reconceptualizing the very nature of the struggle on the shop floor and finding a theoretical middle ground between resistance and surrender.

The Gendered Politics of Feeding

Unraveling AG workers' use of kin terms means starting from two basic facts: the vast majority of production workers at Alima are female, and they make food for babies. These facts are immediately obvious to anyone who glances at the shop floor. What is not obvious, however, is how ideologies of gender and of family relationships make use of these two facts to elaborate a way of determining the value of labor and of laborers that is strongly opposed to the values that management technologies promote.

It is no accident that the majority of AG's manual laborers are female, although people in Rzeszów give different reasons for the feminization of Alima. Some say Alima employed women during the socialist period because the work was "light" and therefore appropriate for physically weaker women. Just what "light" meant is unclear—a woman employed at Alima since 1965 recalled having to lift large wooden crates of filled glass jars and move them around a damp, cold shop floor. But in comparison with the heavy industry going on at the neighboring airplane engine factory, the work at Alima may have been less strenuous.

Certainly, the pay was lower at Alima, and it was less prestigious to work there. Whether men took higher-paying jobs at the airplane factory first, leaving women only the low-paid Alima jobs, or whether Alima jobs paid less because the work was less skilled, or whether Alima's female workers earned less simply because they were women, is unclear (see Fernandez-Kelly 1983). It also may well be the case that the airplane factory jobs were better paying because of the socialist government's preference for heavy industry over consumer-goods production (see Kornai 1992). At any rate, the production line at Alima was characterized by long stretches during which there were few, if any, men on the shop floor. The domination of space by female workers, brigade supervisors, and shop supervisors was punctuated only by the occasional parade of high-ranking male managers or moments when (male) mechanics would emerge from behind the doors of their shops to work on the machines.[4]

It may be that the reason most of the line jobs at Alima were classified as "women's work" is that making baby food in an industrial setting was an extension of women's domestic roles as children's primary caretakers. In Polish culture and tradition, feeding children is the quintessential act of motherhood—and motherhood is the essence of traditional Polish femininity. Even in Catholicism and Polish nationalism, idealized femininity is constructed in terms of maternity. Mary, in her incarnation as the *Matka Boska Częstochowska,* is the protector and symbol of the Polish nation.[5] The Polish Mary's virginity is not emphasized, as it is in other Catholic countries. Rather, what is important is her role as the mother of Christ. She is referred to as the Mother of God, not the Virgin, and held up as the ideal of femininity. A special version of Mary is often seen in religious paintings, medals, and other iconography: the *Matka Boska Karmionca,* or Nursing Mother of God, who is pictured giving her breast to the infant Christ. Feeding the child from her own body, Mary is motherhood divine and motherhood incarnate, feeding the nation as well as the infant (see Long 1996, 40).

Among many of the Rzeszovians I spoke with about gender and motherhood, feeding a child was seen as the most essential act of motherhood because it was seen as part of feminine biological nature. The idea that women "should" or "had to" feed children could be highly problematic. Wojtek and Beata were a case in point. Beata was an administrative assistant at AG who had just been made the logistics manager of the firm. Her husband, Wojtek, was a rising star in the local business community who had a B.A. from City University of New York. Wojtek complained incessantly about having to stay home with his son on weekends while his wife went to the Higher School of Business in Nowy Sącz to earn the degree she needed to continue rising in the company. He argued that since she was the mother of their four-year-old son, she should be home on weekends to cook and care for the family, not off earning an MBA. "Well, he's 50 percent your son," I said, "so shouldn't you do half of the work of taking care of him?" He began to protest, "No! Fathers give only a little bit to the making of children. Look at the difference in size between the egg and the sperm! I gave 10 percent, maximum, to the making of that kid, and so I should only have to do 10 percent of the babysitting!"

Having been in American academic circles, Wojtek certainly knew an

American academic feminist when he saw one and so may have said this just to tease me. However, he was quite serious in his assertion that a woman's duty to feed and grow a child stemmed from her biologically "natural" work of pregnancy and nursing. Strikingly, Beata did not disagree. She may not have been home on Saturdays and Sundays to cook for her son, but she felt she *should* be there. The contradictory imperatives of feeding her child and pursuing an MBA caused her deep emotional distress.

In this view of material practice, maternity "naturally" leads women not only to feed their children but also to create homes for their families. In the most extreme and essentialist form of this argument, women supposedly create homes because it is their biological and spiritual nature to do. It is worth exploring this argument and taking it seriously (if not at face value) because so many AG workers subscribed to it. The argument also provides a particular view of personhood that is radically different from AG's management ideology. Certainly, this idea of personhood is far more successfully naturalized than the ideas put forth in Frugo commercials or quality control protocols or job evaluations. Although it is ostensibly a descriptive theory of domesticity and femininity, this theory of gender and maternal practice is a potent normative theory of both domestic and industrial work—and those who break the rules it prescribes pay dearly.

An article in *Znak,* a Catholic intellectual journal, made this normative theory explicit. Schrade, Wolniewicz, and Lubelewicz, the male authors of the article, begin by making a distinction between "home" and "house." The distinction is perhaps intuitive in English but not in Polish, where *dom* can refer both to a physical structure and to the social institution of a family (Schrade et al. 1996). "Home," they argue, is the place where one feels *u siebie,* in one's own place, outside the public domain: "Home is a place of permanent residence in which the spirit stays. . . . Home is surely a spiritual creation, built on something palpably material, but is penetrated with an immaterial aura" (1996, 91). In this idealized vision, "home" is

a place, one of not many on earth, maybe even the only one, where a person is valued by others as a value in himself (*samoistna*) and as irreplaceable, for whom others are prepared to sacrifice everything. . . . [Home is] where someone is attached to us unconditionally as a concrete, unique, and unrepeatable human being. This relation among the members of a home gives them an internal feeling of worth in and of themselves: probably, we must be something valuable, because others so much and so unselfishly value us. The prime example of this is, of course, the relation of a mother to her own child. (1996, 95)

Schrade, Wolniewicz, and Lubelewicz present an idyllic vision of home as a place where one is valued and loved in the concrete and not in the abstract. Because the authors see the primary model for such relationships as the mother-child relationship, it stands to reason that their vision of "home," as an expanded version of that relation, also derives from feminine biological nature:

> Woman creates a home because that is how she is. . . . Just like the milk with which a mother feeds a child isn't intentionally created by her so that she can breastfeed, but rather is made because it is her biological nature. It isn't the woman as a conscious acting being who makes milk; her female organism creates it as a natural function. The same is true, analogically, with a home: woman creates it not as a conscious acting being, but as a function of her impersonal and general feminine nature—as a certain anonymous spiritual power. (1996, 96–97)

In this view, both home creation and motherhood are ongoing processes. Just as motherhood is not bounded by pregnancy and delivery but requires ongoing nourishing of the child, so building a home is not a single process, completed once and for all. It requires ongoing action. Acquiring food (growing it or buying it), cooking, and feeding are the most important of these actions.

Women workers at AG often brought up a similar if less articulate idea about home creation as a part of female nature. For example, at the same time that they expressed envy and admiration for my travels, they also criticized me sharply for not making a home. Hanna, a shop floor supervisor who often invited me home for dinner, always had a word or two of advice for me. Putting her arm around my shoulder, she would tell me that it was good that I had seen the world but that at my advanced age (28), I should settle down and have a family. She often told me it was "a woman's nature" to do so. If I did not, she warned me, I would be going against my nature and would end up unhappy and alone. Other women had even stronger criticisms. Some called me a *cyganka*, or gypsy—implying that my rootlessness made me slightly bohemian, immoral, or untrustworthy.

Of course, this view of feminine nature is problematic. As feminist scholars have pointed out, motherhood is not merely a biological fact but an activity that is constructed through symbol and practice. Long (1996, 40) notes,

> To be a mother does not mean the same thing in all cultures and times, and equally importantly, the extent to which women are defined as a cat-

egory by the necessity of motherhood is also culturally and historically variable. (See also Allen 1983, 321)

In Poland, different visions of maternity have been competing for decades. Socialist ideology constructed the "worker-mother," who raised children while driving a tractor or working on a shop floor (Einhorn 1993, 51–59). Yet despite women's historically high rates of employment and the fact that most people I interviewed had years of work experience, most of my informants expressed views strikingly similar to Schrade's. They glossed over women's extradomestic employment while focusing on women's roles as mothers and homemakers. Both men and women expressed these views in practice as well as verbally.

The identity of feeding and home creation, and the fact that both of these tasks were done by women, were things I saw in almost every home I visited. The deep cultural and symbolic significance of these acts was not lost on the people who did them.[6] Renata, for example, worked on the juice line at AG. After work each day, she collected her three daughters from preschool, went to the shops to buy food, and then returned to her apartment to begin cooking *obiad,* the substantial afternoon meal. Her husband Jarek, although unemployed or working nights most of the time I was in Rzeszów, did little domestic work. Renata cooked and ate with the children, while Jarek ate by himself in front of the television in another room. When Renata served *obiad* for herself and the three girls in the kitchen, however, only three stools were at the table and only three places were set: Renata spoon-fed her four-year-old daughter, Krysia, from her own plate. Renata told me that if she did not feed Krysia, Krysia wouldn't eat at all. To describe how she must provide food for Krysia, Renata used the term *pokarmić,* the word used for breast-feeding, which implies feeding someone who is not capable of self-feeding, as opposed to *podą jedzenie,* which means to put food on the table in front of someone.

Renata's statement that Krysia would not eat if she were not spoon-fed covered up the real issue, however. It was not that the child could not use a spoon and fork or that she would die of hunger if Mama did not lift the dumplings to her little mouth. It was that Krysia *wanted* Renata to feed her—and so did Renata, because the act provided a moment of emotional closeness and warmth between them. Renata spent half an hour or more feeding Krysia, even though she added more labor to her already overloaded day. Renata's heavy domestic workload is not at all uncommon. In 1984, for example, the average Polish woman spent 30.5 hours per week on domestic chores, while the average Polish man only spent 7.7 hours (Einhorn 1993, 116).

Feeding is so symbolic of home creation that even women without children sometimes do it. Ania, whose house I lived in, was a twenty-six-year-old laboratory technician. She had been married less than a year and did not have children yet. Each night, when she arrived home after work, she made a huge plate of lard-and-paté sandwiches and carefully cut them into small bits. She cooked a big bowl of infant cereal and added heated milk to it. Then, bit by bit, she hand-fed the sandwiches to Jala, a three-year-old German shorthaired pointer. Ania stroked Jala while the dog lapped up the cereal. Mariusz, Ania's husband, looked upon this fondly. However, when he fed the dog, he dumped dry kibble into a bowl or threw the dog some moldy cheese. Ania says that if she did not feed Jala, the dog would not eat. Given that Jala ate what Mariusz gave her, this was clearly not the case. But as Ania fed the dog by hand and Mariusz looked on, the three of them were clearly *u siebie*, at home in their new house. Ania fed Jala not because the dog would starve if she did not but because feeding is what women at home *do*. It was a symbolic rather than a purely functional act, through which Ania built her new home and began to assert her role as *pani domu*, the lady of the house.

A Rzeszów librarian named Katarzyna made it clear to me that many working women hold these ideas about femininity and home creation as deeply felt tenets. Katarzyna is an atypical Rzeszovian: among all the women I met, only Katarzyna insisted that her husband clean the kitchen: "He needs to work around here because I work all day, too, and because he has to set an example for our sons, so they do not grow up to be cretins who lie around the house all day waiting for some poor woman to serve them." Grzegorz, Katarzyna's husband, affectionately referred to her as the "House Commando," due to her well-known bossiness and insistence that her husband and children do domestic work. Katarzyna relished the title. Yet, for all her insistence on an equal division of household labor, she also insisted not only on doing all her own cooking but also on growing and canning her own fruits and vegetables. She was a sharp critic of Alima-Gerber, believing that giving children industrially prepared foods was almost reason enough to have a woman declared an unfit mother. The crux of her argument was not just that industrially prepared foods were unhealthy (although she said that too) but that they weren't *tasty*. Her children, she said, just did not like them. They preferred her homemade foods and juices. The reason that AG products did not taste as good to her children is simple in her eyes: it was because she did not make them.

Everyone has her own way of cooking. The dumplings I make are different from the ones my neighbor makes, and even different than the ones my sister makes, even though we grew up in the same household. My *bigos* is different than anyone else's. And that's what my children like: the way *I* cook. Because my cooking is unlike anyone else's, when I give it to my children or my guests, I'm giving them a part of myself, a part of my personality. . . . Feeding your children, feeding them the food that you grew, that you cooked, feeding them by hand—it is a moment of real caring between mother and child, just like holding them or rocking them. That's why we do it.

For Katarzyna, feeding her children is not an abstract act. It is not some mother giving some food to some child. It is she, Katarzyna, giving her baby the food she grew and cooked. The acts of growing, cooking, and feeding create persons not only in the physical sense but also in the sense of concrete, unique, and irreplaceable beings who are intrinsic components of the "home." Katarzyna believes her food is unique. It is not just calories and vitamins, not just an abstract emanation of an impersonal feminine nature, but hers and hers alone. She sees it as an emanation of her unique personality, which she freely and lovingly gives to her children, even though she works until she is exhausted each night and has little time for herself.

For Katarzyna, her food is more than just a part of her personality. It is part of her *person*, her physical being, as well as her soul. Breast milk is part of her body, which she gives to her babies. Other foods, however, are also a part of her body and her person, although one step removed from the literalness of breast milk. Through her physical labor in her garden and in her kitchen, she makes food for her family. This bodily labor makes her fruits and vegetables also part of her body and a part of her unique self, which she gives to her children.

This gift of bodily substance, including *sila* or the energy contained in labor, means that in Katarzyna's mind, while she and her children are unique, they are not individuals—at least not in the bounded, impermeable, singular sense of that term. The transference of the body's energy to another body via food means that mother and child are inherently social beings, at least in the Polish Catholic worldview. Katarzyna sees her children as literally "flesh of her flesh," grown through her gifts of body, and hence neither totally separate from her nor alien to her. They are distinct from her and from each other (she says that they are "so similar to each other, but yet each one is so different"), but they are parts of her. Just as Strathern (1988, 13) posits for Hagen children in New Guinea, these Polish children are "packed with sociality," the "plural and composite site of the relationships that produced them," even if in this case the relationships are contained within the home and family rather than being seen as stemming from "generalized society," as in Strathern's analysis.

As Katarzyna gardens and cooks, she believes she is creating not just the persons of her children but her own person as well. Growing and cooking rescue her from bureaucratic anonymity and make her into a "unique and irreplaceable person." Katarzyna herself puts it somewhat differently. Trying to explain why Gerber food just was not "tasty," she pointed to a cake she had baked, which was sitting on the table in front of us. It was gorgeous, covered in purple-pink frosting and wreathed in coconut, with small gleaming heaps of black currants on top as decoration. She said,

> You just can't buy something like that in a bakery. And that is not just because I baked the cake, but because the currants come from my own garden. I grow them every summer, can them, and save them for the dead of winter. I love being in the garden. There, I feel like a real person, not just like a number or a *szara istota* [a generic "gray being"] in the middle of gray concrete, running to work, clean, sleep, and then get up and do it all over again. For most of the time, I'm nobody, just an *istota*, just a part of the machine in this artificial world. But in my garden plot, I'm a real person. I am connected to the world. I can be there all day, planting and weeding. Sometimes I just sit. I think that is why these currants taste so good, not like that stuff in jars.

It would be easy to listen to Katarzyna's almost mystical declarations about the food she grows and cooks, and to hear her agreeing with the same essentialist and stereotypical discourse that Schrade and company propose. And, in fact, she read the article and agreed with it. But does this mean that she is merely justifying her subordination, or that she is helping to mask the double burden of wage work and housework that Polish women face? To the contrary, Katarzyna is acutely aware that she bears almost the entire burden of social reproduction in her house (and lets her husband hear about it almost constantly). Yet, she still finds all the baking and canning somehow liberatory—or at least, oppressive in a way that is preferable to the oppression she feels from wage work and the capitalist market.

In contrast to feminist scholars like Einhorn (1993, 117), who argue that women's self-esteem and sense of worth will suffer if they only have domestic employment, Katarzyna sees her domestic work as the antidote to the feelings of worthlessness and inauthenticity she gets from her wage work in the library. In extolling the virtues of homemade food, she criticizes a social system that she feels treats people as abstractions, each of which is similar to another. Jarred food is food made by "the system" (in this context, it is irrelevant to her whether it is the socialist or capitalist system) for *szare istoty*. In the creation and giving of food, she too becomes "unique and irreplaceable," not by virtue of her individuality but by virtue of her relationships to other people. Via her relations to her labor and her family, she becomes what she feels is a whole social being, instead of an abstract source of labor or consumption, which is how she feels she is regarded most of the time in the marketplace and in her workplace.

The reason gardening and home canning feel liberating and somehow "authentic" to Katarzyna, even though they create a great deal of work for her, is related to the symbolism this kind of work had during the socialist period. Under socialism, most urban Poles either had a *działka* (a small private plot of land) or worked on the land of a rural relative in exchange for some of the crop. This was no mere hobby. The intense shortages made family subsistence production on uncollectivized land an absolute necessity. Even Alima workers, who had allotments of Bobo Frut and who worked around apples and carrots and imported apricot purée all day, often had to work nights and weekends in the garden and in the kitchen to make fruit juices at home.[7] This gave the *działka*, like the kitchen, a deep symbolic and social meaning in addition to its purely economic function.

Work in the *działka* was hard labor, but it was work for oneself and one's family. The *działka* became domestic space, a part of the "home," even if it was not physically adjacent to the house or apartment. "Organizing" or buying building materials, people built small sheds on their garden plots that look like small houses. These sheds have windows, often curtained, and small porches where weary gardeners can have a drink of tea and sit in the shade of the grape vines growing up the trellises.

As a part of "home," *działka* production became a practical—if not always intentional—critique of the socialist system. As part of domestic rather than public space, it was part of the great ideological divide between "us" and "them," the system or the powers that be.[8] On the one hand, it was labor that people were forced into by socialism's inability to provide adequately for the population. On the other hand, however, it was pleasurable, because it was work done in a private social space, among family and friends. Just like within the boundaries of the home, one could be one's "real self" there, freed from the surveillance and self-monitoring required in the workplace and in other public domains. Women's labor in the *działka* took on the same political coloration as their work in the house: by creating a space bounded off from the intrusions of the state, they carried out a practical domestic resistance.[9] Canning fruits and vegetables at home stood as a strong critique of industrial and hence socialist production—even when it was intended more as necessary provisioning than political activism.

More than a decade after the fall of communism, most Rzeszovians still spend summer Saturdays planting and weeding out in the *działka,* often several kilometers from home, even though there are no shortages. Those on the lower end of the socioeconomic scale do it for economic reasons. The average income in Rzeszów is lower than in other parts of Poland, about 700 złoty a month, or $250. Food costs are comparable to those in the United States or Western Europe. For many shop floor workers, homemade food is an economic necessity rather than just a pleasant diversion. For those who have more money, however, the *działka* is more a place for pleasure and relaxation than a way to cut down on grocery bills. These people rebuild the little shed houses in the gardens and decorate them elaborately. Some of the sheds even have full-sized stoves and television sets, where gardeners can have a complete meal and catch the soccer matches. Clearly, at least some of the people with extra income are diverting it into the *działki,* not into buying more industrially produced food in order to escape the labor of planting, weeding, picking, and canning. They do it for the reasons Katarzyna does: because there they feel *u siebie.* There, they are persons feeding other persons and not either abstract "social needs" to be met by state-owned factories or anonymous "consumers" who give their złoty to boost private firms' profits.[10]

This ideology places "home" in opposition to the public domains of workplace and market and is built on and around the idea of motherhood. It implies a vast gulf between public and private domains, one in which women's labor is systematically devalued in the workplace because it is overvalued in the home. This is one of the legacies of the socialist era. Especially during the 1980s, most people perceived the primary division in society to be between state and society (Marody 1993, 859). Because the socialist state was seen as attempting to replace all social relationships with the one between the individual and the state, citizens saw it as constantly invading the private sphere (Marody 1993, 861). In that context, the home was one of the only genuine loci of "civil society," and women's homemaking roles were seen as inherently political (Goven 1993; Long 1996).

Indeed, many Eastern European scholars as well as writers in the popular press criticize and reject Western feminism because they feel that it discounts the important role women played in maintaining the sheltered, nonstate, private space of the home (Marody 1993; Drakulic 1992). Moreover, since the state promoted the emancipation of women (in theory, if not in practice), opposing the state meant opposing feminism as well (Leven 1993; Hauser et al. 1993). The social identity of woman/worker/wife/mother was therefore a double-edged sword. On the one hand, it saddled working women with the double burdens of full-time employment and a second full-time occupation as homemaker. Policies like long maternity leaves and restrictions on the types of jobs that women or mothers could do were ostensibly to "protect" women but also barred them from important or lucrative jobs. On the other hand, the political and social values placed on those roles made them sources of power and worth for women. In Poland, this ideology was (and is) supported and reinforced by Catholic nationalism, particularly through Marian devotion (Hauser, Heyns, and Mansbridge 1993; Long 1996).

Strategic Essentialisms

The sharp divide that workers like Katarzyna or scholars like Marody make between public and private suggests that the domains of home and work are sharply bounded. Indeed, many people at AG told me, "Work is work and life is life," suggesting that they conceive of their working lives as utterly distinct from their other activities. Following this potent ideology developed under socialism, it would be easy to create an analytical divide between the public and private domains, but this would not be entirely accurate. Women at AG, particularly those on the shop floor, do not completely separate their work and their home lives and do not maintain utterly distinct home and work identities. Most of the Alima-Gerber shop floor workers continually refuse to be considered merely as abstract sources of labor, as "workers," but demand to have their identities as women and mothers recognized as well. They work in the factory explicitly as mothers, and their work provides them with an alternate basis from which to value both the products they make and themselves as producers. At the same time, because they work as mothers, women on the shop floor are more easily subjected to and accepting of the discipline imposed by the quality control process. Revaluing themselves and their labor by bringing ideologies of motherhood into the factory in one sense gives them room to maneuver within the new structures of discipline and value but, in another, subjects them to ever more stringent control.

Since Bobo Frut was introduced in 1968, women on the shop floor have been told repeatedly that food for children must be of the best quality, with no defects in production. If even one mistake is made, they are told, a small consumer could suffer serious harm. The workers have taken this very much to heart; they follow the strict and often bothersome quality control protocols laboriously and exactingly. For example, one day my brigade was assigned to fermentation testing. Each pair of us was given five pallets of Bobo Frut (11,525 bottles) to test during one eight-hour shift. Each bottle had to be pulled from its tray, turned over, and hit on the bottom with a rubber tube to determine if the bottle had been properly sealed. A properly sealed and pasteurized bottle would make a distinctive sound when hit—*shik, shik.* A defective bottle made a hollow sound—*thunk thunk.* Each bottle had to be hit twice and then returned to the pallet or set aside as defective.[11] My share of the bottles (720 an hour) seemed enormous, so I set to work quickly. To save time, I grabbed two bottles at once in my left hand, while beating them with my right hand. Suddenly, another hand shot over the pallet and grabbed my wrist. "You can't do that. The bottles could knock together and make a clinking sound, and you might think they were good when they were defective. And if a baby drinks that fermented juice, it could die!" said Bogusia, one of my coworkers. Coworkers commonly disciplined one another to maintain quality standards. Rather than waiting for a supervisor to spot the infraction or running to tell a supervisor about it, more experienced workers often corrected the less experienced, particularly those from the temporary agency. The rationale was almost always repeated and almost always the same: if we do not uphold quality control standards, a baby could become sick.

This seems logical, even obvious. But why do production workers choose to uphold the quality control standards and protocols when it would be much easier not to? And why do they choose that particular rationale rather than another? They might argue that if customers buy defective products, they will be unsatisfied and will stop buying AG products, and this might have a negative effect on the firm's profits. They might argue that creating defective product means wasting bottles and caps and labels as well as juice, and this costs money that might otherwise go into wages and other social benefits. Instead, they always emphasized children's safety and, in doing so, participated in their own disciplining.

The workers' gender and the construction of femininity in Poland leads them to interpret what they do as mothers preparing food for children rather than as industrial workers making an abstract commodity. In part, their interpretation derives from the specific and concrete nature of the product itself, baby food. Under the gendered division of labor in state socialism, women were often relegated to performing, in their paid work, "jobs which can be seen as an extension of their unpaid domestic roles, namely feeding, caring for, serving, or cleaning up after men and children" (Einhorn

1993, 124). Industrial production of baby food by women, of course, is the most obvious extension of gendered domestic labor into the extradomestic world. At a more general level, however, the idea of an industrial worker working *as a mother* was part of the ideology of state socialism, regardless of the industry in which she worked. Women were conceived of as "worker-mothers," while men were simply "workers" (Einhorn 1993, 5).

Of all the women I knew on the AG shop floor, only two were not mothers. Because motherhood is such a valued status, AG production workers do not make a rigid division between work and home. Rather, they work very much *as mothers*, acutely aware that via their industrial production they are stepping into the critical role of producing children's food, which is the defining act of motherhood.[12] Because they are constantly envisioning the unknown little consumers of the products they make, they constantly focus on the use value of the product, not on its exchange value. They make food for babies as mothers, not profits for Gerber as laborers. The production of use values in this concrete sense gives the work intrinsic value. This was underscored by something the director of the quality control labs, a woman in her late thirties, said to an all-female group of medical sales representatives: "This is work you can be proud of. If it were cigarettes or alcohol we were making, something that harmed people, I'd feel differently. But we are making things to help children grow up strong and healthy, and I'm proud to be doing that."

Of course, the workers at Alima do not work just out of the goodness of their hearts. They work to earn money in the form of wages. Wages, though, are also not just exchange values, in the sense that they become abstract sums of money given in exchange for labor. Rather, because inflation was still high enough that it makes little sense to hold money in its liquid state, people tended to think in terms of the concrete objects that money could buy rather than of money as an abstract value. By working and earning wages, shop floor workers were indirectly producing food and "caring" for their families, just as they did when they *directly* earned the food that they made in the factory as partial compensation for their labor. Just as Bobo Fruts were a valuable good that could be exchanged for other objects of value, so did money become. Money was not fully an abstract and universal means of exchange but rather a commodity like others—albeit one of the only commodities still in acute shortage.

Jadzia, who runs the pasteurizer on the day shift, is an example of a woman who works in the factory to produce food for her own children as well as for anonymous consumer-children.[13] She is the thirty-eight-year-old mother of three children, aged six, sixteen, and seventeen. She lives with her children, her husband, and her husband's mother on a small farm outside of Rzeszów. While Jadzia and her husband both work blue-collar industrial jobs, her mother-in-law tends the youngest child and the farm, which provides milk, eggs, poultry, and vegetables. The family used to sell what they produced on the farm. Fruits and vegetables went to Alima, and the cow's milk went to the local dairy. Since Alima-Gerber and the dairy both demand large production lots, however, the family has lost its agricultural contracts. Now the farm's produce is only for family consumption.

Jadzia is passionate about her job at the pasteurizer, insisting that procedures be followed by the book and taking defects in product quality as a personal affront. When I asked her why she worked, she said that for her, it was either factory work or field work. Her equivalence of the two kinds of work is striking: she clearly believes that one is equivalent to the other, because in both cases her labor provides for her family. Her mother-in-law's farm labor provides staples, while her own labor allows the family to purchase commercially produced things like soda pop, cookies in packages, fashionable jeans for the teenagers, a telephone, and a newly renovated kitchen. For Jadzia, her labor is a means of provisioning her family, just like her weekend labor in the fields and in the kitchen. Even better, it allows the family to consume more prestigious consumer packaged goods rather than rely on home-grown food (see also Long 1996, 42). Jadzia finds self-esteem and fulfillment in her job outside the home, not because it is something other than being a mother but because it is a way of carrying out her maternal responsibilities in a manner she finds interesting (cf. Einhorn 1993, 117).

For many working mothers, wage labor is a sacrifice that one makes for one's children, in order to "invest" in them. In this sense, wage labor is another way of providing children not only with tangibles such as food, which they need for growth, but also with intangibles like violin lessons, the all-important English lessons, or a costly private course at one of the now ubiquitous "schools of management." For the lucky few, a mother's labor will also provide extremely costly food and housing while the child studies at a more prestigious university than the ones in Rzeszów. These are the critical elements of class mobility in Rzeszów. Just as food ensures that the child will grow physically, intangibles like education, which are earned through shop floor labor, are—when there are more possibilities for class mobility than in the recent past—a way of ensuring that the child's and the family's social status also grows.

On the shop floor and to me, working mothers continually argued that their maternal status entitled them to special consideration from their employers. Under socialism, special treatment for all mothers was standard practice. Paid sick leave during pregnancy for those who needed it and shifts to less physically taxing work during pregnancy for those who stayed at work, paid maternity leaves after birth with the guarantee of a job to return to, paid leave to take care of sick children, and an additional stipend attached to a mother's wages were all parts of the socialist maternal welfare package. Since 1989, these benefits have begun to erode, both formally and in practice. Maternity leave is shorter, and many women fear that if they take sick leave during pregnancy or take many days off to care for ill children, they will be deemed "unreliable" and placed at the top of the list for the next round of layoffs. A situation of full employment lets women safely take advantage of the benefits to which they are legally entitled. When unemployment is high and people must compete openly to retain their jobs, however, benefits that exist on paper cannot necessarily be enjoyed in practice.

In the face of eroding formal benefits to mothers, some women use their status as mothers to demand particular, personal consideration from their managers. The most extreme case I saw of this was not at AG, but at Sanepid, the local food-inspection station. Ania (the woman who fed her German shorthaired pointer by hand) and a coworker, Alicja, were both hired on six-month trial contracts as laboratory technicians. The understanding was that at the end of six months, only one of them would be offered a permanent contract, while the other would be laid off.

Alicja's strategy during the competition was to continually assert her right to the job, not on the basis of her merit in the laboratory but on the basis of her need. She was the mother of three children, while Ania was childless. Alicja's labor went to the growing of children, while Ania's only went to frivolities and self-indulgences like dogs. Alicja particularly emphasized the issue of food to illustrate how her work was essential for children while Ania's was not. When Ania mentioned that she had pets, Alicja replied (in a loud voice so all could hear), "You have pets? And do you cook for them or give them canned food? You give them milk? You give them canned food? Special food for *animals?* Well, obviously, you're rich. And why not? You do not have kids." Alicja even looked askance at Ania's eating food like oranges and kiwis. "Tropical fruits? When you have children, you will not be eating tropical fruits. You will not be eating fruits at all. Oh no! Those children will eat everything you have. You will not be eating oranges and kiwis; sometimes you will not have food to put in your mouth. You'll sacrifice everything to those children, just like we do!"

Alicja's final jab was to place Ania in the category of daughter-receiver, while positing herself as mother-giver. She told Ania, "Women without children should go on unemployment insurance. They do not need the money, so why work? Their mothers will help them. Of course, not every mother is in a position to give her children money. But most are. So women who are young and childless can be unemployed." Alicja here asserts that her physical labor in the lab, the product of her bodily activity, is converted into food for children.[14] In this way, her labor nourishes, just as Katarzyna's labor in the *działka* does. Because of this, she implied, her labor has more value than does Ania's, and so she should be given the permanent contract. (Whether this gambit worked is unclear. Just before Sanepid was about to decide whether to lay Alicja or Ania off, Ania got a better-paying job in AG's quality control laboratories. Alicja kept her job at Sanepid.)

This kind of argument provides a system of statuses, values, and images that is very different from the work station valuations and employee evaluations devised at AG. The work station valuations posit a person who is individual and who exists only in the workplace. Relations to others in the company and activities, relationships, and obligations outside the firm are not among the criteria that determine the value of labor. The employee evaluations further subdivide this bounded individual, making internalized qualities and states of mind, rather than actions carried out with or vis-à-vis others, the basis of value. Alicja's demands that her maternal obligations become the basis for determining the value of her labor turn this system inside out. She talks about the value she produces in terms of not only her present productive labor but also her reproductive labor and the improvement in her children's future productive labor that her present contributions ensure. Her salary reproduces not only her own labor (as she believes Ania's does) but also labor in general via her children. The value she gives in exchange for that salary is therefore higher than what Ania gives, at least in Alicja's mind. To assert this alternate basis of value, she has to continually assert her multiple social identities: not just individual laborer in the workplace reproducing her own self, but socially embedded laborer in the home reproducing labor via her children. She carries her domestic world into the workplace in order to prove her worth.

At AG, workers often demand that their multiple social statuses both inside and outside the domains of work be taken into account and that both their reproductive and productive labor be seen as sources of value within the company. As the generalized benefits that socialism gave on the basis of statuses derived from outside the workplace erode, workers increasingly make these demands in the form of requests for personal consideration. They do this by making appeals not just to managers qua managers but to the aspects of managers' persons that come from outside the workplace, including their parenthood.

For example, Stasia, for whom the division supervisor arranged the job at the labeling machine, became pregnant again. She was living in a one-room apartment with her husband and five children—a situation that everyone in the brigade acknowledged as particularly difficult. The pregnancy was a surprise, since Stasia had bribed her gynecologist to tie her tubes after her last caesarean section. When Stasia learned of the impending arrival of her sixth child, she had an emotional outburst on the shop floor. Weeping and raging, she let it be known in no uncertain terms that she did not want to be pregnant and that she was afraid of losing her job.[15] As her difficult pregnancy progressed, Stasia made it clear that she was continuing to work rather than taking sick leave because she feared that if she left, she would not be able to return. She was miserable and uncomfortable, and she had to leave her labeler often to run to the bathroom.

After a few weeks of this, Kasia, one of the shop forewomen, began to apply one of the periodically enforced disciplinary rules to Stasia. In an effort to cut down on Stasia's absences from her machine, Kasia insisted that Stasia sign in and out of a "break book" every time she went to the bathroom. Once, when Stasia came back from break six minutes late because she had stopped in the bathroom after lunch, Kasia was standing there with a watch, threatening to "write Stasia up." Workers greatly feared these "write-ups," because they believed management would use the write-ups to determine whom to dismiss in the next round of layoffs. In spite of this risk, Stasia patently refused to register her bathroom trips:

> I told her, "Christ, you've been pregnant seven times. Can't you remember what it is like to be pregnant? That when you have to go to the toilet, you simply have to go? Does that not give you any sympathy for me?" But you know, Kasia never managed to carry a baby to term. She tried and tried, but she miscarried every time. It made her completely mentally ill, completely crazy, and devoid of sympathy. That's why she runs around screaming in that high-pitched voice. She couldn't have a baby, so she's insanely jealous of anybody who is pregnant, and she just wants to see us suffer. It is inhuman.[16]

Stasia chalked up her failure to escape intensified discipline to Kasia's failed maternity, suggesting that Kasia enforced workplace discipline because she was somehow an incomplete human being whose field of social action was unnaturally limited to the workplace. In the end, however, Stasia prevailed. She appealed again to Jolanta, who is the mother of two adult sons. As a mother and as "the good mother of the crew," Jolanta transferred Stasia to a job packing boxes—a job off the line, where Stasia could go to the bathroom without disrupting production. By considering her own maternity and Stasia's maternity in a workplace context, Jolanta stood figuratively not only as Stasia's mother but also as the mother of all her subordinates. This role significantly increased her moral authority on the shop floor, but on terms outside capitalist business rationality.[17]

Clearly, personalistic ideologies do not entirely replace the maternity benefits women had under socialism. Some women are even afraid to take advantage of the benefits that remain (like sick leave during a pregnancy) for fear that they will be considered unreliable workers and will be more likely to be dismissed. The same philosophy prevails among those who are opposed to maternal benefits at the national policy level. Even feminists argue that as long as women have special benefits under the labor code, they will be less likely to be hired or promoted, because they will be seen as inherently unreliable—more likely to take time off for childrearing and children's illnesses and less likely to put in the long hours and travel schedules that some prestigious jobs require (Einhorn 1993, 47). The idea of women as "mother-workers" in a context where men are not also "father-workers" clearly disadvantages female workers. Yet, in the face of direct discrimination, some women workers use their gender and kin status to foil attempts at labor discipline and to gain some autonomy in their jobs.

Workers also use their family statuses to protect their jobs. They made these kinds of demands on Mr. Jagielski, when he interviewed the temporary workers to determine who would be laid off and who would get a permanent contract. When he put aside the notebook containing the point-scale evaluations and began to ask employees about their domestic situations to determine whose *family* could best cope with unemployment, he considered labor as an integral part of a laborer with multiple social relations rather than as a detachable part of an internally divisible individual laborer who is bounded within the workplace. He determined the value of their labor in terms of reproductive use values as well as productive exchange values. When one of his employees commented to me that he did not need the notebook because he "knows us as a father knows his children," she indexed precisely the idea of the person that is contained in Schrade's description of the person inside the home or in Katarzyna's description of her children: unique and irreplaceable, valued for one's specific and entire self.

By using kin terms to describe workplace relations, women on the shop floor revalue their gender. By doing so, they call for radically different kinds of relations between the public and private spheres and between the firm and its employees.[18] That demand creates an analogy rather than an opposition between "home" and "workplace." If the firm must stand in some sense as home, then the firm, in the concrete persons of its managers, must relate to the employees as parent to child. In addition to valuing the person as a parent does a child, the firm's managers must provide caring in both material and immaterial forms, without calculated exchange. This, of course, was part of the ideology of socialism, in which the state assumed the role of parent, determined the needs of the citizens qua "children," and doled out the "care," largely via the workplace. Benefits like vacations in the mountains, concerts, and even the monthly allotments of soap and towels were not calculated compensation for labor but were the gifts of the parent-state to its child-populace (Verdery 1996, 64).

In asking for these benefits now, within the framework of a capitalist business that is supposedly divorced from the state, employees are asking the firm to become the equivalent of the parent-state and to provide for their well-being. They want the firm to see them in multiple social roles and contexts—not only as workers but also as men, women, parents, and (metaphorical) children. They want the company to acknowledge that these roles and contexts create particular needs, and they want the company to meet those needs.

The importance that many employees attach to having the firm recognize their gender and family status was never clearer to me than on International Women's Day. A holiday that was strongly promoted by the socialist government as part of its drive to create equality for women, Women's Day was supposed to be a symbolic acknowledgment of women's labor both in the factory and in the home. In socialist Poland, the custom was for the firm to give small presents to its female workers in recognition of their services. At Alima, gifts from the firm included flowers and candy, as well as more costly items, such as tablecloths or cloth napkins. Male coworkers, too, often brought flowers and chocolates. These presents were a form of "care" given in symbolic compensation for women's labor.

In 1995, my first Women's Day on the shop floor, changing traditions led to conflict and hard feelings. Along with the (female) assistant to the director of production, I suggested that the director, who was a man, remember the holiday by giving shop floor workers flowers or candy. His assistant and I believed that a display of gratitude might smooth over some of the hard feelings that had been raised in the ongoing labor negotiations. At first, he agreed. A few days later, however, he changed his mind. He said that Women's Day was a Communist holiday, and he had no intention of upholding it now. He later unbent slightly: his assistant, along with several of the other female secretaries, arranged coffee and cakes for some of the female employees—but only for the women who were managers under his supervision. The director of quality control, a few of her high-level subordinates, some of the women from the planning, import, and export departments, and the secretaries were all invited. Of the women on the shop floor, only those employees who were division supervisors or shop masters were invited. Lower-ranking women, from shop forewoman to manual laborer, were neither invited nor recognized in any other way.

When Stasia, the labeler, heard about this, she was infuriated. "Well! I guess we're not women! Right, we're not women, we're just niggers! We're just slaves!" This switch from gender categories to highly loaded and negative racial ones indicated her firm belief that by refusing to recognize her *gender,* the firm was refusing to recognize that she was a *person.* In her lexicon, "niggers" and "slaves" are unpersons, human beings used to provide power, like draft animals.[19] Stasia's anger came from the clash of two systems of personhood. She demanded that her status as a woman—and later, her status as a mother—be acknowledged publicly. She believed that she was not just an object, anonymous and alienable labor power, a pair of hands that could be replaced by any other. Rather, she asserted that her personal social status be acknowledged via the flow of gifts between her and the firm. She sees her labor as a woman's and a mother's, and she demands that the firm reciprocate in the same categories.

One might think that the use of kin terms is part of an "egalitarian" ideology. However, although this kind of *znajomości* demands concessions, return gifts, and mutual obligation on both sides, it does not preclude hierarchy. It builds hierarchy and fosters inequality. However, it builds hierarchy in a sharply different way than the individualizing, impersonal systems of personhood contained in job evaluations or even niche marketing do. When a state-owned enterprise, as an institution, gave presents on Women's Day, the institution became both masculine and a parent. The firm as father-employer gave gifts to the daughter-workers. The gift-giving therefore was of a dual nature: while it honored and valued women and their labor, it also organized a sharply hierarchical gendering of labor that disadvantaged women. Women's Day also had a paradoxical effect, in many cases. Because it honored women's extradomestic work, but because there was no equivalent holiday for men, it covertly assumed that women's extradomestic labor was somehow *extra,* an added function separate from their necessary and proper domestic roles. Because women's work outside the home was something the state and male workmates had to be grateful for, the holiday made their work seem somehow additional and unnatural, rather than a taken-for-granted part of adulthood for both sexes. This, of course, is part of the ideology that makes it easier for firms to lay off women workers or to pay them seventy groszy for every złoty a man makes (Einhorn 1993, 122).

However, the hierarchy that Women's Day draws and reinforces is valuable to female workers because it is an important part of vassalage—and this is why they invoke it. There is a distinction here between "vassalage" and the "slavery" that Stasia uses to characterize the impersonal relations of capitalism. The kinds of relations that are built up when gender and parental status are made explicit parts of the employee-employer relationship do create subordination. Differences in power, position, and agency are fully recognized, whether the employee-employer bond is redefined as female-male (as in the case of Women's Day) or as child-parent (as in the case of the "good mother of the shop floor"). This kind of subordination demands reciprocity, however. Just as a liege lord is responsible for his vassals' well-being, kinship metaphors attempt to make the father-firm recognize employees' needs, provide care for them, and attend to the continual maintenance of the relationship by giving gifts. Shop floor workers and some middle managers fight to remain vassals because they see "wage slavery" as the only alternative. However unfair vassalage is, it gives them more room to maneuver as they seek benefits from the firm and its managers. Employees at Alima-Gerber do not fight for "freedom" or "equality" or any other such lofty goals. They accept a subordinate status, seeing that as normal and natural. But they do fight to determine the *kind* of power relation in which they are subordinate. For many of them, the state of vassalage—bolstered with Catholicism's and Polish nationalism's gendered expectations—is preferable precisely because it allows them to demand certain material and social advantages.

The Wedding Banquet

The use of kin terms is more than a way to determine the kind of hierarchy within the firm. Workers also use the gendered division of labor and gendered domestic roles to think about their relationships to the firm and the firm's obligations to them. Rather than accept a view of personhood that conceives of them as atomized individuals who interact with the firm only by selling their labor power, workers insist that their relationship to the firm is a multifaceted *social* (not contractual) relationship. This view not only implies reciprocal exchange but also an enduring partnership. Workers also use gender and kin terms to think about their firm's new place in the global economy and to conceptualize their position within the international division of labor. Here, gender and kin imagery is a means through which workers acquiesce to their subordination in the national and transnational economies.

When Gerber's purchase of Alima was announced, the press discussed the transaction not as a sale, but as a romantic relationship. Headlines in national newspapers announced "the marriage of Alima and Gerber." Using the marriage metaphor, the press described the privatization as a union between a poor but beautiful Polish bride and a rich, older, American husband. They emphasized what both sides brought to the marriage: Alima brought its years of experience in quality production and a highly skilled workforce, and Gerber brought technology, access to world markets, and most important, money. Like a bride price to the bride's father, Gerber brought millions of dollars to the state treasury. Gerber promised to invest millions more in "setting up house" (Zatorski 1992; *Nowy Świat* 14 February 1992; *Gromada Rolnik Polski* 19 February 1992; Andrys 1992). As one national paper phrased it:

> She: About 40 years old. Hard working and enterprising. In 1968 she decided to start producing baby food, which was later known all over Poland as Bobo Frut. . . . Since 1980, in spite of the economic situation she invested a lot in her own development. Thanks to that, she was able to produce 25,000 tons of tasty baby food. . . .
>
> He: 70 years old. Very rich. A world leader in production of baby food, clothes and baby care products. He supplies 70% of the US market. He dreams of a similar success in Europe. He came to the conclusion that this goal could be achieved with the help of his enterprising partner. . . .
>
> It is possible that Alima-Gerber will be as powerful in Europe as its shareholder in the US. We can only wish them a prosperous hundred years [a traditional wedding toast]. Those who know life say that marriages of convenience lack the beauty of love, but they are also much more stable. The partners know what to expect from one another and they disregard details which might lead to conflicts in a more emotional relationship (Rychlewski 1992).

The marriage metaphor was strengthened when the two companies decided to celebrate their new relationship. A huge warehouse at Alima-Gerber in Rzeszów was cleared out and decorated. All the employees, along with government officials and Gerber personnel, were invited to show up in their finest attire. On the appointed day, when the tables were set and the warehouse transformed into a banquet hall, Al Piergallini, the CEO of Gerber, arrived in a chartered Tupolov jet (Zatorski 1992; *Nowiny* 16 February 1992; Sawicki 1992). With him, he brought waiters and chefs from the prestigious

Marriott hotel in Warsaw, which had already become the symbol of Western capitalism in Poland. The Marriott staff rolled out carts of sumptuous food. There were trays upon trays of fancy sandwiches, whole salmons, beautifully arranged delicatessen meats, and gorgeous bite-sized hors d'oeuvres. As each guest arrived, he or she was given a glass of champagne to toast the merger.[20] The guests wore their best clothes, and a videographer roamed the room, filming the party. When it came time for the ceremonies, Piergallini and Czartoryska, the presidents of the two firms, gave speeches and exchanged gifts. Alima presented Gerber with a large crystal vase—a traditional wedding present. Gerber, slightly missing the metaphor, presented Alima with a crystal apple, a symbol of fruit production. Unbeknownst to Gerber executives, who did not recognize the cultural code, the party looked just like a *wesele,* the traditional Polish wedding banquet. The comely Polish bride had snared a rich and powerful husband, one who could fly in and out in a chartered jet and transport magnificent banquets as if by magic. With the exchange of the crystal gifts, the deal was sealed, symbolically as well as legally.

Because privatization was a totally new phenomenon (Alima being one of the first handful of companies privatized in Poland), it was complex and difficult for employees to understand. What would the ramifications of privatization be for them and for their families? Not only was the marriage metaphor a way of making an incomprehensible and uncertain situation more understandable, it was also a strategy for binding Gerber into an enduring relationship that entailed specific obligations. In this sense, kinship terminology was not a "leftover" or a relic of tradition but a cultural resource deployed actively in the present. For example, when Gerber gave company stock to each employee in accordance with the deal it had negotiated with the Ministry of Privatization, it brought the marriage to the personal as well as the institutional level. It was as if, through the gift, Gerber told employees, "With this stock certificate, I thee wed." Along with the eighteen-month moratorium on layoffs and changes in agricultural contracts, this calmed employees' fears that Alima would be liquidated by Gerber. For employees, the crystal gifts sealed an enduring relationship between Alima and Gerber and therefore ruled out the possibility that the company would be closed or sold to another owner. They believed that the stocks sealed a relationship between employees and the firm. This marital relationship was in no way damaged when Gerber offered to buy back the stock at an increased value: it merely transformed the stocks into money, which could immediately be converted into useful household objects. In this way, Gerber-the-husband was merely investing in the workers' homes, much as it was doing in the factory-home. Workers also used the marital metaphor to assert that they came as active partners to the corporate union, rather than being sold like geese, slaves, or a part of the factory's machinery.

Although the marital metaphor implied partnership and union rather than sale, it did not preclude hierarchy. Employees believed Gerber had the right to change the plant or AG's corporate strategy, just as the husband in a traditional Polish patriarchical family has the right to make decisions about the wife's actions and about the family's strategy. By conceptualizing themselves collectively as a "wife," the shop floor workers acknowledged they were less powerful than Gerber—a statement that does not seem to amount to "resistance." But in using the metaphor, workers were making claims on Gerber. In a traditional Polish marriage, the couple's resources should be pooled and used to meet the family's needs without individual calculation on the part of either partner, and the husband must ensure that the wife is provided for. Gerber's installation of the quality control labs, the new boiler system, and the wastewater treatment plant (the first three major investment projects, carried out almost immediately after privatization) made it seem as if Gerber was meeting its husbandly obligations. Husband Gerber made a decision about what was right for the couple and then gave freely of his money to provide for the couple's needs. This was accepted as a matter of course by employees, who even found it a strong sign that the relationship would be an enduring one.

In thinking about what the creation of "Alima-Gerber" meant, both employees and the Polish press drew an analogy to the hundreds of mail-order bride operations that were springing up all over the Eastern Bloc. Just as beautiful but poor Eastern European women were being introduced to marriage-minded American men, and then were marrying them and going to the United States where they would be financially supported, Alima had been introduced to Gerber, who was now providing for her needs. Of course, it was not the best of all worlds. Many employees pointed out to me that just as it would have been preferable for Polish women to marry Polish men, it would have been preferable for Alima to stay in Polish hands. However, circumstances being what they were, Alima, like other impoverished Polish women, was making the best of things and had found a rich and not-bad-looking American to take care of her. It seemed to be the best hope for the future. As Gerber poured investments into the plant, it seemed more and more as if Alima had picked a good husband.

The problem in all of this reframing of the Alima-Gerber relationship was that although many Alima employees understood the relationship as a marriage, Gerber and its managers had no idea that this metaphor was at work. Perhaps if Gerber managers had been able to converse with shop floor workers or read the press accounts of the banquet, they might have been more aware of the context they were entering into. After all, marriage metaphors are used to describe corporate mergers in the United States as well. (But even if they had understood the metaphor, it was unlikely that Gerber managers would have understood the moral claim workers were making on them, which depended on both socialist and Solidarity ideologies to be so powerfully meaningful.) To the firm's executives, however, the privatization was a purchase. Further investments were part of a business deal, not contributions to a marriage. Since Gerber officials had never been to a Polish wedding, they completely missed the symbolism of the privatization banquet. While they acted in a way that was symbolically interpretable to Poles, they did it without realizing the cultural context of their actions.

The same was true of the stocks. Although Gerber had to give 40 percent of the stocks to employees at preferable prices under the terms of the 1991 privatization law, they voluntarily gave employees the money to purchase the shares. Gerber officials, especially Piergallini, saw this action in a completely different context than did Polish employees. By helping employees purchase stocks, they saw themselves as making employees into *owners,* not wives. Placing this action into the context of American management jargon, Gerber officials believed that employee-stockholders would "take ownership" of their work and their actions, calculating the effects of their labor in terms of increases in the values of their shares and therefore in terms of their own financial benefit (see Wasson 1993). The stocks were supposed to be "motivating," because they would tie individual action to concrete monetary rewards.

Gerber officials imagined that "taking ownership" would not only encourage Polish employees to work harder and increase their productivity (thereby avoiding the Communist curse of lazy, unproductive workers) but also to take individual responsibility for the production process. Since the Americans believed low productivity, lack of individual responsibility, and a dearth of initiative led to the economic collapse of communism, they thought that getting employees to "take ownership" would rectify some of the basic flaws in the system as it existed in the firm. Of course, their view assumed that Polish employees were individuals who assessed the value of labor strictly in terms of money, who constantly carried out cost/benefit analyses in terms of their own personal gain, and who could be motivated to act independently of their social groups by the "carrot" of an increase in stock price. All of these assumptions about human nature were made on the basis of American cultural values, habits, and social institutions (like stock markets), none of which necessarily applied in the Polish context. It soon became clear that employee stock ownership did not create competitive individuals but instead allowed employees to assert that their "ownership" entitled them to a voice in management decisions similar to the one a wife has to influence a husband's decisions in the home. This assertion led Gerber to buy up the shares quickly, so that it ended up owning 98 percent of the company.[21]

The conflict between the way that Gerber saw the relationship and the way that Alima employees conceived of it remained submerged as long as Gerber was investing large amounts in the firm and in the employee wage fund. After two years of huge investments, Gerber began to slow down its investments of both money and management expertise. This slowdown coincided with Gerber's increasing problems in the United States. As Gerber withdrew from the French market and abandoned its Czech and Hungarian ventures, it decided that its globalization strategy was a failure. Now Gerber had little motivation to continue making large investments in AG, and the Polish company found itself forced to sink or swim in the domestic market. Gerber needed AG to begin producing profits rather than continue to be a drain on the corporate bottom line, because it was negotiating with foreign buyers for its own takeover, and AG could not be seen as a liability.

Unaware of Gerber's problems, AG employees saw the investment slowdown and the "voluntary" layoffs as a betrayal of the commitments Gerber had made at the "wedding" (Kapuścinski 1995). This sentiment became more intense when Gerber announced its own sale to Sandoz. Having promised investments, job security, and a radiant future based on global exports, Gerber was now abandoning its Polish bride and running after other, richer partners. Anna, a worker in Division 4, scoffed, "If Gerber was a husband, he was not a very good one. He's left his Polish bride and gone off with a Swiss whore!" The appearance of Gerber's "affair" and betrayal was made even stronger when it was revealed that Sandoz had no idea that AG even existed until after it had purchased Gerber. Employees were deeply worried by this. They began, once again, to talk about the possibility that Alima might be sold or closed. In doing so, they had to reconceptualize the institutional relationships between the two firms: now, instead of being a wife, Alima was property that could be alienated or disposed of as the owner saw fit. This was a kind of subordination with very different implications from that implied by the marriage metaphor.

Reciprocity in a Capitalist Market

One of my last conversations at Alima was with Monika, an English-speaking college-educated worker in the planning department. In a voice that ranged from forlorn to bitter, she told me about the lesson her (Polish) boss taught her when she asked him for a raise. Although she believed that her work was important and that she was doing it well, her boss refused to increase her salary. She commented,

We're all unable to make changes in our salaries. It all depends on what your value to the company is. They have a point system which measures this now, tells exactly what your work is worth to the firm. [My boss] taught me, "This is your job. You do not have to do it—if you do not like it, quit. We'll find somebody else to do it. But do not complain about your tasks or your salary." I felt bad. I'd like to feel I'm important, that my job is important, and I'd like to be appreciated. Does not everyone want to feel that they are appreciated? But it happens. . . . It is not just about money. People want to feel they are valuable. But we are told that we do a certain job for a certain amount of money, and if we do not do it, they can always find someone else.

Monika had been told that her job and her performance of it could be calculated and that employees were compensated with an amount of money directly proportional to their value. Here again, the central relationship is between two forms of property, not between two persons: employees alienate their labor and exchange it for the firm's money. In the way that Monika portrays her boss's thinking, labor is an anonymous and general commodity, like money. If the employee as provider of the labor is unsatisfied with the exchange, he or she may leave. The firm will then contract with another supplier of an identical commodity. As Monika's boss told her, "We can always find somebody else."

But is it true that employers "don't appreciate" workers and "can always find somebody else"? Are Polish employees in the postsocialist era doomed to be just *szary istoty*, the anonymous providers of abstract labor that can be fully compensated for with a wage? In practice, are postsocialist workers just assets or liabilities, the sums of qualities totaled in a column? The use of kin metaphors suggests that in fights and discussions and compromises hammered out on the shop floor, workers were parrying the demands brought by American management to become flexible, calculable, and commodified. Drawing on symbolic resources from the socialist period, they were struggling toward new forms of capitalist personhood.

Kin metaphors are compact symbols that index a whole set of relations and constructions of personhood and move them into the workplace. If AG shop floor workers work as mothers, if their products are the products of a mother-worker, and if they are compensated as mothers or daughters, then by constructing themselves as mother-workers they are constructing themselves as socially embedded. Their labor is a valuable part of a socially embedded person, never fully alienable and never fully compensated for by wages. Rather, as Mauss (1950) pointed out, gifts demand reciprocity. By invoking kin terms, then, employees demand certain kinds of considerations and benefits from the firm.

By using kin terms, workers also demand that management expand their criteria for valuing work. Trapped between socialism (which most people remember as difficult and degrading) and the new structures of capital (which are radically disempowering most nonmanagerial employees), workers use kin metaphors to index a different philosophy. In seeking to transfer ideologies of gender and kin—in particular, those of home and motherhood—to the workplace, employees mobilize the structures of *znajomości,* or "connections." By doing so, they seek to maintain the distinction between persons and things, to assert the primacy of labor over capital, to constitute themselves as the subjects of work rather than its objects, and to insist they are persons rather than property. Kin terms construct the production process as a relation between persons mediated by the exchange of objects, rather than as a relation between objects (machinery, money, or baby food) mediated by persons. Just as Alicja did when she said she should get the Sanepid job because she was a mother, workers bring these forms of social personhood into the workplace in an attempt to recontextualize and revalue their labor. They do so to preserve jobs, wages, and workplace autonomy.

This form of embedded personhood is a stark contrast to the individualizing, commodifying constructions of personhood found in the Frugo commercials or the job evaluation protocols, which were used to divide persons from social contexts. The Frugo advertisements, in which those who were of a "lower" social class and an "advanced" age were associated with socialism, attempted to free white-collar workers from the historical taint of socialism and the associated economic rigidity. Quality control techniques equated persons and products and took the separation of person and social context even further. By turning attention from social structures and relationships within the firm and toward the inner world of the psyche, the quality control metaphor posited a bounded individual who could be internally divided into qualities. The use of kin terms reverses this notion, invoking an image of the person as somehow porous or interpenetrated with the personhood of others, which travels in the form of the gift.

It is tempting to see these daily symbolic quarrels as resistance. For an anthropologist, depicting AG's employees as carrying on Solidarity's struggle for labor rights would uphold some of the key values of the discipline. It would dignify workers by highlighting their agency, creativity, and spirit. The situation, however, is much less clear-cut than a simple dichotomy of power and resistance. By using terms like "wife" and "child" to describe themselves, workers assert that they are acting subjects, not merely inputs to production. At the same time, though, workers who use those terms constantly recognize and even naturalize their subordination. To become the "wife" to a multinational corporation is to continually acknowledge—and accept—the unequal distribution of power in the relationship. Polish workers occupy a gray zone somewhere between fatalistic acceptance of the changes in their working lives and romantic resistance to new forms of capitalist power.

Just how successful were workers' demands for reciprocity from management? Did the use of these metaphors have any material effects? On the one hand, by asserting expectations and obligations that were ostensibly grounded in "natural" or "biological" social roles, workers may have limited the firm's field of action in many ways—including the kinds of benefits it could give (or not give) to various sorts of employees, whom it could hire or fire, and whether or not it could retain trained employees. That things were not worse—that the firm decided to hold voluntary compensated layoffs, for example, instead of just abruptly firing people—suggests the strategy was at least partly effective. Fodor's (1997) finding that women's unemployment rates are lower than expected suggests Alima's experience is more indicative of a general trend in which the cultural legacies of socialism have regulated and shaped labor markets.

On the other hand, employees' use of kinship terms was not totally successful. There were layoffs, and the subsequent restructuring reduced employees' autonomy, job security, and bargaining power. Negotiations with management did not give workers back the political power they enjoyed in the 1980s, when Solidarity was strong, and did not liberate them from the heavy hand of capital. But then again, nobody on the shop floor ever expected that would happen, anyway. Alima's employees were not struggling against capitalism. Even as they tried to create labor relations they could live with, they fully accepted marketization, privatization, and the presence of multinational corporations. They were not fighting against their subordination. Rather, they were fighting to determine the way in which they would be subordinated.

6 Power and Postsocialism

In the years since 1989, Poland has been widely hailed as one of the great successes of postsocialist economic transformation (*Economist* 5 September 1998; *Economist* 13 February 1999; Wagener 2000). Some of the praise is based on quantitative economic measures. Throughout the 1990s, growth in GDP hovered at about 5 percent annually, making Poland the only country in the Eastern Bloc to have a higher per capita income than in 1989 (O'Rourke 2000).[1] After a period in the early 1990s in which hyperinflation reached 500 percent annually, inflation slowed to about 11 percent. By 1999, unemployment had fallen to around 13 percent from an estimated high of almost 20 percent (CIA 1999; Główny Urząd Statystyczny 2000). However, lurking beneath these supposedly objective measures is more ideologically driven praise. Poland, along with the Czech Republic and Hungary, are often praised for how *similar* they have made their economies, polities, and societies to those of the West.

Sometimes the accolades are for adopting specific features of Western European law, as when Brussels issues proclamations rewarding Poland for adopting most of the European Union's *acquis communautaire,* or body of common law. Other times, the rewards come in the form of certifications, as when factories that adopt rigorous quality control procedures are granted ISO 9000 certificates by the International Organization for Standardization in Geneva. Overwhelmingly, the idea that *change for the good* equals *more like Western Europe or the United States* has become the backbone of the "transition" in Poland. The idea of convergence, or getting back on the "road to Europe," has been the driving metaphor of the postsocialist transformation.

In this book, I have argued that a major element in the push for convergence has been the installation of a set of regulatory technologies and productive practices that were taken out of their original context—the transition from Fordism to post-Fordism in the United States and Western Europe. Bringing these managerial techniques to Poland, as well as to some of the other postsocialist countries, was a major element in a grand project of spatial transformation. Postsocialist reformers from both outside and inside Poland who wanted to reintegrate Poland into "Europe" were, in fact, striving to create a "technozone," or a homogenized space cutting across the geographical and social divisions the cold war created (cf. Barry 2001, 58). By refashioning Poland to ensure that it shared the same technical practices and ways of organizing work post-Fordist countries in the West used, postsocialist reformers sought to increase the flow of ideas, capital, and goods across Poland's Western border.

This project is not unique to Poland by any means: it is part of a regional project to make Western Europe a more unified and intensely regulated technological zone. As the European Union expands, it is also seeking to intensify the regulatory and technical interconnections between its member states. Some of this process is official and takes place through additions to the *acquis communautaire* and through the creation of new EU institutions. It is also part of the larger neoliberal project to knit distant corners of the globe together, not just through intensified trade but through common bodies of regulation (e.g., through the spread of IAS committee regulation or through audit-based food-safety regulations written by global organizations like Codex Alimentarius and endorsed by the World Trade Organization).

Only some of these technical practices are spread through formal regulation, however. Much of the process of technological interconnection is informal and social, carried out through the spread of "best practices" of measurement, management, and manufacture. Technical practices like audit, accounting, quality control, and niche marketing exemplify these less formal—but no less important—forms of technological interconnection. A closer look at these practices shows that they are more than just expedient devices for making production more efficient or for facilitating cross-border trade. Because they carry along new models of social relations and encapsulate notions of what it means to be a person, installing them in a postsocialist environment is also, at root, an attempt to make fundamental changes in the cultural notions that underpin economy and society in Poland.

The advent of these new technologies in Poland and the new concepts of personhood they inculcate add up to a substantively new form of power in Eastern Europe. Saying that these techniques are part of the operation of discipline and power rather than just politically neutral technical devices makes it possible to challenge the idea that Poland's postsocialist transformation is an unmitigated success. Do postsocialist changes add up to "success" if they foster inequality and disempower the very workers who struggled against the socialist state? Is the transition a success if it fosters the same kinds of corrupt or informal relations that the socialist system did? In this book, I have argued that in eradicating the institutions of state socialism, neoliberalism and post-Fordism have damaged or destroyed some of the most socially valuable aspects of the socialist era. This is not an apologia for socialism. It is an argument which asserts that state socialism, taken as a life-world, had some positive aspects that many people wish to see preserved, including forms of economic equality, social relations, and embedded personhood. It is also an argument that says Polish workers' struggles over power and subjectivity present models for thinking about other ways to be a person, for organizing work, and for creating social communities in places outside Poland as well.

It is utopian to think that the practices of a few shop floor workers in a baby food factory in Poland might add up to a liberatory ideology. But it is possible to imagine that people in the United States and Western Europe, like Alima-Gerber's workers, might use these ideas to find a form of subordination that suits them better.

From Redistribution to Regulation

The shifts in managerial practice that Alima's experience exemplifies are part of a very specific moment in Eastern European history. When neoliberal economic reform first held sway in the early 1990s—the "liberal moment," as Holc (1997) labels it—the vision of the acting subject as an autonomous individual was reintroduced in Poland.[2] The goal of the social order was narrowed to the radical individualist notion of "liberty," and the definition of "liberty" was narrowed to mean "economic freedom" (Holc 1997, 415). Merely talking about these ideas, however, was not sufficient to make them the governing principle of the new political-economic order. They had to be implemented and naturalized and, most of all, made into practices that seemed so mundane that they were beneath notice. Through management and marketing techniques, companies like Alima attempted to constitute employees and customers as autonomous, choice-making subjects who could audit themselves and then act upon their constituent parts. It did so to sell more product, to change the labor market it had to deal with, and to extract value from laborers more efficiently.

Disciplining economic actors through new managerial technologies is part of an attempt to produce a new form of person and a new mode of subjection. Just as the Frugo advertisement showed, the hyperactive flexible bodies that are the goal of post-Fordist managerial techniques are presented as a contrast to the bodies that the socialist system often tried to produce. State socialist biopower often centered on immobilizing people: the state placed sharp restrictions on people's ability to travel, made labor mobility almost impossible by causing severe housing shortages, and trapped people for hours at a time in interminable lines for basic food products. In constantly seizing time and immobilizing bodies, the socialist state attempted to make its subjects docile by destroying most opportunities and capacities for independent initiative and planning.

> Not knowing when the bus might come, when cars might be allowed to circulate again, when the exam for medical specializations might be given, or when food would appear in stores, bodies were transfixed, suspended in a void that obviated all projects and plans but the most . . . spontaneous. (Verdery 1996, 49)

New managerial techniques, coupled with neoliberal ideas about autonomy and activity, promise to create a different kind of person: one who is active, mobile, and endowed with the ability to choose. The idea of "flexibility" and the making of the flexible worker are thus proposed as the antidote to socialism—a kind of freedom counterposed to the constraints of communism.

More important, the introduction of new managerial technologies also marks a shift from power based on *redistribution* to a kind of power based on *self-regulation*. In chapter 4, I described the systems of *znajomości* and vassalage that both created hierarchy and cross-cut it during the socialist period. These systems operated on the principle of redistributive power: people inside the socialist system acquired power through the ability to reallocate goods. Anyone who could decide who got more and who got less of something desirable and otherwise unattainable made recipients into dependents (Verdery 1996, 25). This made the Communist Party center—which was the head of the pyramid of redistribution—enormously powerful but also made people who could hoard resources outside official channels and informally redistribute them powerful as well.

In the postsocialist era, power operates quite differently. Now, the central motif of power is not redistribution but dispersed self-regulation. People and institutions govern themselves by monitoring themselves constantly and altering their behavior to comply with norms set informally (e.g., in advertisements or in "best practices") or formally (e.g., by international accounting standards or international quality control procedures). These norms are often presented as neutral, scientific, and expedient. But they are also forms of power that impinge on how people conceive of themselves, conduct themselves, and organize their daily lives. New disciplinary technologies are almost always presented as "empowering" and liberating. Accounting standards promise to help executives "see" their companies more clearly and, hence, to give them more power to run them efficiently. Niche marketing holds out the promise of allowing people to choose what kinds of persons they will become by choosing the products they consume. Quality control techniques promise to give managers the power to control the qualities of each unit that comes off the line so minutely that they can overcome even nature's variations and create a standardized product. Employee evaluation programs promise to allow employees to control every aspect of their personalities and capacities, and to "improve" themselves constantly to gain advantage in the labor market. In each case, self-regulation is presented as a way of giving power and autonomy to individuals (firms and persons), not as a form of constraint.

These promises of empowerment—along with images of choice and autonomy—echo the calls for freedom and choice of the first postsocialist reformers, who were themselves neoliberals. They promised that the postsocialist transformation would bring both national sovereignty (i.e., freedom from economic and political policy dictated by the Soviet Union) and individual freedom. But both of these "freedoms" have turned out to be a part of social and economic regulation. Although the motives for introducing new managerial techniques were largely based on corporate self-interest, putting these ideas about persons into practice forged an important link between the emerging market economy and the means by which individual behavior is regulated and made consonant with that economic structure (cf. Aglietta 1987; Boyer 1990; Harvey 1989; Jessop 1984, 1990). Thus, the construction of the self-managing, choosing individual at places like Alima is not just the conceit that makes liberal political and economic theorizing work (cf. Holc 1997, 406). It is an integral means of regulating social actors so that the capitalist-democratic political economy runs smoothly and coherently.

Miller and Rose (1990, 24) suggest that the linchpin of regulation is the naturalization of the autonomous individual through management technology or, in Miller and Rose's terms, "the language of the enterprise":

The language of the enterprise has become so significant, we suggest, because it enables a translatability between the most general *a priori* of political thought and a range of specific programmes for administering the national economy, the internal world of the firm, and a whole host of other organizations from the school to the hospital. But further, it enables such programmes to accord a new priority to the self-regulating capacities of individuals. . . . At the level of the macro-economy, the argument that an economy structured in the form of relations of exchange between discrete economic units pursuing their undertakings with confidence and energy will produce the most social goods and distribute them in the manner most advantageous to each and to all has not spelt an end to programmes for the "government" of economic life. Rather, it has given rise to all manner of programmes for reforming economic activity in order to construct such a virtuous system, and to a plethora of new regulatory technologies that have sought to give effect to them. (1990, 24)

The idea that economies are regulated or "governed" through the creation of autonomous "choosing" subjects is a paraphrase of the main thesis of this book: that the creation of specific forms of personhood is a central aspect of social regulation, which shapes and is shaped by macroeconomic structures. In a sense, what is happening at the individual and microsocial levels replicates what is happening at the national political-economic level. Just as Poland is supposedly "free to choose" whether it will join the European Union or participate in the global economy but in fact is compelled to do so because the only alternative is economic disaster, so too are individuals apparently more autonomous yet more stringently regulated than ever before. If marketers can successfully convince mothers that they can "freely" choose between buying commercial baby food and poisoning their children, the choice is certainly constrained by the allocation of scientific authority to the baby food producer. Likewise, people of working-class backgrounds may be "free" to choose where they will be employed, but because of the personal characteristics ascribed to them by new human resource techniques, they are certainly not "free" to choose to become sales representatives or marketers. Becoming "free" has thus made people less free than ever before or—freedom being hard to quantify—differently unfree. Economic regulation, private property, and the constitution of the person as an individual are inextricably linked in both ideology and practice, which leaves people with little choice as to the kinds of *persons* they will become.

Invisible and Distorted Subjects

The idea that there is nothing natural about the calculative actors who inhabit a marketplace is the antithesis of the assumption at the heart of neoliberal economic theory (see Barry 2001, 82). Neoliberalism sees subjects as either "invisible" or "distorted" (Holc 1997, 423). "Invisible subjects" are rational actors whose behavior is determined only by the forces of the market. Economists' models usually assume that such actors exist in the real world, rather than exploring the possibility and conditions of their existence. In contrast, liberal economic theory uses the label "distorted subjects" to refer to people with populist beliefs, strong ethnic identities, short-term personal economic ties, personalistic ties, or commitments that outweigh market logic (Holc 1997, 423). Neoliberalism changes the autonomous self-regulating individual into an unmarked category and turns other forms of personhood into deviations or "distortions" of the norm.

My discussion of the differences between *menadżerowie* and *kierownicy* in chapter 3 was an example of the way the idea of "invisible" and "distorted" subjects was being created and naturalized. *Menadżerowie* were supposedly rational actors who could apply new capitalist technologies and rationality without being hampered by "socialist-style" connections or mentalities. According to the Polish and foreign managers I interviewed, however, *kierownicy* were irreparably distorted by the experience of state socialism. Their positions in the socialist system of "vassalage," combined with their habit of activating social networks in order to carry out managerial action, made them "too inflexible" to become the invisible subject of market rationality.

A similar idea of the individual has emerged in anticorruption rhetoric in Poland, as it is used by institutions such as the World Bank and the Polish Sejm, as well as among shop floor workers. The idea of "corruption" condemns the network of favors and reciprocal exchanges, labeling it immoral and, in some cases, illegal. Anticorruption rhetoric thus stands as a widespread condemnation of embedded personhood and the personalization of economic relations, and a naturalization of the autonomous, rule-governed individual (Krastev 1998; Granovetter 1992).

Naturalized concepts of personhood and internalized processes of self-regulation make up a new form of power in Eastern Europe precisely because of their invisibility. Socialist power was, if anything, overt. It rested on visible displays of force (as in the infamous May Day parades, which demonstrated military might). It depended on the very public knowledge that anyone, anywhere, could be under surveillance (Horvath and Szakolczai 1991). If information was kept from the general public—and it was—there were also many public acknowledgements of the existence of secrets. These secrets served to make the power of the state to withhold information more visible. Most significantly, the bare fact of central redistribution made power extremely visible:

Under state socialism, the central appropriation of surplus is transparent and therefore has to be legitimated. Here the state is the self-declared appropriator of surplus. It is the transparent oppressor and exploiter, making its appearance in production as a triple alliance between managers, union, and party. The very visibility of the agents of state domination requires an ideology which justified central appropriation. (Burawoy and Lukács 1992, 147)

State socialist enterprises tried to justify the power of the state through a series of workplace rituals: "communist shifts" and "voluntary Saturdays," brigade competitions and interfactory contests to meet the Plan, and endless production campaigns. These were designed to transform socialism's overt ideological claims into bodily practice and lived experience. But as Burawoy and Lukács (1992, 147) point out, these rituals actually forced workers to act out a kind of socialism that they knew was false. While socialist propaganda trumpeted that the socialist system had created equality, anyone who worked in a state-owned enterprise had to deal with the injustice, shortage, and irrationality that the Plan created on a daily basis. This made the presence of the state in everyday life highly visible.

The post-Fordist managerial technologies that have been imported to Eastern Europe try to make power invisible by first dispersing it and then embedding it in the very constitution of working people. Power no longer operates by relying on external surveillance. The panopticon-like system of wiretaps, informers, and secret police that characterized socialist power is no longer necessary. Instead, new managerial technologies make power invisible by seeking to make "invisible subjects." By stripping workers of their social context, devaluing their personal connections, making their family relations irrelevant, and dismissing their moral beliefs about interpersonal obligation, new management technologies attempt to make Poles into the market-rational invisible subjects of post-Fordist neoliberalism. Because these "privatized individuals" are supposed to make themselves hew to the norms set out for their economic behavior, they need only comply with the demand for auditable performance (which evaluates their self-checking mechanisms, not their actual performance) in order to become self-disciplinarians. As the market subjects of flexible capitalism, they embody the new economy in their everyday action and in their beliefs about themselves as producers of value. The privatization of persons thus also privatizes regulation, making subjects—not the state—the agents who ensure that their behavior is consonant with the reproduction of the economic order.

The new invisible power manufactured and installed by post-Fordist management techniques is not evenly distributed, by any means. Some types of people are able to determine the qualities of the acting subject while others are powerless to do so. Those who have access to technologies of audit, accounting, TQM, statistical process control, factor analysis, and niche marketing—and the power to make other people "choose" to enact them—can make others into particular kinds of people and assign value to different kinds of workers, their labor, and the products they make. Those who dictate the use of these techniques constitute others—or require them to constitute themselves—as "privatized individuals;" that is, subjects easily treated as objects, subjects with divisible qualities that can be "worked on," and subjects who, through the relentless process of self-audit, treat themselves as objects to be worked on.

Negotiating Personhood

As persuasive and pervasive as new management technologies and the privatized individual have become in the global economy, the "liberal moment" and the liberal individual are not uncontested. In this regard, Poland is a special case, in which a powerful concatenation of local knowledges, including the long tradition of organized labor activism, the cultural and ideological resources gained during the socialist period, and the philosophies of the Polish Catholic Church, give Polish workers resources to renegotiate their objectification and impoverishment. Alima workers object to being treated as property, as "geese" or "slaves," in their terms, rather than as full persons. They insist that they are the subjects of labor (although perhaps subordinated ones), not its objects.[3] In doing so, they follow the Polish pope in insisting on the primacy of relationships between human beings over relations between persons and things (John Paul II 1981, 101; Dumont 1985, 104). Although the arguments that AG workers present have strong Marxist overtones, the workers neither ground their assertions in Marxism or advocate a return to state socialism.[4] Rather, they find arguments against their "privatization" in the idea of creating a collective moral balance sheet, rather than in creating balance sheets of their own personal qualities. Most important, they find alternate ways of constituting human persons in the practice of reciprocity, which was elaborated during the socialist era.

AG workers challenge the privatization of persons in three ways. First, they insist that work should be for persons, rather than the other way round (see John Paul II 1981, 106). They believe that the most important consideration in the production process is moral, not financial. They argue that their product should benefit the people who make it as well as the mothers and children who consume it. This, they assert, is more important than that the work benefit the firm's owners. When a laboratory worker says that she should have her job because she has children to support, or when a manager throws out the evaluations and decides which family can best afford a lay-off, both parties are making a moral decision to value the person who works over the profits the worker produces.

Second, AG workers emphasize that production is a relation between people rather than a relation between persons and things. They emphasize the production of use values over the production of exchange values. When worker/mothers uphold quality control standards because "a baby might get sick and die" if they do not, they are thinking in terms of the production of use values, which is intrinsically a relation between persons, albeit one mediated by an object, the product. This view of labor, which sees work as an action by one person for another and workers as the subjects of labor, contrasts sharply with the structures of Fordist or even post-Fordist capitalist management, in which persons are processes that can be "reengineered" to increase quality and productivity. In post-Fordist management, persons qua processes can be isolated, analyzed, taken apart, fixed, pressed back into service, or replaced with identical "parts" if necessary. The worker here is the object of labor, much as semi-finished goods or machines are. The workforce, like other forces needed for production, is an instrument for the production of exchange values. In a relation where money is converted into capital and back again into money, the acting subject is capital, not a person.

Third, AG workers also renegotiate their "privatization" by insisting on the social nature of capital. Like both Marx (1978, 207) and Pope John Paul II (1981, 118–19), AG workers assert that capital is the product of human labor and so should benefit those who worked to produce it. AG workers made this assertion when they argued that their labor gave them ownership rights in the firm. Although Gerber believed its purchase of the employees' stock terminated those ownership rights, that employees symbolize Alima's relationship to Gerber as a marriage shows that they think quite differently. The ongoing labor of both partners in a marriage gives both of them rights to their collective wealth and rights to make joint decisions in the home. Similarly, many workers continue to believe their ongoing labor gives them rights to share in the fruits of success and rights to a voice in company decisions, even if they are less powerful than management. It is a blow when management asserts that they do not have such rights.

AG workers do not oppose the privatization of the firm, nor are they reactionary defenders of "socialist legacies." The critical issue for AG workers is not who owns the plant per se but who gets to use it and for whose benefit (cf. John Paul II 1981, 125). In accordance with Catholic social teaching, AG workers believe the dignity of labor and the person as subject of labor can exist under both private and social ownership of the means of production. What is important is who works, how they work, and to whose benefit they work. Production as a relationship between persons can exist under private or collective ownership. However, AG workers do oppose the privatization of persons. They do so by refusing the concept of the person as an asocial monad with divisible qualities. They see this "autonomous subject" as someone who is disconnected from the common good and as a potential threat to the collective welfare. At AG, workers expressed those sentiments by labeling those whom they did not see as embedded persons "outsiders," "foreigners," or simply "them."

By insisting on their own embeddedness, they are also insisting on being the subjects of their labor. The idea that human persons are self-constituting as laboring subjects is precisely what Katarzyna expresses in her separation of *człowiek* (person) and *szara istota* (gray being). In her garden and in her kitchen, Katarzyna is the subject of work. She is not a "subject" in the abstract, though, but is woman, wife, and most of all, mother. She is subject by virtue of the person-to-person relationship that she creates by producing for others and transferring part of her self to them. Only when she is an object of labor, an abstract worker or consumer who is not embedded in a social context, does she feel she is a *szara istota*. Industrially produced baby food, produced by capital for profit rather than by mothers for children, makes her into the object of labor—at least in her mind.

It might be possible to dismiss these ideas as sour grapes from a working class whose power is diminishing. It might be easy to see AG workers' ideas as outmoded or reactionary, or as nostalgic looks back at what now appears as "the radiant past" (to use Michael Burawoy's term). It might be easy to see embedded personhood as a set of traditional ideas about personhood that stand in the way of progress, economic change, and a better standard of living for everyone. However, these ideas should matter both to people involved in Eastern European economic change and to critics of neoliberal capitalist societies. First, ideas about embedded personhood affect politics in Eastern Europe, which are swinging dramatically between neoliberalism and "personalist" philosophies like the ones described here. This swing between philosophies affects issues from privatization to abortion rights to European Union accession (see Holc 1997; Gal 1994; Zbierski-Salameh 1998; Swain 1993; Hann 1993a and 1993b). It has undeniable material effects, because ideas about embedded personhood are translated into governmental regulations, such as the labor code and privatization programs, and into institutions like trade unions and political parties. Personhood, in short, enters into debates about economic transformation in very specific and concrete ways.

Debates about social regulation have profound effects on the global economy. Changes in the form of the state, the legal structure, the business environment, or firms' ability to extract value can have profound effects on foreign firms' willingness to invest in Poland and the amount of capital they take away. These problems of capital flow profoundly shape how Poland will enter the global economy as well as regional political and economic organizations like NATO and the European Union. Polish politicians often find themselves subject to intense external pressure when the World Bank, the International Monetary Fund, or the European Bank for Reconstruction and Development make loans conditional on Poland's instituting fiscally conservative policies and cutting back on social welfare. At the same time, large numbers of internal constituents whose political preferences are based on embedded personhood and ideas of reciprocity may demand that the state increase its redistribution of wealth. The contradictory sources of pressure lead to political turmoil and, by blocking or facilitating international loans, further shape multinational capital flows.

More philosophically but more importantly, Polish debates over personhood and social embeddedness are debates over the emancipatory potential of different socioeconomic systems. The transition from socialism, in this sense, is a moment in which two strong sets of ideas about economy, society, and person are opposed. The contrast opens up the possibility of critique: from this perspective, the embedded and integrated personhood that Polish shop floor workers advocate is not mere nostalgia for a socialist or mythic precapitalist past but an alternative to the deeply fragmented subject now typical in the heartland of market democracy. Employees in workplaces from American high-tech firms to British universities to German car factories are experiencing ever greater demands at work and at home, finding themselves individually as well as collectively disempowered, and discovering that the corporation demands access to their emotions and psyches while providing ever fewer benefits. More and more, people in the market democracies find themselves increasingly alienated from their families, neighborhoods, and work communities. The kinds of subjectivity and social relations that Polish production workers offer provide the opportunity to rethink the consequences of these isolating and privatizing practices: the products people in market societies buy and the self-audits they perform, the kinds of moral balance sheets they construct, the stocks they invest money in, and the relationships they invest time in. The study of Polish workers, who have unique historical, cultural, and religious resources with which to contest their subordination, opens a window through which to criticize and perhaps change new structures of domination.

Notes

Chapter 1. The Road to Capitalism

1. Many of the principles of "scientific management" predated Taylor, including the idea of breaking down craftwork into specialized and repetitive jobs and the idea of reducing each job to a series of movements. Taylor, however, was the first to formalize the system and to popularize it. Other industrial engineers of the Progressive era, including Frank and Lillian Gilbreth, Carl Barth, and Henry Gantt, came up with forms of scientific management. I thank Martha Lampland for reminding me that Taylorism and scientific management are not synonymous.

2. The model I draw of state socialism here is based largely on the work of Janoś Kornai. The model, which he calls the "classical" model of state socialism, largely ignores the changes in centrally planned economies wrought during the reforms of the 1960s, 1970s, and 1980s. Because it does not account for reform, the model also largely ignores the divergences among the countries in the Bloc. These divergences were highly significant by the 1980s, when, for example, Romania was undergoing draconian import substitution measures while Hungary was transforming major portions of its economy. Nonetheless, I agree with both Kornai and Verdery (1996) that the model describes the basic *tendencies* of socialist economies and hence the basic economic processes they shared. Shortage might have been more severe in one place or time than another, and reforms may have granted a little more autonomy to firms in some countries and decades, but the basic problems of central planning plagued all the countries of the region, at least until the collapse of the Communist system.

3. Piotr Sztompka, an influential Polish sociologist, even went so far as to diagnose Polish society as suffering from "civilizational incompetence" stemming from the "fake modernity" of socialism (Sztompka 2000).

4. I owe this idea to Michael Power.

5. The director of human resources was himself writing about new management practices, and his work was showing up in national newspapers and magazines as well as scholarly books. I believe he let me into the plant because he saw me as a source of intellectual companionship—something he felt he sorely lacked in Rzeszów. AG's president was also aware of my presence in the company. As I found out only after fieldwork was completed, however, Gerber executives back in Michigan did *not* know I was there. Gerber's public relations department was later quite upset to find out I had spent nearly two years inside their Polish subsidiary.

6. In this book, I do not disclose *any* information that might influence either AG's or Gerber's competitive standing in the marketplace. (Any proprietary information that I may have had in 1995–97 is now outdated, at any rate.) I do, however, include information that might be embarrassing to particular managers. For that reason, I have given pseudonyms to all the employees I discuss, with the exception of the CEO of Gerber. Assigning pseudonyms to either AG or Gerber, however, seems pointless to me. Because the specifics of the AG privatization are so unique and because so few players are in the baby food market, anyone who could benefit from knowing the name of the company would easily recognize the firm I portray.

Chapter 2. Accountability, Corruption, and the Privatization of Alima

1. A pseudonym.

2. All unattributed quotes in this book are from personal interviews and conversations with the author.

3. The term "accountability" translates awkwardly into Polish and doesn't have the same sense as it does in English. *"Księgowość,"* or bookkeeping, expresses the economic sense, whereas *"odpowiedzialność,"* or "answerability," expresses the moral sense. Nonetheless, because the *procedures* of accounting were used to address both economic and moral issues, "accountability" sums up the Polish problem well. See also John Borneman's (1997) book, *Settling Accounts.*

4. Balcerowicz was not the only advocate of this theory. See also see Klaus and Ježek 1991; Balcerowicz 1995, 6, 131; Kornai 1995, 14, 22–25, 29; Schrader 1994, 263; Winiecki 1993, 135; Streissler 1991; and Kovács 1991.

5. Many commentators argued that Eastern Europeans already *knew* these fundaments of private business. There was thus some empirical basis for assuming that repealing laws against private economic activity would lead to the development of a market economy (Koźminski 1993, 55), because so many Eastern Europeans displayed entrepreneurial aptitude when private trading was tolerated at the periphery of the first economy.

However, the neoliberal equation of the second economy with a market economy and the assumption that relaxing restrictions on private enterprise would allow the second economy to expand at the expense of the first was problematic. Although Eastern Europeans did engage in economic activity outside the scope of central planning, that activity was not necessarily fully governed by market principles. In particular, private enterprises that depended on materials acquired from the first economy or had SOEs as customers were sheltered from market forces. When socialist entrepreneurs bought inputs made in SOEs, those inputs were price-controlled and subsidized. When traders used trains or buses, the state subsidized ticket prices and, hence, the transportation costs of goods. Factors like these meant the "private sector" in socialist Eastern Europe was in many ways more like the socialist state sector than like a Western market economy. Entrepreneurs did not necessarily face hard budget constraints or assume the risks that an ideal-typical capitalist would.

When the second economy did not immediately expand to fill the space left by the demise of the socialist first economy, and when state-owned enterprises did not immediately restructure despite liberalizing measures that exposed them to market forces, scholars and policy makers began to consider a constructivist approach to economic transformation.

6. Employees very often gender Alima as female and use metaphors about "marriage" to describe their company's relationship to Gerber (see chap. 5).

7. However, once several foreign firms were interested in buying Alima, it was discovered that although there were no claimants to the *firm,* which had originally stood on a piece of land in the center of Rzeszów, there were more than sixty claimants to the *land the firm stood on,* where Alima was moved in the 1960s. When Gerber finally purchased Alima, it left $4 million of the money it owed to the Polish state treasury in escrow in a

London bank. If and when the land claims were settled, the state treasury would receive the money; if the land claims were not disqualified, the money could be used by Gerber to purchase the land. As of early 1997, the bulk of the claims still had not been settled, and the money remained in London.

8. Kornai disagrees with this proposition vehemently: "It is ethically paradoxical to mix slogans of fairness and quality into a program of capitalist privatization" (1995, 89).

9. Although Lewandowski was, in essence, a champion of trade sales because he believed they were the quickest route to technology transfer, he also strongly advocated a program of mass privatization (Lewandowski and Szomburg 1989). He felt it was a means of giving each citizen a personal stake in the success of economic transformation, which might ensure popular consent for more large-scale economic transformation and create political legitimacy for the Solidarity government (see also Dobek 1993, 79–80).

10. In straight-line depreciation, an asset depreciates the same amount each year over its useful lifespan. The value of a machine that is supposed to last ten years, then, is discounted by 10 percent each year. Accelerated depreciation takes technological obsolescence into account and frontloads depreciation in the first few years after the purchase. In the United States and Western Europe, for example, insurance companies use accelerated depreciation, which is why the book value of new cars declines so much in the first few years after they are produced.

11. Poovey (1998, 56) argues that the formal precision of the system, not correspondence to real events, is the basis of accounting's claims to truth and virtue. As long as the books balance, she says, it's immaterial whether the entries correspond to real transactions and objects. I disagree. Revelations from recent accounting scandals, such as the Enron case, which prove that accounts are the socially constructed results of negotiations between managers, accountants, and auditors, destroy the credibility that accounting might confer.

12. Although specific new techniques of sampling and audit are unique to post-Fordist organizations, the idea that public disclosure of a firm's activity can blend the economic and moral senses of accountability dates from the beginning of the double-entry bookkeeping system. By opening their books to inspection, sixteenth-century merchants represented themselves as trustworthy men of virtue (Poovey 1998, 59).

13. This problem became one of the most heated at Alima. Between 1993 and 1997, the firm used more and more imported tropical fruits and fewer domestically grown ones, especially in the production of Frugo (see chap. 3). Even as late as March 1997, Alima's contracting farmers were complaining to the local media that Alima's production decisions were ruining their livelihoods.

14. This kind of voluntary compensated layoff has become a model for other firms in the region. The glassworks at Jarosław, one of AG's suppliers, offered its employees up to sixteen months' salary to quit. According to a member of the firm's marketing department, however, the glassworks did not get the same turnout as AG and had to turn instead to *involuntary* compensated layoffs.

15. It is extremely difficult to gauge the real effect of the Alima layoffs—as well as the layoffs from other regional firms—on the local community. Recent research suggests that more than half of the 2.3 million people registered nationally as unemployed are in fact not seeking work: 7 percent are working illegally, 14 percent are unable to work (e.g., mothers at home with small children), and 25 percent show no activity whatsoever in

seeking work (*Gazeta Wyborcza* 1997). Given the nature of the problem, it is difficult to assess the reliability of these statistics. An employee of the Rzeszów *Urząd Pracy* (Employment Office) judges that the majority of her clients are also not genuinely seeking work.

To rectify this situation, the Rzeszów area unemployment office designed new regulations: after one year of unemployment benefits, clients had either to go to public-works jobs or take a job arranged by the Employment Office. The state subsidized the salaries for these jobs, which created a new situation: a low-cost labor base of workfare workers. Employers preferred the workfare employees, and so when the workfare employee's time was up, the employer would fire them, and they would return to the unemployment rolls. Employers would then accept a new batch of workfare participants. Rather than creating new jobs, this program has made it more difficult for unskilled workers to find full-time, long-term employment (Krystyna Moczuk, pers. comm.).

16. The temporary workers were also much cheaper than full-time permanent employees; some earned as little as 2.5 million old złoty a month (about $100).

17. Another factor that led the firm to change the number of its suppliers was an overall change in the product line. In response to market research and sales results, AG began focusing more on developing products made either from imported fruits and vegetables like banana and orange, which are not grown in Poland, or from specific varieties of fruit, like sweeter Golden Delicious apples, which had not been grown in the Rzeszów area before. This was terrible for planters who had invested both money and labor in planting crops like black currant, which now was only being purchased in very small quantities, or strawberries, which AG was not buying at all. Some contractors received loans to cover the costs of changing crops, but others simply lost their contracts. Farmers watched AG import crops like carrots, which they grew themselves. AG asserted that it simply could not purchase carrots in Rzeszów that met the Polish government's standards for heavy metal contamination and so imported them from France. Local farmers who could not produce carrots that met those standards also lost their contracts.

18. See Kostera (1996), who discusses the affinity between religious proselytism and the work of business schools and consultants.

19. At first, Gerber sent two of its managers to act in the capacity of company president. After a long search, however, the firm hired a thirty-nine-year-old Polish executive away from Coca-Cola Polska to run the company. The new manager of quality control was a Polish woman in her thirties who had been trained at Rutgers University, in New Jersey. She was brought in to supervise the installation of the new laboratory and to train both laboratory and shop floor employees in Gerber's quality control procedures. The old personnel department was reorganized, and a new manager was brought in to create a "human resources" department. Significantly, the new department was not called the "Dział Kadr," or Personnel Department; this name was given to the old department responsible for doling out employee benefits and other forms of "social care." The new director attempted to use the English term "human resources" to describe his division, but this was rapidly polonized to "Dział do Spraw Pracowników," or "Employee Affairs." This new "human resources" director was a lawyer in his early forties who had worked for many years in the United States, including at the Monterey Defense Language Institute and at the Library of Congress. He soon hired a new director of personnel and created training, recruitment, and public relations departments.

20. Whether Gerber actually bought the assertion that Jones was immoral—or even cared—is unclear. It is also unclear whether Jones's affair was the sole problem precipitating his firing. However, several Gerber managers reiterated the idea that Jones had become a liability, suggesting that whatever Gerber's top executives thought of his performance or his personal life, they clearly decided he was more trouble than he was worth.

21. Lampland (1995) has argued that labor was already commodified under the socialist system, largely thanks to Fordist innovations like work points, which were adopted by socialist enterprises. Although this is not the place for an extended debate, I would assert that if labor was a commodity under socialism, it was a very different kind of commodity precisely because it was embedded in an economy of shortage. Hence, whether the privatization of persons in postsocialist Eastern Europe is an original commodification or a recommodification is irrelevant. The point is that the privatization of enterprises marked a fundamental shift in conceptions of both persons and labor.

Chapter 3. Niche Marketing and the Production of Flexible Bodies

1. Alima's director of operations gave this figure in a speech to Division 4 (baby food) workers.

2. AG marketers provided these figures during the Frugo launch presentation.

3. As Schrum points out, the category of "teenager" did not exist until after World War II. It was a deliberate invention of marketers and magazine publishers, who used the pages of magazines like *Seventeen* to convince young women to consume new products.

4. Two AG employees gave me this interpretation, in response to my complaints that I didn't understand why everyone else who viewed the ads laughed uproariously.

5. Although many foreign-made and domestic products were aligned with capitalist forms of being and belonging, some products were marketed with an image of indigeneity. An interesting twist on this practice was in an advertisement for Lee jeans, an American brand. Making a pun on *Litwo Ojczyzna Moja* (Lithuania, my fatherland), the opening lines of a famous nationalist poem by Adam Mickiewicz, the jeans company used the slogan *"Leetwo Ojczyzna Moja,"* incorporating the product name and thereby associating itself with an Eastern European national identity rather than foreign capital.

6. Ironically, the Gerber managers believed there was very little interdepartmental communication, when in fact there was a great deal. As I describe in detail below, the socialist economy of shortage meant that production managers were constantly scrambling to produce *something* with the materials they had on hand and to acquire new inputs for the next round of production. This required a great deal of informal coordination with raw materials ordering, operations management, and facilities management, not to speak of plan bargaining with the central planners who drew up production quotas.

7. This company name is a pseudonym, as are all the personal names in chap. 3.

8. Similarly, the Polish term for "management," *zarzadzanie,* is now often replaced with the polonized English term, *menadżment* (Kostera 1996, 160).

9. I use the masculine pronoun advisedly. See n. 10 below.

10. Their connections with ministries and other higher-ups may be covertly valued.

In most cases, when ex-Communists are hired, it is said to be for their "knowledge of the culture," rather than for their ties to the bureaucracy.

11. My reference to "gendered" magazines is not accidental. It seems to me that the image of the *menedżer* is definitely an image of a man. The effect on female managers, however, is a topic that I have yet to research.

12. At the same time, of course, the requirements and qualifications for managers also increased. Although "attitude" sufficed to qualify a prospective manager for a new job in the immediate postsocialist period, when few people knew much about capitalist management, real experience and specialized training soon became prerequisites for managerial work.

13. AG has a very strict age limit for newly hired salespeople: they must be under thirty-five. Iwona, the recruitment specialist, says that older people just "don't have the strength" to do the job.

14. There is also a pragmatic issue at work here, for both production workers and sales representatives. Because of the overall shortage of housing and the expense of renting or of buying a new apartment, it is extremely difficult for Polish employees to relocate in search of better job opportunities. This would make it hard for production workers, who lived in Rzeszów, to move to cities where sales reps were needed.

15. Rigidly specified procedures, formalized in written documents, are standard operating procedure in most food-processing firms in the West. It was unlikely that the binders at AG were deliberate insults to shop floor workers. Nonetheless, at AG, just as in American firms, managers assume that workers do not have the craft knowledge to do the job and deny them the right to control their own labor.

16. Even this kind of flexibility has its associations with capitalism and socialism. Restrictions on firings and layoffs are seen as legacies of the socialist era. New restrictions have been included in the 1996 labor code, which was written while the SLD—the post-Communist left-wing party—was in power.

17. One day, my job was to hack fifty-kilo blocks of frozen butter into little chunks, which were being added along with salt to a vat of baby food. When I asked the head of product development, who was testing a new recipe, why we were adding so much fat and salt, she said that Polish babies, like other Poles, had a taste for it and wouldn't eat the low-fat, salt-free recipes Gerber devised. This idea of national tastes is part of a global niche marketing strategy that Gerber uses not only in foreign markets but also within the United States as part of its niche marketing strategy based on ethnicity. For example, the Gerber "tropicals" line was developed to reach Hispanic-American consumers.

18. E.g., it takes longer to switch from meats to fruits than from one kind of fruit to another, since new machines must come on line. Changing bottle sizes is the most time-consuming task, because mechanics must manually reset parts on all the machines.

19. I owe this point to Katherine Verdery.

20. Thanks to Michael Burawoy for reminding me of this.

21. The rich literature on gifts, favors, and "connections" during the socialist period is discussed at greater length in chaps. 4 and 5. For more complete descriptions, see Wedel 1986; Ledeneva 1998; and Yang 1994.

22. Of course, salesmen give gifts to clients in capitalist societies as well. This fact blurs the distinction between capitalist/money societies and socialist/gift societies that I have drawn here. What is important here, however, is that the salesmen, the clerks, and the

marketing department all classified the exchange of gifts as a particularly *socialist* practice—and this is what made it controversial.

23. Casual racism—including anti-Semitism and bigotry against blacks—is so noncontroversial in Poland that one of the local coffee shops in Rzeszów was called "Murzynek," or "Little Nigger Boy." Nobody I asked was shocked in the least by it. "It's the name of a brand of coffee" was the only explanation I ever got when I asked how a café might come to have such a racist name.

Chapter 4. Quality Control, Discipline, and the Remaking of Persons

1. I owe this phrasing to Katherine Verdery.

2. For an almost archetypical story of a firm that was seen as "too rigid" but was supposedly made "more flexible" through the application of quality control, see Kearns and Nadler's (1992) description of Xerox in the 1980s.

3. The irony of this statement is, of course, that the U.S. government gives massive subsidies to American farmers, including Gerber's suppliers. In postsocialist Poland, however, farmers received virtually no subsidies from 1990 onward.

4. The actual quality assurance protocols are Alima-Gerber's proprietary knowledge and a significant part of AG's competitive edge in the marketplace. For that reason, I have made my description of them vague enough that they do not provide anything but knowledge common to others in the industry.

5. In Poland, it is most often mothers, not fathers, who feed children. Feeding a baby is an integral part of the definition of good motherhood (see chap. 5). Hence, here, I follow the usage of both Alima and Gerber employees and speak of mothers rather than parents.

6. Examples of the number of points assigned to different jobs include company archivist, 111 points; laboratory technician, 123–35; senior accountant, 166; pilot line technician, 168; planning specialist, 191; director of quality control laboratory, 243; brand manager, 325; and head engineer, 340. (This information comes from the contract between AG and its employee unions.)

7. In fact, in many cases the salaries awarded to new hires (i.e., in the marketing or training divisions) actually exceeded the salaries of other middle managers in departments like export, where the majority of personnel had been in the firm for many years.

8. While AG officials did not divulge their salaries to me, a Gerber official confirmed that they were comparable to what managers at the Fremont headquarters made.

9. No AG personnel attended this course, although AG has close connections to the training company and has used their services in the past.

10. The power of these courses to construct a bounded self and then reach deeply inside it is difficult to convey but hard to overestimate. I came to the course as an observer, assuming that I would maintain a certain emotional distance from the proceedings. When it was my turn to present a difficult scenario with my "boss," I was forced to replay my response at least five times. At one point I exploded in anger, and by the end of the exercise I was in tears and my body was shaking.

11. One mechanic told me that he made a metal sled for his daughter and tried to take

it out the factory gates. When he was caught, he used his personal contacts with another gate guard to get the sled through and to avoid punishment.

12. Outsourcing of services like the cafeteria and security is another way to attack *znajomości*. The director of human resources told me that one reason that gate guards are now hired by an independent security firm rather than by AG is that close personal relationships between guards and workers facilitated theft. Now, guards are socially unrelated to the workers and, if they develop close contacts, can easily be replaced by persons without such relationships.

13. Jolanta's *private* name-day celebration, at home, was even more sumptuous. She prepared a six- or seven-course dinner, with wine and vodka, for a group of about fifteen of her closest friends.

14. These relationships were in fact crucial to the success of my research. At the beginning of my stay, a shift supervisor informed every member of my brigade that I was a spy sent from Gerber and that they were not to tell me anything at all. When I entered the lunchroom, it fell silent. Workers actually turned their backs to me when I attempted to ask questions. Only later, when Pani Jolanta heard the rumor, did she tell all her *znajomy,* including the shift supervisor who had originally accused me, that I was *nasza dziewczyna,* or "one of us," and could be trusted. She demonstrated this by inviting me to her home. Why Jolanta helped me, I don't know, but her intervention literally saved my project. I acknowledge here an enormous debt of gratitude to her.

15. The principle of equality is extremely important in this context. At the same party, Danusia presented me with a silver chain and a silver jewelry box that she had purchased by taking up a collection among the members of my brigade. Pani Jadzia, a particular friend of mine, refused to donate to the collection because she had bought me a farewell gift—an expensive gold bracelet—earlier. Danusia was furious. She saw Jadzia's gift as an opportunistic attempt to create closer *znajomości* with me than other workers had.

16. At one point I may have (inadvertently) saved a friend's job by talking with the director of production for the whole firm. We were discussing the layoffs of monthly contract workers. I told him that I did not believe there were significant differences in the loyalty and productivity of these workers vis-à-vis permanent workers. "To fire Jadzia would be a big mistake," I said. "She takes her job more seriously than anyone on the line, and she feels personally responsible for product quality." When Jadzia was one of the workers who was not only not fired but offered a more permanent contract (to AG rather than through the temp firm), she credited me. This may have contributed to the belief that I had powers of intercession that I in fact did not have. Jadzia herself called me later and asked me to help her get an interest-free loan from the company, by moving her name from one hundred twenty-seventh on the list to first. She had a difficult time accepting that it was not in my power to do that (see chap. 5).

17. Gracjana maintains that she is the only worker at AG without *znajomości* and is therefore less privileged and unable to defend herself from attacks by management. The story appears to be more complicated, however. Her mother-in-law works for the firm, and her husband did work for the firm when she was hired.

18. My work on the Mormon charity system (Dunn 1996) makes this point.

19. I am grateful to Michał Buchowski for this idea.

Chapter 5. Ideas of Kin and Home on the Shop Floor

1. While unemployment statistics from the socialist period should, of course, be taken with a grain of salt, figures from other Eastern Bloc countries suggest the percentage of women in the workforce was even higher. Slovakia, for example, reported that 84 percent of working-age women were employed outside the home (Fodor 1997, 474), while East Germany reported that 91 percent of working-age women were either employed or in vocational training. This was in contrast to West Germany, where only 55% of working-age women were employed or in training (Einhorn 1993, 116).

2. Fodor argues that women's unemployment is low because many women were highly educated in disciplines like accounting, which had become very important in the postsocialist era. But this does not explain why working-class women are not disproportionately affected by unemployment, either.

3. This data comes from David Ost, whose forthcoming book, "Anger and Democracy: The Transformation of Post-Communist Poland" (Cornell University Press), describes labor's loss of power in more detail.

4. The overwhelmingly feminized nature of the shop floor may be one reason that my discussion of gender portrays it as something borne only by women. I spent most of my time with women on the shop floor and was only rarely admitted into the male domains of the machine shops or the wastewater treatment plant. David Ost (pers. comm.) suggests that the use of gender and kin terms at Alima is somewhat unique to it and to other firms in the food sector. He says that workplaces in other sectors were shaped much more extensively by Solidarity's masculinized vision of heavy industrial labor. This may very well be true. Without spending more time on male-dominated shop floors (something quite difficult for a female anthropologist to do), I am unable to tell just how different the Alima case is and must await comparative ethnography. However, a competing vision of labor based on notions of maleness would not change my basic argument here.

5. Clearly, religion, gender, and nationalism are important factors in the construction of maternity. See Long 1996; Verdery 1996; Einhorn 1993; Funk and Mueller 1993; Goven 1993 and Hauser; Heyns and Mansbridge 1993.

6. Almost without exception, every woman I spoke with complained about how little her husband did around the house. Interestingly, the wives always phrased this in terms of how little their husbands helped them, which presupposed that the task was the wife's and that a husband could only "help." Only one of my acquaintances—Katarzyna, whom I discuss below—ever postulated that her husband had to do a certain amount of domestic work because he was coproprietor of the establishment.

7. Domestic production of fruits and vegetables on the *działka* is, of course, another example of a means of compensating for the failures of the official socialist economy.

8. The concept of *działki* was introduced in the nineteenth century by Germans trying to lure peasant labor off the farm and into the industrial workplace. The garden plot was supposed to ease the psychological transition from rural to urban life (Anne Camilla Bellows, pers. comm.).

9. See, e.g., Long's (1996, 44–46) discussion of the *Matka Bohaterska,* the figure of the "mother-heroine" who passed down Polish language, culture, and tradition to her children under the partitions of Poland, when such teaching was forbidden by the occupying powers. Long asserts that this figure partly defined women's roles during the

Solidarity movement. Women were marginalized to provisioning roles rather than allowed to become active participants in the protests on the streets.

10. I heard this sentiment not only from avid gardeners like Katarzyna but also from other members of their families who came to the *działka* to relax, sit in the sun, do a bit of gardening, and eat some of the produce grown there.

11. Discerning the difference between fermented and unfermented bottles required a good deal of mētis, especially when the fermentation had not progressed to such a degree that the characteristic *thunk, thunk* sound was very pronounced. This kind of post-production testing goes against the tenets of TQM and of Gerber's own quality control process. The situation arose because microscopic defects in the bottles and caps couldn't be found until the juice had fermented in the bottle.

12. See Long (1996) on how women's political activism in Gdańsk was shaped much in the same way; see also Einhorn 1993, 5.

13. Jadzia is the same woman who attempted to build *znajomości* with the division supervisor, by buying name-day greetings, and with me, by buying a gold bracelet.

14. Perhaps the reason that Alicja could make her demands in this extreme form was precisely because she worked at Sanepid and not at AG. Sanepid, as an arm of the Polish state, is still an SOE. This makes it more vulnerable to demands based on the needs of workers rather than on their contributions to the enterprise.

15. Although Stasia did not want to be pregnant, the idea of having an abortion was never raised. At the time she became pregnant, the SLD (post-Communist party) government had once again legalized abortion under certain circumstances, after six years of no legal abortion in Poland. However, the doctors at every hospital in Rzeszów signed statements that they refused to provide abortion services under any circumstances. To get an abortion, Stasia would have had either to contact the local government, which would have sent her to a private clinic for an abortion, or go to another city. In any case, Stasia is a devout Catholic and would not have an abortion, even though she had covertly attempted to have herself sterilized.

16. Stasia's further proof that Kasia's failed maternity made her psychologically ill came in the form of a rumor. She said that after Kasia's seventh miscarriage, which was late in the pregnancy, Kasia saw a baby in a store and, believing that it belonged to her, took it home. She narrowly avoided kidnapping charges, at least according to Stasia. A kindly doctor arranged for Kasia to adopt the child of an unwed teenage mother, so in one form or another, Kasia achieved the status of "mother." But it is not a full status, even though Kasia was both pregnant and raised a child. In Kasia's defense, I have to add that her attempt to enforce greater discipline on Stasia came as part of an overall push on the shop floor to increase productivity and to cut down on absences and extended breaks. This did not come directly from Kasia, but from managers.

17. When Jolanta took maternity into account, she was extremely consistent about it. Renata asked Jolanta to give her five vacation days (which are paid at 100 percent of regular salary) to care for Krysia when she had a cold. Jolanta insisted that Renata take parental leave days, which are paid at 80 percent of regular salary.

18. This phenomenon is not unique to Eastern Europe. Hochschild (1997) asserts that men and women in American corporations often see home as work and work as home. In the American case, however, employee-parents often come to work to *escape* domestic labor and to connect both socially and emotionally with their workmates. Eastern Eu-

ropeans, especially women, do not seem to see the workplace as a refuge in quite the same way. Rather, Eastern European women often see their relegation to domestic work as a welcome refuge from the socialist "double burden" of domestic work and paid employment, while persons of both genders see the home as a refuge from the state or "the system."

19. Again, racist remarks aimed at Blacks, gypsies, Jews, and many other minorities are unfortunately commonplace in Poland, which is basically a monoethnic country. However much such slurs horrified me, they simply did not carry the same shock value for other Poles. (My acquaintances often told Jewish jokes in polite company, for example. They thought the small carvings of Jewish musicians with grossly caricatured noses in Cepelia craft shops, which were repugnant to me, were funny and cute.) While racial and ethnic relations are a matter of discussion and debate in Poland—particularly in the context of Holocaust studies and Polish-Israeli relations—ethnic slurs are not usually socially condemned. Stasia probably did not intend her statement to be as strong as it would appear when translated into English.

20. Like a parent with an adolescent child, Gerber rationed the liquor. As one of the party planners told me, employees were given only one glass of champagne because Gerber executives feared the workers would become inebriated and spoil the dignity of the occasion.

21. The reasons not all employees sold their shares to Gerber are complex. Some farmers held shares in the belief that this would give them more bargaining power when agricultural contracts were negotiated. Of all the employees I knew well, only Jolanta, the division supervisor, held her shares. Her husband believed that none of them knew the real reason that Gerber was buying up shares. Since they didn't stand to lose anything by holding the shares (since Gerber had given her the money to buy them), they might as well hold on to them until the situation was clearer.

Chapter 6. Power and Postsocialism

1. By the end of 1999, Poles enjoyed an average per-capita income that was 130 percent of 1989 levels. Ukraine, at the other end of the spectrum, saw per capita incomes fall to 50 percent of their 1989 levels (O'Rourke 2000).

2. I say "reintroduced" because Polish intellectuals were exposed to these ideas during the late eighteenth century, when the conceptual foundations of liberalism were being discussed throughout Europe. Whether those ideas ever made it to other social groups in Poland, however, is an open historical question.

3. For example, when they conceptualize themselves as wives rather than slaves or machines.

4. Alima workers do not advocate reinstating state socialism, nor do I. However, many others throughout the Eastern Bloc do advocate a return to some form of state socialism. This line of thought is perhaps strongest in Belarus and Russia.

Bibliography

Aglietta, Michel. 1987. *A Theory of Capitalist Regulation.* London: Verso.

Aitken, Hugh. 1960. *Scientific Management in Action: Taylorism at the Watertown Arsenal.* Princeton: Princeton University Press.

Allen, Jennifer. 1983. "Motherhood: The Annihilation of Women." In *Mothering: Essays in Feminist Theory,* edited by Joyce Treblicot, 315–30. Totowa, N.J.: Rowman and Allanheld.

Aktualności. 1995a. Employee newsletter, Alima-Gerber S.A., March.

———. 1995b. Employee newsletter, Alima-Gerber S.A., October.

Amin, Ash, ed. 1994. *Post-Fordism: A Reader.* Oxford: Blackwell.

Amsden, Alice, Jacek Kochanowicz, and Lance Taylor. 1994. *The Market Meets Its Match: Restructuring the Economies of Eastern Europe.* Cambridge: Harvard University Press.

Anderson, David. 1996. "Bringing Civil Society to an Uncivilized Place: Citizenship Regimes in Russia's Arctic Frontier." In *Civil Society: Challenging Western Models,* edited by Chris Hann and Elizabeth Dunn, 99–120. London: Routledge.

Andrys, Piotr. 1992. "Wyswatani" (A couple brought together by a matchmaker). *Zielony Sztandar,* Rzeszów, 11 March.

Appel, Hilary. 1995. "Justice and the Reformulation of Property Rights in the Czech Republic." *Eastern European Politics and Societies* 9, no. 1: 22–41.

Asad, Talal. 1993. *Genealogies of Religion: Discipline and Reasons of Power in Christianity and Islam.* Baltimore: The Johns Hopkins University Press.

Bailey, Derek T. 1988. *Accounting in Socialist Countries.* London: Routledge.

Balcerowicz, Leszek. 1995. *Wolność i rozwoj: Ekonomia wolnego rynku* (Freedom and development: Free market economy). Krakow: Wydawnictwo Znak.

Barlik, Ewa. 1996. "Wartosciowanie pracy" (Valuing work). *Rzeczpospolita,* Warsaw, 27 March, C3.

Barry, Andrew. 2001. *Political Machines: Governing a Technological Society.* London: Athlone Press.

Bauman, Zygmunt. 1992. *Intimations of Postmodernity.* London: Routledge.

Berg, Andrew, and Olivier Blanchard. 1994. "Stabilization and Transition: Poland 1990–1991." In *The Transition in Eastern Europe,* edited by Olivier Blanchard, Kenneth J. Froot, and Jeffrey D. Sachs, 51–91. Chicago: University of Chicago Press.

Błaszczyk, Barbara, and Marek Dąbrowski. 1993. *The Privatization Process in Poland 1989–1992: Expectations, Results, and Remaining Dilemmas.* London: Centre for Research into Communist Economies.

Borda, Maria, and Stuart McLeay. 1996. "Accounting and Economic Transformation in Hungary." In *Accounting in Transition,* edited by N. Garrod and S. McLeay, 28–42. London: Routledge.

Borneman, John. 1997. *Settling Accounts: Violence, Justice and Accountability in Postsocialist Europe.* Princeton: Princeton University Press.

Boyer, Robert. 1990. *The Regulation School: A Critical Introduction.* New York: Columbia University Press.

Braverman, Harry. 1974. *Labor and Monopoly Capital.* New York: Monthly Review Press.

Brenner, Robert, and Mark Glick. 1991. "The Regulation Approach: Theory and History." *New Left Review* 188: 45–120.

Brown, Kate. 2001. "Gridded Lives: Why Kazakhstan and Montana Are Nearly the Same Place." *American Historical Review* 6, no. 1: 17–48.

Burawoy, Michael. 1979. *Manufacturing Consent.* Chicago: University of Chicago Press.

——. 1985. *The Politics of Production.* London: Verso.

——. 1998. "Industrial Involution: The Russian Road to Capitalism." In *À la recherche des certitudes perdues: Anthropologie du travail et des affaires dans une Europe en mutation,* edited by Birgit Müller, 11–57. Berlin: Centre Marc Bloch.

Burawoy, Michael, and Janos Lukács. 1992. *The Radiant Past: Ideology and Reality in Hungary's Road to Capitalism.* Chicago: University of Chicago Press.

Casper, Steven, and Bob Hancké. 1999. "Global Quality Norms within National Production Regimes: ISO 9000 Standards in the French and German Car Industries." *Organization Studies* 20, no. 6: 961–85.

CIA. 1999. *World Fact Book.* http://www.odci.gov/cia/publications/factbook/pl.html.

Comaroff, John, and Jean Comaroff. 1991. *Of Revelation and Revolution.* Chicago: University of Chicago Press.

Csaba, Laszlo. 1995. *The Capitalist Revolution in Eastern Europe.* Aldershot: Edward Elgar.

Czegledy, Andre. 1996. "New Directions for Organizational Learning in Eastern Europe." *Organization Studies* 17, no. 2: 327–43.

Dicken, Peter. 1992. *Global Shift: The Internationalization of Economic Activity.* New York: Guilford.

Dickson, Peter R., and James L. Ginter. 1987. "Market Segmentation, Product Differentiation and Marketing Strategy." *Journal of Marketing* 51: 1–10.

Dobek, Mariusz. 1993. *The Political Logic of Privatization: Lessons from Great Britain and Poland.* Westport, Conn.: Praeger.

Drakulic, Slavenka. 1992. *How We Survived Communism and Even Laughed.* New York: Harper and Row.

Dumont, Louis. 1985. "The Christian Beginnings of Modern Individualism." In *The Category of the Person: Anthropology, Philosophy, History,* edited by Steven Collins, Steven Lukes, and Michael Carrithers, 93–122. Cambridge: Cambridge University Press.

Dunn, Elizabeth C. 1996. "Money, Morality and Modes of Civil Society among Mormons." In *Civil Society: Challenging Western Models,* edited by Chris Hann and Elizabeth Dunn, 27–49. London: Routledge.

——. 2000. "Accounting for Change." In *Critical Approaches to Eastern European Management,* edited by Mihaela Kelemen and Monika Kostera, 38–64. London: Harwood.

Dyakonov, Sergei. 2002. Interview transcript, archived at Russian Archives Online. http://www.russianarchives.com/rao/catalogues/trans/yfs/yanks_serg_1.html.

Easton, George. 1993. "An Overview of Total Quality Management." Unpublished ms.

Economist. 1995. "Paradox Explained," 22 July, 52.

——. 1998. "Flickers of Economic Light," 5 September, 47.

——. 1999. "Converging Hopes," 13 February, 74.

Einhorn, Barbara. 1993. *Cinderella Goes to Market: Citizenship, Gender, and Women's Movements in East Central Europe.* London: Verso.

Fernandez-Kelly, M. Patricia. 1983. *For We Are Sold, My People and I: Women and Industry in Mexico's Frontier.* Albany: State University of New York Press.

Fodor, Éva. 1997. "Gender in Transition: Unemployment in Hungary, Poland and Slovakia." *Eastern European Politics and Societies* 11, no. 3: 470–99.

Fogel, Daniel, and Suzanne Etcheverry. 1994. "Reforming the Economies of Central and Eastern Europe." In *Managing in Emerging Market Economies: Cases from the Czech and Slovak Republics,* edited by Daniel Fogel, 3–33. Boulder: Westview.

Foucault, Michel. 1979. *Discipline and Punish: The Birth of the Prison.* New York: Vintage.

Frydman, Roman, and Andrzej Rapaczynski. 1994. *Privatization in Eastern Europe: Is the State Withering Away?* Budapest: Central European University Press.

Funk, Nanette, and Magda Mueller, eds. 1993. *Gender Politics and Post-Communism: Reflections from Eastern Europe and the Former Soviet Union.* New York: Routledge.

Gal, Susan. 1994. "Gender in the Postsocialist Transition: The Abortion Debate in Hungary." *Eastern European Politics and Societies* 8, no. 2: 256–86.

Garson, Barbara. 1975. *All the Livelong Day: The Meaning and Demeaning of Routine Work.* New York: Penguin.

Gazeta Wyborcza. 1997. "Ilu jest bezrobotnych w Polsce?: Milion prawdziwych, milion falszywych" (How many unemployed in Poland? A million real ones, a million false ones). Warsaw, 22 January, 1.

Gestern, Aleksander. 1996. "W kręgu różnych kultur i mentalności" (In the domain of different cultures and mentalities). *Rzeczpospolita,* 26 April.

Główny Urząd Statystyczny. 1999. *Mały Rocznik Statystyczny.* Warsaw: GUS.

Goven, Joanna. 1993. "Sexual Politics in Hungary: Autonomy and Anti-Feminism." In *Sexual Politics and the Public Sphere: Women in Eastern Europe after the Transition,* edited by Nanette Funk and Magda Mueller, 224–40. New York: Routledge.

Granovetter, Mark. 1992. "Economic Action and Social Structure: The Problem of Embeddedness." In *The Sociology of Economic Life,* edited by Mark Granovetter and Richard Swedburg, 53–81. Boulder: Westview.

Gromada Rolnik Polski. 1992. "Małzenstwo Alimy z Gerberem" (The marriage of Alima to Gerber). Warsaw, 19 February.

Grosfeld, Irena. 1991. "Privatization of State Enterprises in Eastern Europe: The Search for a Market Environment." *Eastern European Politics and Societies* 5, no. 1: 142–61.

Hammer, Michael, and James Champy. 1993. *Reengineering the Corporation: A Manifesto for Business Revolution.* London: Nicholas Brealey.

Hann, C. M. 1993a. "Property Relations in the New Eastern Europe: The Case of Specialist Cooperatives in Hungary." In *The Curtain Rises: Rethinking Culture, Ideology and the State in Eastern Europe,* edited by Hermione DeSoto and David Anderson, 99–119. Atlantic Highlands, N.J.: Humanist Press International.

———. 1993b. "From Production to Property: Decollectivization and the Human-Land Relationship in Contemporary Eastern Europe." *Man* 28: 299–320.

Haraszti, Miklos. 1977. *A Worker in a Worker's State: Piece Rates in Hungary.* London: Pelican.

Harvey, David. 1989. *The Condition of Postmodernity: An Enquiry into the Origins of Cultural Change.* Oxford: Basil Blackwell.

Hauser, Ewa, Barbara Heyns, and Jane Mansbridge. 1993. "Feminism in the Interstices of Politics and Culture." In *Gender Politics and Post-Communism: Reflections from Eastern Europe and the Former Soviet Union,* edited by Nanette Funk and Magda Mueller, 257–73. New York: Routledge.

Hausner, Jerzy, Bob Jessop, and Klaus Nielsen, eds. 1995. *Strategic Choice and Path Dependency in Post Socialism: Institutional Dynamics in the Transformation Process.* London: Edward Elgar.

Havel, Václav. 1985. *Living in Truth.* London: Faber and Faber.

———. 1993. "The Post Communist Nightmare." *New York Review of Books* 40, no. 10: 8–13.

Henderson, Richard I., and Kitty Lewis Clarke. 1981. *Job Pay for Job Worth.* Atlanta: Georgia State University.

Hirsch, Joachim. 1984. "Fordism and Post-Fordism." In *Post-Fordism and Social Form,* edited by Werner Bonefeld and John Halloway, 8–34. London: Macmillan.

Hochschild, Arlie Russell. 1997. *The Time Bind: When Work Becomes Home and Home Becomes Work.* New York: Henry Holt and Company.

Holc, Janine. 1997. "Liberalism and the Construction of the Democratic Subject in Postcommunism: The Case of Poland." *Slavic Review* 56, no. 3: 401–27.

Holy, Ladislav. 1992. "Culture, Market Ideology and Economic Reform in Czechoslovakia." In *Contesting Markets: Analyses of Ideology, Discourse and Practice,* edited by Ray Dilley, 231–42. Edinburgh: Edinburgh University Press.

Horváth, Agnes, and Arpad Szakolczai. 1991. "Information Management in Bolshevik-type Party-states: A Version of the Information Society." *Eastern European Politics and Societies* 5: 268–305.

Hoskin, Keith. 1996. "The 'Awful Idea of Accountability': Inscribing People into the Measurement of Objects." In *Accountability: Power, Ethos and the Technologies of Managing,* edited by Rolland Munro and Jan Mouritsen, 265–82. London: Thomson.

Jameson, Fredric. 1991. *Postmodernism, or, the Cultural Logic of Late Capitalism.* Durham: Duke University Press.

Jessop, Bob. 1984. "Regulation Theory, Post-Fordism, and the State: More Than a

Reply to Werner Bonefeld." In *Post-Fordism and Social Form,* edited by Werner Bonefeld and John Holloway, 69–91. London: Macmillan.

——. 1990. "Regulation Theories in Retrospect and Prospect." *Economy and Society* 19, no. 2: 153–216.

John Paul II. 1981. "Laborem Exorcens." *Origins* 11, no. 15: 225–44.

Johnson, Simon, and Gary Loveman. 1995. *Starting over in Eastern Europe: Entrepreneurship and Economic Renewal.* Cambridge: Harvard Business School Press.

Kanter, Rosabeth Moss. 1977. *Men and Women of the Corporation.* New York: Basic Books.

Kapuścinski, Pawel. 1995. "Alima i Gerber—małżenstwo w trudnych czasach" (Alima and Gerber, a marriage in hard times). *Życie Gospodarcze,* Warsaw, 8 August, 24–25.

Kearns, David, and David Nadler. 1992. *Prophets in the Dark: How Xerox Reinvented Itself and Beat Back the Japanese.* New York: Harper Collins.

Kemp-Welch, A. 1983. *The Birth of Solidarity: The Gdańsk Negotiations, 1980.* London: Macmillan.

Kennedy, Michael, and Ireneusz Bialecki. 1989. "Power and the Logic of Distribution in Poland." *Eastern European Politics and Societies* 3, no. 2: 300–328.

Kharkordin, Oleg. 1999. *The Collective and the Individual in Russia: A Study of Practices.* Berkeley: University of California Press.

Klaus, Václav, and Tomás Ježek. 1991. "Social Criticism, False Liberalism, and Recent Changes in Czechoslovakia." *Eastern European Politics and Societies* 5, no. 1: 26–40.

Kornai, Janoś. 1992. *The Socialist System: The Political Economy of Communism.* Princeton: Princeton University Press.

——. 1995. *Highways and Byways: Studies on Reform and Postcommunist Transition.* Cambridge: MIT Press.

Kostera, Monika. 1996. "The Missionaries of Management." In *À la recherche des certitudes perdues: Anthropologie du travail et des affaires dans une Europe en mutation,* edited by Birgit Müller, 153–82. Berlin: Centre Marc Bloch.

Kovacs, Janos Matyas. 1991. "From Reformation to Transformation: Limits to Liberalism in Hungarian Economic Thought." *Eastern European Politics and Societies* 5, no. 1: 41–74.

Koźminski, Andrzej. 1992. *Po wielkim szoku* (After the great shock). Warsaw: Panstwowe Wydawnictwo Ekonomiczne.

——. 1993. *Catching Up?: Organizational and Management Change in the Ex-Socialist Bloc.* Albany: State University of New York Press.

Krastev, Ivan. 1998. "Dancing with Anti-Corruption." *East European Constitutional Review* 7, no. 3. http://www.law.nyu.edu/eecr/vol7num3/special/corruption.html.

Kubik, Jan. 1994. *The Power of Symbols against the Symbols of Power: The Rise of Solidarity and the Fall of State Socialism in Poland.* University Park: University of Pennsylvania Press.

Laba, Roman. 1991. *The Roots of Solidarity.* Princeton: Princeton University Press.

Lampland, Martha. 1995. *The Object of Labor: Commodification in Socialist Hungary.* Chicago: University of Chicago Press.

Lawrence, Paul, and Charalambos Vlachoutsicos. 1993. "Joint Ventures in Russia: Put the Locals in Charge." *Harvard Business Review,* January–February, 44–45.

Ledeneva, Alena. 1998. *Russia's Economy of Favours: Blat, Networking, and Informal Exchange.* Cambridge: Cambridge University Press.

Leven, Bozena. 1993. "The Status of Women and Poland's Transition to a Market Economy." In *Women in the Age of Economic Transformation,* edited by Nahid Aslanbeigui, Steven Pressman, and Gale Summerfield, 27–42. London: Routledge.

Lewandowski, Janusz, and Jan Szomberg. 1989. "Property Reform as a Basis for Social and Economic Reform." *Communist Economies* 1, no. 3: 257–68.

Long, Kristi S. 1996. "Mothering Solidarity: Maternal Imagery and Activism." *Ethnologia Polona* 19: 39–52.

MacPherson, C. B. 1962. *The Political Theory of Possessive Individualism.* London: Oxford University Press.

Major, Iván. 1993. *Privatization in Eastern Europe: A Critical Approach.* London: Edward Elgar.

Marcus, George, and Michael M. J. Fischer. 1986. *Anthropology as Cultural Critique.* Chicago: University of Chicago Press.

Marody, Mira. 1993. "Why I Am Not a Feminist." *Social Research* 60, no. 4: 853–64.

Marriott, McKim. 1976. "Hindu Transactions: Diversity without Dualism." In *Transaction and Meaning: Directions in the Anthropology of Exchange and Symbolic Behavior,* edited by Bruce Kapferer, 109–42. Philadelphia: Institute for the Study of Human Issues.

Martin, Emily. 1992. "The End of the Body?" *American Ethnologist* 19, no. 1: 121–40.

——. 1994. *Flexible Bodies.* Boston: Beacon Press.

Marx, Karl, and Friedrich Engels. 1978. *The Marx-Engels Reader.* New York: Norton.

Maurer, William. 1999. "Forget Locke? From Proprietor to Risk-Bearer in New Logics of Finance." *Public Culture* 11, no. 2: 47–67.

Mauss, Marcel. 1950. *The Gift: The Form and Reason for Exchange in Archaic Societies.* New York: Norton.

McDonald, Kevin. 1993. "Why Privatization Is Not Enough." *Harvard Business Review,* May–June, 49–60.

Miller, Peter, and Nikolas Rose. 1990. "Governing Economic Life." *Economy and Society* 19: 1–31.

Ministry of Privatization. 1991. *Proposed Program for Mass Privatization.* Warsaw.

Mintz, Sidney. 1982. "Choice and Occasion: Sweet Moments." In *The Psychobiology of Human Food Selection,* edited by Lewis M. Barker, 157–69. Westport, CT: Avi.

Morawski, Witold. 1992. "Uncertainties on the Road to Markets and Democracy." *Sisyphus* 2, no. 8: 34–46.

Munn, Nancy D. 1986. *The Fame of Gawa: A Symbolic Study of Value Transformation in a Massim (Papua New Guinea) Society.* Cambridge: Cambridge University Press.

Nagengast, Carole. 1991. *Reluctant Socialists, Rural Entrepreneurs: Class, Culture and the Polish State.* Boulder: Westview.

Newman, Katherine. 1999. *Falling from Grace: The Experience of Downward Mobility in the Age of Affluence.* Berkeley: University of California Press.

Nove, Alec. 1993. *The Economics of Feasible Socialism.* London: Allen and Unwin.

Nowiny. 1992. "*Tupolewem do Alimy na obiad*" (To Alima by Tupolev for lunch). Rzeszów, 16 February.

Nowy Świat. 1992. "Gerber—przez Polske do EWG" (Gerber—to the EEC via Poland). Warsaw, 14 February.

Offe, Claus. 1985. *Disorganized Capitalism.* Oxford: Oxford University Press.

Ong, Aihwa. 1987. *Spirits of Resistance and Capitalist Discipline: Factory Women in Malaysia.* New York: State University of New York Press.

O'Rourke, Breffni. 2000. "EU: How Much Does Membership Reduce National Sovereignty?" RFE/RL, 23 March. http://www.rferl.org/nca/features/2000/03/F.RU.000323155933.html.

Pancer, Andrzej. 1985. *Zakładowe systemy wynagrodzania* (Systems of workplace compensation). Warsaw: Panstwowe Wydawnictwo Ekonomiczne.

Pankov, Dmitri. 1998. "Accounting for Change in Belarus." *Management Accounting* 76, no. 10: 56–58.

Pearce, Jone, and Michal Čakrt. 1994. "Ferox Manufactured Products and Air Products and Chemicals: A Joint Venture." In *Managing in Emerging Economies: Cases from the Czech and Slovak Republics,* edited by Daniel S. Fogel, 85–102. Boulder: Westview.

Perlez, Jane. 1993. "In Poland, Gerber Learns Lessons of Tradition." *New York Times,* 8 November.

Peters, Tom. 1992. *Liberation Management.* New York: Knopf.

Piore, Michael J., and Charles Sabel. 1984. *The Second Industrial Divide: Possibilities for Prosperity.* New York: Basic Books.

Polanyi, Karl. 1944. *The Great Transformation.* New York: Rinehart.

Poovey, Mary. 1998. *A History of the Modern Fact: Problems of Knowledge in the Sciences of Wealth and Society.* Chicago: University of Chicago Press.

Power, Michael. 1997. *The Audit Society: Rituals of Verification.* Oxford: Oxford University Press.

Quaid, Maeve. 1993. *Job Evaluation: The Myth of Equitable Assessment.* Toronto: University of Toronto Press.

Radio Free Europe/Radio Liberty. 2000. "Corruption Seen Everywhere." In *RFE/RL Poland, Belarus, and Ukraine Report* 1, no. 29: 29 December.

Rayport, Jennifer. 1995. "Russian 'Indianists': A Romance with the Image of the North American Indian." *Anthropology of East Europe Review* 13, no. 2. http://condor.depaul.edu/~rrotenbe/aeer/aeer13_2/rayport.html.

Rychlewski, Czesław. 1992. "Alima w objeciach Gerbera: Małżenstwo z rozsadku"

(Alima in Gerber's embrace: A marriage of convenience). *Glob 24,* Warsaw, 26 February.

Sachs, Jeffrey. 1993. *Poland's Jump to the Market Economy.* Cambridge: MIT Press.

Sahlins, Marshall. 1985. *Islands of History.* Chicago: University of Chicago Press.

Sampson, Steven. 1996. "The Social Life of Projects: Importing Civil Society to Albania." In *Civil Society: Challenging Western Models,* edited by Chris Hann and Elizabeth Dunn, 121–42. London: Routledge.

Samuelson, Paul A. 1976. *Economics.* New York: McGraw Hill.

Sawicki, Tomasz. 1992. "Obiad Amerykanski" (American lunch). *Kurier Polski,* Warsaw, 24 February.

Schoenberger, Erica. 1988. "From Fordism to Flexible Accumulation: Technology, Competitive Strategies, and International Location." *Environment and Planning D: Society and Space* 6: 245–62.

——. 1997. *The Cultural Crisis of the Firm.* London: Blackwell.

Schrade, Ulrich, Bogusław Wolniewicz, and Jan Lubelewicz. 1996. "Dom jako wartość duchowa" (Home as a spiritual value). *Znak* 4: 90–108.

Schrader, Klaus. 1994. "In Search of the Market: A Comparison of Post-Soviet Reform Policies." In *Privatization, Liberalization, and Destruction,* edited by László Csaba, 259–84. Aldershot: Dartmouth.

Schrum, Kelly. 1998. "'Teena Means Business': Teenage Girls' Culture and Seventeen Magazine, 1944–1950." In *Saints, Sinners and Material Girls: Twentieth Century American Girls' Culture,* edited by Sherrie Inness. New York: New York University Press.

Scott, James C. 1985. *Weapons of the Weak: Everyday Forms of Peasant Resistance.* New Haven: Yale University Press.

——. 1998. *Seeing Like a State: How Certain Schemes to Improve the Human Condition Have Failed.* New Haven: Yale University Press.

Shore, Cris, and Susan Wright. 2000. "Coercive Accountability: The Rise of Audit Culture in Higher Education." In *Audit Cultures,* edited by Marilyn Strathern, 57–89. London: Routledge.

Siwek, Stanislaw. 1992. "Tajna prywatyzacja" (Secret privatization). *Dziennik Polski,* Krakow, 22 January.

Sochaka, Renata, and Jean-Louis Malo. 1996. "Emerging Capital Markets, Securities Regulation and Accounting: A Systems Perspective." In *Accounting in Transition,* edited by Neil Garrod and Stuart McLeay, 28–42. London: Routledge.

Sonntag, Krystyna. 1992. "Obiad w Amerykanskim stylu" (Lunch American style). *Życie Gospodarcze,* 8 March.

Sosnowska-Smogorzewska, Lidia. 1992. "Fruitful Sale?" *Warsaw Voice,* 1 March, 1.

Staniszkis, Jadwiga. 1991. "Path Dependence and Privatization Strategies in East Central Europe." *Eastern European Politics and Societies* 6, no. 1: 17–54.

Stites, Richard. 1989. *Revolutionary Dreams: Utopian Vision and Experimental Life in the Russian Revolution.* Oxford: Oxford University Press.

Strathern, Marilyn. 1988. *The Gender of the Gift.* Berkeley: University of California Press.

———. 1999. "Bullet Proofing." Paper presented at the Seminar in Political Thought and Intellectual History, Faculty of Philosophy (May), Cambridge University.

———. 2000. "New Accountabilities: Anthropological Studies in Audit, Ethics and the Academy." In *Audit Cultures,* edited by Marilyn Strathern. London: Routledge.

Streissler, Erich W. 1991. "What Kind of Economic Liberalism May We Expect in 'Eastern' Europe?" *Eastern European Politics and Societies* 5, no. 1: 195–201.

Swain, Nigel. 1993. "The Smallholder Party vs. the Green Barons: Class Relations in the Restructuring of Hungarian Agriculture." Unpublished ms.

Szakolczai, Arpad, and Agnes Horvath. 1991. "Political Instructors and the Decline of Communism in Hungary: Apparatus, Nomenclatura, and the Issue of Legacy." *British Journal of Political Science* 21, no. 4: 469–85.

Sztompka, Piotr. 2000 (1993). "Civilizational Competence: A Prerequisite for Post-communist Transition." http://www.ces.uj.edu.pl/sztompka/competence.htm.

———. 1992. "Dilemmas of the Great Transition." *Sisyphus: Social Studies* 2, no. 8: 9–28.

Tadikamalla, Pandu R., Dagmar Glückanford, and Stephen L. Starling. 1994. "Total Quality Management in Czechoslovakia." In *Managing in Emerging Market Economies: Cases from the Czech and Slovak Republics,* edited by Daniel Fogel, 209–24. Boulder: Westview.

Taylor, Frederick Winslow. 1947. *The Principles of Scientific Management.* New York: Norton.

Tinsanen, Tanno. 1996. *Post-Communist Capitalism and Capital: Foreign Investors in Transitional Economies.* Commack, N.Y.: Nova Science.

Tintor, Janko. 1997. "Company Restructuring and Business Analysis." In *Restructuring Eastern Europe,* edited by Soumitra Sharma, 167–76. Cheltenham: Edward Elgar.

Tymowski, Andrzej. 1993. "Poland's Unwanted Social Revolution." *Eastern European Politics and Societies* 7, no. 2: 169–202.

Van Atta, Don. 1986. "Why Is There No Taylorism in the Soviet Union?" *Comparative Politics* 18, no. 3: 327–37.

Verdery, Katherine. 1996. *What Was Socialism and What Comes Next?* Princeton: Princeton University Press.

———. 1998. "Fuzzy Property: Rights, Power, and Identity in Transylvania's Decollectivization." In *Uncertain Transition: Ethnographies of Change in the Postsocialist World,* edited by Michael Burawoy and Katherine Verdery, 53–82. Boulder: Rowan and Littlefield.

———. 1999. *The Political Lives of Dead Bodies.* New York: Columbia University Press.

———. 2000. "Privatization as Transforming Persons." In *Between Past and Future: The Revolutions of 1989 and Their Aftermath,* edited by Sorin Antohi and Vladimir Tismaneanu, 175–97. Budapest: Central European University Press.

Wagener, Hans-Jürgen. 2000. "Why Has Russia Missed the Boat?" Paper presented at the Wissenschaftskolleg zu Berlin, March 2000.

Warsaw *Voice.* 2000. "Only Fish Don't Take the Bait." Reprinted March 30, 2000 in

Central Europe Online. http://www.centraleurope.com/features.php3?id= 147318.

Warzocha, Adam. 1992. "Sprawy poufne" (Confidential matters). *Nowiny,* Rzeszów, 16 March.

Wasson, Christina. 1993. "'Taking Ownership': The Organization as Marketplace." Paper presented at the Annual Meeting of the American Anthropological Association, Washington, D.C.

Weber, Max. 1958. *The Protestant Ethic and the Spirit of Capitalism.* New York: Charles Scribner and Sons.

Wedel, Janine. 1986. *The Private Poland.* New York: Facts on File.

Welc, Pawel. 1994. "Monografia ZPOW 'Alima' w Rzeszowie (od 1992 r. 'Alima-Gerber SA')" (A monograph on ZPOW 'Alima' in Rzeszów). Unpublished master's thesis, Szkoła Głowna Handlowa w Warszawie, Wydział Społdzielco-Ekonomiczny w Rzeszowie.

Wilczak, Jagienka. 1992. "Tam i z powrotem" (There and back). *Polityka,* Warsaw, 29 October, 4.

Winiecki, Jan. 1993. *Post-Soviet Type Economies in Transition.* Aldershot: Avebury.

Wright, Melissa. 1996. "Third World Women and the Geography of Skill." Ph.D. diss., Department of Geography and Environmental Engineering, Johns Hopkins University.

Yan, Yun-xiang. 1996. *The Flow of Gifts: Reciprocity and Social Networks in a Chinese Village.* Stanford: Stanford University Press.

Yang, Mayfair Mei-hui. 1994. *Gifts, Favors, and Banquets: The Art of Social Relationships in China.* Ithaca: Cornell University Press.

Young, Allegra. 1993. "Gerber Products Company: Investing in the New Poland." Harvard Business School, case study N9-793-069.

Zatorski, Ryszard. 1992. "Wesele Gerbera i Alimy" (The marriage of Gerber and Alima). *Trybuna,* Warsaw, 14 February.

Zbierski-Salameh, Suava. 1998. "Polish Peasants in the 'Valley of Transition.'" In *Uncertain Transition: Ethnographies of Change in the Postsocialist World,* edited by Michael Burawoy and Katherine Verdery, 189–222. Boulder: Rowan and Littlefield.

Zuboff, Shoshana. 1988. *In the Age of the Smart Machine: The Future of Work and Power.* New York: Basic Books.

Żuławnik, Bozena. 1992. "Przed trybunałem bialych niezwolników" (Facing the tribunal of white slaves). *Gazeta Bankowa,* Warsaw, 15 December, 21.

Index

Abortion, 184n15
Accountability, 7, 20, 32, 34, 99, 176n3, 177n12
  applied to persons, 94, 104–18
  fiscal, 28, 38, 40–41
  as goal of privatization, 31–33, 34, 38
  as ideology, 31, 47, 53, 55
  as learned skill, 53
  of managers, 50–54
  as moral imperative, 28–29, 38, 40–42, 54, 57
Accountants, 41–42
Accounting, 7, 31, 41–42, 55, 163, 166, 170, 177n11
  cost, 36
  creating auditability, 40–42
  as epistemological problem. See Epistemology; Epistemological gap
  IAS, 39–43, 57, 99, 163
  illusion of accuracy and, 41–42
  illusion of transparency and, 40–42
  as managerial tool, 36, 170
  net, 41–42
  and self-governance. See Self-regulation
  and social context, 41–42
  socialist, 38–41
  as transforming persons, 31, 55
  US GAAP, 39–44, 57, 99
  See also Audit
Advertising, 5, 58–59, 63, 88
  for Frugo, 58–60, 63–64
  symbols of socialism in, 59, 63–64
  See also Marketing; Niche marketing
Affairs, extramarital, 54, 179n20
Age, 59, 62–64, 180n13
  association with socialism, 54–59, 63–64
  of managers, 54
  of workers, 80, 160. See also Workers
Alima:
  as analog to Gerber, 2
  as exemplar of post-socialist transition, 27
  history of, 10, 133–34
  as outlet for farmers' crops, 96–97. See also Firm; Farmers
  price of, 43
  privatization of, 28–31, 176n7
  as property, 158
  as provider of social welfare. See "Caring"
  as wife, 154–58, 171
Amerikanizatsiya (Americanization), 9
Anderson, David, 62
Appearance, personal, 73, 77

Arbitrariness, 38–43. See also Value
"Arranging," 89. See also Załatwić sprawy
Assertiveness, 116–18, 126
Assets, 40
  managers as, 51, 54
  workers as, 45, 46, 55, 85, 118, 159
Attitude, 22, 70
  as element of democratic governance, 21–22
  managers', 21–22
  See also Mindsets
Audit, 5, 7, 20, 22, 31, 41–42, 55–57, 129, 174, 177n12
  of Alima for Ministry of Property Transformation. See KPMG
  applied to persons, 104–19, 129, 164, 169
  inauditability and, 40–42
  socialist records and, 41–42
  used in quality control, 99
Auditable documents, 42, 53
Autonomy, 13–15, 20–21, 80, 126, 150, 160–68, 172
Automobiles (as objects of dispute), 90

Baby food, 143–44
  as product of the 'system', 138
  as women's work, 134
Balance sheet, 45–47
  moral, 29–30, 32, 37–40, 47, 170, 174
  opening, 39–40
Balcerowicz, Leszek, 3, 4, 34–36, 132, 176n4
Barth, Carl, 175n1
Bauman, Zygmunt, 67
Bellows, Anne Camilla, 183n8
Bielecki, Ireneusz, 120, 124–25
Biopower, 165
Bobo Frut (product), 11, 46, 62, 143, 145
Bodies, 113, 165. See also Embodiment
Borneman, John, 176n3
Braverman, Harry, 13
Breastfeeding. See Feeding
Brown, Kate, 8, 13–14
Bribes, 29, 56. See also Corruption
Buchowski, Micha, 182n19
Budget constraints:
  hard, 34–35, 176n5
  soft, 15, 41
Burawoy, Michael, 129, 169, 172, 180n20
Businessman (magazine), 71–72, 74

Capital, 33–36, 43, 171
  flows of, 6, 18, 173
Capitalism, 9, 20, 21, 161
  Poland as having distinct form of, 8, 20
  road to, 3–6, 162–63
  See also Flexible accumulation
"Caring" (as distribution of goods), 34, 46–47,
    91, 96–97, 145, 151–52, 160. *See also* Redis-
    tribution
Catholicism, 7, 8, 23, 54
Cellular telephones, 72–73
Choice, 21–23, 165, 166–67, 170
Circulation: 6, 18, 129. *See also* Gifts; Networks
Citizenship regimes, 62
Civil society, 142
Class, social, 62, 70, 198
Classes, of production inputs, 97–99
Collectivism, 114, 59, 80, 128–29
Color (as associated with capitalism), 59, 64
Commodification:
  by individualizing workers, 82, 92
  of labor, 54, 81–82, 92, 159, 160, 179n21
  through objectification. *See* Objects
Communism. *See* Socialism
Communist Party, 13, 15, 44, 63–64, 79, 165
Compensable factors, 105–7, 170
Competition, 45, 129
  employees' fears of, 45
  foreign, 35–36
Connections. *See* Networks; *Znajomości*
Consumerism, 63
Consumers, 5, 8, 61–65, 101–3
Consumption, 62–65, 120, 127–28
Control, 13, 16, 99–100, 128
Corruption, 29–33, 39, 42–43, 51–57, 163, 168
  public perceptions of, 30–31
Craft knowledge. *See* Mētis
Cultural imperialism, 73

Demand (as constraint in capitalist
    economies), 36, 63, 87
Democracy, 20–21
Democratic Union, 38
Depreciation, 177n10
Desire, 60–64
Deskilling, 10, 12, 13, 86
Difference, 61–64, 66, 82, 92, 104, 108, 127
  and labor market segmentation, 81–82, 92,
    104–5
  related to motivation, 114
  under socialism, 62–65
Discipline, 8, 13, 19, 41, 47, 94, 118, 129, 143, 144,
    149–50, 164, 166

Dividuals, 125–26, 160
Dress. *See* Appearance
Działki. See Gardens

Easton, George, 100
Efficiency, 9, 10, 12
  gains through deskilling, 10
  as goal of privatization, 31, 34, 38
  lack of, 53, 97
Einhorn, Barbara, 140
Embeddedness, 55, 57, 87, 91, 93, 125–28,
    160–61, 164, 172–73. *See also* Networks
Embodiment:
  of flexible capitalism, 69, 70–75, 76, 165, 169
  of state socialism, 63–64, 165, 169
  See also Bodies
Employee evaluations, 22, 104–12, 123–24
Employees. *See* Managers; Workers
Empowerment, 21–23, 113, 166
Energy. *See* Siła
Enterprising self, 22
Entrepreneurial self, 22, 127–28
Envy, 108–9, 114
Epistemological gap, 42–43
Epistemology, 22, 40
Espionage, 182n14
Ethnography, 23–27
European Bank for Reconstruction and Devel-
    opment, 173
European Union, 162–63, 172
Exchange. *See* Gifts; Markets
Experience, 83, 84, 86
Experiential education, 19
Expertise, 83–86, 123
  Alima's lack of, 51, 103
  as basis for moral authority, 111–12
  in accounting. *See* Accounting
  in marketing, 51
  of production workers, 83–86, 109–12. *See
    also* Mētis
  technical, 51, 103
  of unions, 112

Factor analysis. *See* Compensable factors
Facts, 32
Fairness. *See* Justice
False consciousness, 140
Farmers:
  affected by supplier restructuring, 5, 45, 47,
    96, 155, 177n13, 178n17
  rights in enterprises, 38, 45, 47, 96
  social connections to firm, 47, 146, 155
Favors. *See* Gifts

Feeding, 5, 133–43, 172, 181n5
    breastfeeding, 136, 139
    and home creation, 135–43
    mothers' knowledge of, 102–3
    in Polish culture, 103, 138
    and self-feeding, 137
    as transfer of self, 139–40, 172
    as women's work, 134–41
Fernandez-Kelly, M. Patricia, 101
Firm:
    as family, 90–91
    organization of, 67–68
    as outlet for suppliers' products, 95–97
    as parent, 91, 130. *See also* Parent-state;
        "Caring"
    as product of workers' labor, 37–38
    as profit-making enterprise, 46, 96
    as transforming economy, 6
    value of, 31, 38–39, 43. *See also* Value
    as vehicle for social "care." *See* "Caring"
    See also Alima; Gerber Products Company
Flexible accumulation, 18–19, 61, 66, 169. *See
    also* Post-Fordism
Flexibility, 5, 7, 8, 19, 59, 64–68, 69, 70, 74–78,
        82, 85, 93–93, 159, 165
    based on individuality, 74, 82, 85, 92
    based on mētis, 109, 180n15
    based on universalism, 84–85
    exclusion of workers from category of, 59,
        74–78, 79, 82, 92–93, 180n16
    lack of, 19, 59, 64–68
    as trope in American advertising, 66
Fodor, Eva, 161, 183n2
Ford, Henry, 9, 13
Fordism, 10–14, 16–18, 22, 62, 74, 79, 95, 163, 171
    as macroeconomic formation, 16–18
    organization of firms in, 10–14
    rigidity of, 22, 66–68, 74. *See also* Rigidity
Fordizatsiya, 9
Foucault, Michel, 8, 100–101, 113, 127
Freedom. *See* Liberty
Frugo (product), 58, 59, 61, 63–64, 66, 73, 75, 81,
        160, 165

Gantt, Henry, 175n1
Gardens (*działki*), 141–42, 183n8–9, 184n10
Gender, 7, 8, 132, 143–58, 180n11, 183n5
    domestic work and, 135–38, 153
    essentialist views of, 133–43
    industrial work and, 131–34, 142–44, 152–53,
        183n4
    socialist ideologies of, 130–32, 143, 151–52
    unemployment and, 131–32, 150, 147–58

Generalism, 85. *See also* Universalism
Gerber Products Company, 1, 29, 175n5, 178n19,
        179n6, 185n20
    allocating scientific authority, 102–3,
    changing consumers' eating habits, 5, 101
    history of, 3, 5, 10
    as husband, 154–58, 171
    international strategy of, 1, 36, 55, 158
Gifts, 51, 62, 87–91, 119–28, 160, 180nn21–22
Gilbreth, Frank, 175
Gilbreth, Lillian, 175
Globalization, 6, 8, 18, 173
Governmentality, 6, 7, 21, 118, 126–27
Granovetter, Mark, 55
"Gray being." *See Szara istota*
Grey and Associates, 63–64
Grids, 10, 18

Habitus, 70–75, 87
Havel, Václav, 64
Hay Method, 105
Heinz (H. J. Heinz Company), 28, 33, 36, 38, 40,
        45
Hierarchy. *See* Inequality
Hiring, 22, 69–72, 75–76, 123–24
Hoarding. *See* Shortage–hoarding cycle
Hochschild, Arlie, 184
Holc, Janine, 164
Holy, Ladislav, 64
Home, 135–43, 150, 151
House, 135–43
Human nature, 3, 20, 21, 34, 35

Impersonality, 74
Improvement, 113–19. *See also* Self-improvement
    continuous, 72–73, 95
Income, acceptance of differences in, 53, 107–
        14, 181n7–8
Individualism, 7, 23, 43, 55, 59, 74, 80, 85, 87, 91–
        94, 113–14, 126–29, 157–58, 160, 164, 167–
        73. *See also* Privatization of persons
Industrialization, 9, 13
Inefficiency. *See* Efficiency
Inequality, 34, 82, 152–53, 156, 164. *See also* Dif-
        ference; Income
Inflation, 162
Inflexibility. *See* Rigidity
Innovation, 53
International Monetary Fund, 173
ISO 9000 standards, 162

Jealousy. *See* Envy
Job valuation. *See* Work station valuation

John Paul II, Pope, 23, 170–71
Justice, 32–37, 43

Kennedy, Michael, 120, 124–25
Kierownik, 70–75, 168
Kinship, 7, 8, 133–61
  metaphors of, 130–33, 183n4
  See also Motherhood
Kornai, Janós, 175n1, 177n8
Kostera, Monika, 178n18
Koźminski, Andrzej, 52–53
KPMG, 39–40

Labor, 104–12, 128, 160, 171
  as accounting number, 47–49
  as artifact of social relations, 47–48, 55–56,
    128, 142, 159, 171
  as bodily substance. *See Siła*
  as commodity, 47–48, 54–55, 59, 75, 81, 128,
    159–60, 179n21. *See also* Commodification
  congealed in products, 37–38, 128
  discipline of, 7, 149
  experience of, 10–18
  as growing children, 136, 139–40, 146–48
  markets in. *See* Markets; Labor
  organization of, 10–12, 56–57, 82
  as owned by individuals, 128
  privatized persons and, 127–28,
  separation of mental and manual, 10–18,
    79
  socialist ideologies of, 128
  women's. *See* Gender
  See also Work; Value
"Language of the enterprise," 166–67
Lampland, Martha, 175n1, 179n21
Layoffs, 48, 51–54, 84, 123–24, 131–32, 155, 161,
  177–78n15, 183nn1–2
Lenin, V. I., 9, 13
Leśniak-Moczuk, Krystyna, 46
Lewandowski, Janusz, 28–30, 34, 36–39, 42, 44,
  56, 177n9
Liabilities:
  Alima's assets as, 39–41
  ignored in socialist accounting, 40
  managers as, 53–55, 118
  pre-war property claims, 36
  workers as, 45, 85, 118, 159
Liberal moment, 164, 170
Liberty, 21, 127, 164–67, 173
Long, Kristi, 136, 183, 183–84n9
"Look." *See* Appearance
Lott, Merrill, 105
Lukács, János, 129, 169

Managers, 5, 8, 70–75, 120, 178n19, 180n11
  as assets, 51, 54
  expatriate, 51, 70
  firing of, 53, 70. *See also* Layoffs
  as liabilities, 53–55, 118
  local, 54, 70
  as parents, 130
  participant observation with, 26–27
  of state–owned shops, 89
  transformation of, 51–53, 70–75, 81
  western business experience and, 54, 71
  youth of, 54
  See also Kierownik; Menadżer
Marketing, 36, 51, 63, 74, 79, 87–91, 179n5
  budget for, at Alima, 87–91
  See also Niche marketing
Markets:
  multiple, 62–74
  as predicted outcome of privatization, 4,
    34–35, 176n5
  as subjects of government, 62,
  See also Niche marketing
Martin, Emily, 19, 66, 92
Mary (mother of God), 134
Marxism, 132, 170–71
Mass consumption. *See* Consumption
Mass production, 62
Mauss, Marcel, 160
Menadżer, 70–75, 168, 179n8, 179n10. *See also*
  Managers
Mentalities. *See* Mindsets
Merit pay, 85, 93, 104, 123–24. *See also* Income
Mētis, 17, 109–12, 129, 180n15, 184n11
Mickiewicz, Adam, 179n5
Miller, Peter, 127, 166
Mindsets, 22, 91
  of managers, 70–75, 51
  socialist, 89
  See also Attitude
Mintz, Sidney, 61
Modern, as personal quality, 72
Modernity, 6, 8, 18
Modernizing projects, 6, 18
Money, 145
Moral authority, 111
Morality, 38, 54
  as goal of privatization, 31, 36–38
Motivation, 112–18, 120
Motherhood, 134–61, 183n5, 184n16
  and benefits, 146–50, 184n17
  and Catholicism, 134
  and feeding. *See* Feeding
  and home creation, 135–43

as ideology in quality control, 143–45
and socialism, 137
as rationale for hiring, 145–48, 171
as threat to employment, 140, 149–50
in the workplace, 130–61
Movement, 59, 64, 66, 76–77, 80, 84, 165

Name-day celebrations, 121–22, 180n17
National tastes, 180n17
Natural units, 41–42
Needs, 61
Neoliberalism, 7, 18, 35, 67, 118, 163–69, 172, 176n5, 185n2
Networks, 8, 19, 51–57, 62, 70, 85–93, 119–29, 160, 168, 181–82n11, 182n14, 182nn16–17
as artifacts of shortage economy, 57, 74, 85, 87–88, 93. *See also Znajomości*
Niche marketing, 5, 7, 58, 61–93, 128, 163, 166, 170, 180n17
in consumer products, 58, 61–64
and gifts, 88. *See also* Gifts
as hallmark of post-Fordism, 61, 64–75, 83, 166
in labor, 74, 81–82, 85, 128
Nomenklatura, 33

Objectivity, 95, 104–5, 108–9, 121, 123
Objects, 95, 103
creating relations among persons, 95, 139, 170–71, 174. *See also* Gifts
people as, 10, 45, 54, 56–57, 87, 90–91, 94–95, 170–71
Ong, Aihwa, 12
OPZZ (*Ogólnopolskie Porozumienie Związki Zawodowe*), 44
Orientalism, 92
Ost, David, 183nn3–4
Outsourcing, 182. *See also* Temporary labor
Ownership, 157–58. *See also* Stocks

Panopticon, 91, 151
Parent-state, 91
Participant-observation. *See* Ethnography
Participatory management, 20
Passivity:
associated with socialism, 63–64, 127
of author, 25
of bodies, 10, 19, 59
of informants, 25
of workers, 10, 19, 25, 31, 59, 80, 132
Performance evaluations. *See* Employee evaluations
Personal connections. *See* Networks

Personhood, 8, 20, 21, 91, 125–29, 152, 159–64, 167, 172
ambiguity of, 87–91
capitalist, 20, 63–64, 70–74, 76, 87, 159, 163, 166–67
created in niche marketing, 63–64, 76, 81, 128. *See also* Niche Marketing
created through labor, 139–41
defined via job evaluation. *See* Employee evaluations; Work station valuation
and economic change, 161–67, 172–73
multiple forms of, 126–27
socialist, 7, 63–65, 74, 87
transferred via exchange, 139
See also Persons; Subjectivity
Persons, 160
as asocial monads. *See* Individualism
created through feeding. *See* Feeding
defined by work station evaluation, 108–19
as having divisible qualities, 94, 114, 126–28, 170
as having interior spaces, 115–19, 126–28, 170
as natural maximizers, 34
as owners of themselves, 126, 128–29
as processes, 94, 115, 118, 171
as the product of social relations, 125–29, 139–40, 160
See also Personhood
Persuasion, 110–11
Piece rates, 12–13
Piergallini, Al, 3, 29, 46, 54, 154, 157
Plan (state socialist economic document). *See* Planning, central
Plan bargaining, 42
Planning, central, 10, 14–18, 175n2
and product quality, 97
See also Shortage
Polanyi, Karl, 81, 54
Poovey, Mary, 177n11
Post-Fordism, 7, 12–18, 20, 22, 31, 61, 66, 68, 81, 92, 114, 118, 163, 165, 169, 171, 177n12. *See also* Fordism; Flexible accumulation
Post-socialism, as moral order, 30–31
Power, 15, 17, 18, 23, 45, 46, 101, 118, 120, 128, 163–74,
anthropological framings of, 132
masked by "control," 100–101
obscured by job station valuation, 108–9, 166
of workers, 17, 31, 44–45, 170
Power, Michael, 175n2
Private domain, 140–43

Privatization, 5, 29, 31–33, 37, 46, 155–57, 161, 173
    of persons, 31, 55, 80–82, 87, 92
    as a reorganization of meaningful worlds, 32
Process, 94, 99
Product array, 16–17, 84, 95
Production, 23, 120, 170, 172
    coordination of, 84–87
    logs, 100–101
    as relation among people, 171–72
    under socialism, 7, 83–85
Productivity, 9, 20. *See also* Efficiency
Professionalism, 88
Property, 33, 55
    persons as, 55. *See also* Objects; Workers as
        geese; Workers as slaves
    private, 4, 20, 33, 47, 55
    rights through labor. *See* Labor; Workers as
        owners of state property
    state, 33
Protestant Ethic, 53
Public domain, 142–43

Quality, 19, 94
Quality control, 7, 19, 20, 93, 143, 163, 166,
        178n17, 181n4, 184n11
    as disciplining consumers, 101–3
    as labor discipline, 20, 94, 100–101, 114–16,
        143–45, 160, 180n15
    upheld by workers, 143–44

Racism, 181n23, 185n19
Rationality, 9, 21–23, 35, 59, 100, 107–8, 123
Reciprocity, 88–89, 152–53, 158–61, 170, 173. *See
        also* Gifts; Networks; *Znajomości*
Redistribution, 91, 165, 168–69. *See also* "Car-
        ing"
Re-engineering, 171
Regulation, 6–7, 161–74. *See also* Self-
        regulation
Resistance, 23, 31, 156, 160
    anthropological framings of, 132, 161
    domestic work as, 141–42
    and Solidarity. *See* Solidarity
Responsibility, 7, 52
Resumés, 71
Rigidity, 19, 59, 66–68, 74, 78–79, 82, 160, 168,
        181n2
Risk, 22–23, 40
Rose, Nikolas, 127, 166
Rzeszów, 1–9, 28, 33, 39, 44, 54, 58

Sales representatives, 5, 24–25, 75–81, 85, 87–93,
        123

Sandoz, 158
Scale, 14–15, 62
Schrade, Ulrich, 135–36, 140
Schrum, Kelly, 179n3
Science, 100, 102–3, 109, 112, 166–67
Scientific Management, 10, 175n1. *See also* Tay-
        lorism
Secrets, 168
Segmentation of markets, *See* Niche marketing
Self-improvement, 113–19, 126–27, 166
Self-regulation, 7, 20, 23, 41, 113, 127, 129,
        165–70
"Shock therapy," 3, 35
Shortage:
    economy of, 8, 15–17, 36, 42, 51, 62, 64, 68, 84,
        119, 175n2, 179n6, 179n21
    -hoarding cycle, 5, 16, 165
Siła (energy), 139
Small batch production, 17, 19, 61, 82–84,
        180n18
    as hallmark of flexible production, 19, 61, 83
    under socialism, 17
Socialism, state, 7, 9, 15, 22–23, 62–64, 118,
        175n2, 185n4
    alternate interpretations of, 82
    bases of distribution in, 125
    cultural legacies of, 4, 8, 87, 119–28, 143, 157,
        159, 161, 170
    as economic system. *See* Shortage, economy
        of
    as foil for identity formation, 63–64, 74, 92,
        142–43, 160–61, 170
    organization of production in, 7, 9, 13–16,
        62–63, 98, 82, 92
    power in, 118, 128–29, 168–69
    as symbol, 63–64, 74, 82, 85, 87
    See also Planning; Shortage
Solidarity (trade union), 4, 8, 17, 31–32, 44, 57,
        80, 104, 111, 128–29, 132, 157, 160, 183n4,
        183–84n9
Soviet Union, 8, 13
Specialization, 85
Społeczeństwo (society), 120
Spółka Usługe Rożne. See Temporary labor
Środowisko (social circle), 119, 122, 126
Stalin, Josef, 9
Standardization, 5, 17, 20, 94–99
Stasis, 59, 64–66, 76–78
Statistical process control, 99, 170
Stocks, 43, 46–48, 155–58, 171, 174, 185n21
Storming, 16
Strathern, Marilyn, 125–26, 129, 139–40
Strikes, 17, 32, 44, 133

Subjection, patterns of, 8, 140, 153–54, 158–64,
 170, 174
Subjectivity, 8, 20, 132, 172–73
 as integral to capitalism, 6, 20, 172
 as key to transition, 6, 170–74
 vs. objectivity, 95, 171–74
 See also Personhood
Subjects, 168–70
Subordination. *See* Subjection
Subsidies, 35, 39, 176n5, 181n3
Supplier relations. *See* Farmers
Supply (as constraint in socialist economies),
 36, 59, 62–63, 87
Surveillance, 100–101, 118, 168–69
Szara istota (gray being), 140, 142, 159, 172
Sztompka, Piotr, 53, 75, 175n2

Taylor, Frederick Winslow, 10, 13, 175n1
Taylorism, 10–13, 20, 175n1
 in Malaysia, 12, 101
 in Mexico, 12, 101
 in the United States, 12
 in the USSR, 13
 See also Scientific Management
Technology, 35, 36, 38, 45, 94, 103
Technozones, 163
Teenagers, 61–64, 179n3
Teilorizatsiya, 13
Tempo of work, 9, 16
Temporary labor, 49–50, 84, 123–24, 178n16
Total Quality Management, 19, 94, 98–99, 100,
 170, 184n11
 as controlling persons, 94, 100–101, 180
 See also Quality control
Training, 51, 77–84, 115–19, 123
"Transition" from socialism, 6, 8, 9, 22, 52–53,
 162–63, 173

Ubezwłasnowolnić, 45, 48
Unemployment. *See* Layoffs
Unions, 29–33, 48, 104, 111–12, 132
 See also Solidarity; OPZZ
Universalism, 84–85
U siebie, 135, 138, 142

Value:
 exchange, 145, 171
 of labor, 23, 31, 54, 75, 80–81, 84, 104–12, 159,
 160. *See also* Labor
 and motherhood, 146–49
 multiple frameworks of, 8, 34, 38, 46, 55, 111–
 12, 159, 160
 relative, 43

of state assets, 31–39, 42–43
 use, 145, 171
 See also Arbitrariness
Vassalage, 120–26, 153, 165, 168
Verdery, Katherine, 175, 180n19, 181n1
Vertical integration, 10, 19

Wages, 146–47. *See also* Income
Wałęsa, Lech, 132
Weber, Max, 53
Wedding banquet, 153–58, 171, 185n20
Welfare state, 67
"We See A Difference" (advertising campaign),
 102–5
Women, 23, 136–53
 work and, 133, 143–53. *See also* Gender; Work
Women's Day, 151
Work, 21–23, 170–72
 claims to ownership based on, 37–38, 47, 48
 control of process of, 17, 18, 84–87. *See also*
 Autonomy
 domestic, 135–46, 183n6, 184–85n18
 gendered, 145–46
 organization of, 8, 9, 13, 18, 23. *See also* Production, coordination of
 for persons, 170
 as research method, 23–25
 as resistance, 142
 as self-fulfillment, 21, 140–41
 as social relation, 146, 153–58
 as transfer of qualities among objects, 91
 See also Labor; Workers; Workplace
Workers, 5, 8, 10, 12, 24–25
 age of. *See* Age
 as assets, 45–46, 55, 85, 118, 159
 as children, 130, 150–51, 159, 161
 discrimination against in work station evaluations, 108–9
 disqualified from non-manual jobs, 78–81,
 180n14
 as geese, 45, 54, 155, 170
 as liabilities, 45, 85, 118, 159
 as machines, 10, 155
 as mothers, 137, 143–53, 159, 160, 171. *See also*
 Motherhood
 as "negroes," 90, 152
 as objects, 10, 45, 54, 56–57, 87, 90–91, 94–95,
 152, 160
 as owners of state property, 44–48, 155,
 157
 power of, under socialism, 17, 31, 44–45
 as processes, 94
 as property, 158–59, 160, 170–71

Workers (*continued*)
  rights to information, 44, 155
  as "simple people," 78–81
  as slaves, 45, 54, 90, 152–55, 170
  voice in managerial decisions, 18, 44–47
  as wives, 155–58, 161
  as women, 143–53
Workplaces, as constructing subjectivity, 20–21, 143–44, 150, 184n18
Work station valuation, 108–9, 151–53, 181n6
World Bank, 168, 173
Wright, Melissa, 81–82

Youth, 58–59. *See also* Age; Niche marketing

Załatwić sprawy (arranging things), 119–20, 126
Zielony Sztandar (newspaper), 29
Zjednoczenie Przemyslu Owocowo-Warzywnego (ZPOW), 10–11, 15
Znajomości, 93, 118–29, 152, 160, 163, 165, 182n12, 182nn16–17